Contents

Foreword

Last spring I was browsing through a catalog looking for a tough rucksack for summer day hikes in the Shenandoah Valley. I found what looked like a good cowhide bag with a leather strap and ordered it. In September I received something that resembled a suede purse much more than it did a rucksack! My disappointment was lessened by the fact that I have been able to use that "purse" as a briefcase. But, you must admit, the use I get from it is quite different from that which was orginally intended.

I share this story because it seems clear to me that when a client sets to work with the interior designer it is like my search for a good rucksack. I knew what I wanted and how I wanted to use it. When the product was delivered (late) I used it for a purpose different than I originally intended and different from that for which the product was designed. Frequently building users complain that what they received was not what they thought they were getting, was not on time, and now that it is completed, it is being used for something else entirely. I have begun to think of this situation as the "suede purse dilemma."

The Challenge of Interior Design offers interior designers a way to cope with the "suede purse dilemma." It does this by demystifying many of the more complex considerations in interior design. This book sets the stage for a design process that accurately addresses the needs of the client, and allows clients to (metaphorically) use the rucksacks they buy for briefcases, or even rainhats, as their circumstances change.

Walt Kleeman begins the process of demystification by a clear statement of several general problems in interior design. These problems are rooted in law, physics, anthropometrics, ergonomics, communications theory, symbolism, and human behavior. He follows this description of the interdisciplinary nature of good interior design with illustrations of how such problems can be addressed in facilities for the elderly, the mentally ill, the office worker, the home-owner/renter, the student, and even the astronaut. Finally, the author shows, by case studies, the application of his approach to the "suede purse dilemma" in practical terms.

Most architects and interior designers will agree that a usable text on this subject is hard to find. I have used *The Challenge of Interior Design* in manuscript form and I can attest to its high utility. What is more, I have found the data-based materials to be valid. Validity and utility, an excellent combination in any book.

Robert G. Shibley, Architect
Consultant on Environmental
and Organizational Change

Preface

This book is written from the standpoint that the design of interiors for the optimum use and comfort of human beings must proceed from an expanded base. The research already accomplished and recorded in many disciplines, some of which might seem to be unrelated to interior design, must be evaluated and considered as to the relevance it may possess. This is the challenge of interior design.

A ten-year search by the author has identified thirty disciplines (and/or subdisciplines, depending on how they are counted) that contain information useful to the interior designer. Listed alphabetically, they are: acoustics, anthropology, anthropometry, architecture, art, cartography, computer science, demography, ecology, engineering, ethology, geography, gerontology, home economics, human factors engineering (called ergonomics outside the United States), illuminating engineering, industrial design, landscape architecture, law, linguistics, medicine, operations research, opthalmology, optics, orthopedics, physiology, psychiatry, psychology, sociology, and urban planning.

Additions to the above list will come as new material is discovered and becomes available. Meanwhile, a new term is needed to include interior design and its expanded base. The term "interior ergonomics" has been chosen because of the inclusive definition of the word "ergonomics" by the Ergonomics Society (London, *Applied Ergonomics* 1, no. 1, 1969):

> . . . the study of the relation between man and his occupation, equipment and environment, and particularly the application of anatomical, physiological and psychological knowledge to problems arising therefrom.

It would be very pleasant to say that there is one study in each of the disciplines above which is definitive, and that any designer can take a limited number of studies, put them together, and then design any space or building so that it is behaviorally correct.

Unfortunately, that is not possible with the material now available. However, the studies cited in this book tell us as designers that there are behavioral implications in every one of our designs. Interior design can produce environmental habitability, a very important goal in terms of human well-being. The condition of the ultimate environment, the interiors where we live, love, work, and play, cannot help but be one of the most important factors in our survival as rational, functional human beings.

A great many people have helped with the writing of this volume. It began as a Project Demonstrating Excellence in partial fulfillment of the requirements for a doctoral degree in the Union Graduate School, and the critical help of Dr. Roy P. Fairfield, my committee chairman, and of Dr. Warren James and Dr. Edward Ostrander, my adjunct professors, was essential, as was the help of my student peer members, Dr. Helene Newman and Dr. Richard Leuba.

My son Christopher typed the original manuscript, and my daughter Elissa searched through libraries for references that were difficult to find.

I am especially indebted to H. T. E. Hertzberg for his unfailing help and constructive criticism throughout the project. Sam A. Sloan, Dennis E. Green, and Dr. Robert Sommer, my colleagues on the GSA-FAA office design project, helped in numerous ways, as did my coworkers at arc (architecture/research/construction), especially Robert Reeves.

Kiyo Izumi and Dr. Humphry Osmond have been unique sources of inspiration for this work.

Jerry Nielsen, Robert Shibley, Dr. Richard G. Coss, Dorothy Eastline, Cathy B. Allgeier, Dr. Francis Duffy, Lorraine Hiatt, Thomas O. Byerts, Don Conway, Dr. Alton J. De Long, and Jack Hockenberry have been indispensable in offering critical suggestions.

I should also like to pay tribute to the late Dr. Darell Boyd Harmon, an early pioneer in this field, who stimulated and taught me so much.

Sam A. Sloan, arc, the National Aeronautics and Space Administration in the person of Bill Mayes, Oxford Pentaflex Corp., and Jack Hockenberry of Steelcase, Inc. all generously furnished photographs that I could not have obtained otherwise.

I thank all of them for their help, but I alone am responsible for what follows.

Walter Kleeman, Ph.D., FASID, IBD, CSI, IDEC

"An interior (or a building or a city) that carries too heavily and forever the professional signature of its designer, and permits no contribution from its users, may be a fine monument, but it is nevertheless a tomb."

Inscape, ed. Sir Hugh Casson (London: The Architectural Press, Ltd., 1968)

I *General Problems in Interior Design*

1 *Interior Architecture by Consent Decree and Court Order*

As an interior design consultant for mental hospitals and mental retardation sites in three states, I am convinced that mental patients are being hurt, not helped, by the design of the settings where they are sent for treatment, and that they cannot by themselves influence these designs.

Patients have participated in the designing process, but for this partnership to be fruitful, they must want to do so and invite the designer's help instead of having the designer's services imposed on them. This involves first enlisting the help and participation of the staff. The designer can then talk with the staff and patients, interpret and evaluate his or her combined findings, and finally present the evolved design to the powers that be in a way that helps the patients achieve what they want and need.

As for the powers that be, funds for the designer and physical improvements come from remote sources, for example, a state board of mental health and mental retardation. It is the patient, however, who is the user and whose needs and wants are paramount; the patient is the real, the user client, while the board is the paying client.

This is not, however, merely a matter of distinguishing between the user client and the paying client; it is also a matter of the designer helping patients who by the very nature of their difficulties are in no condition to respond, project, demand, evaluate—in short, to fend for themselves. The designer must therefore be the patient's design agent, intercessor, and advocate.

In varying degrees, this kind of advocacy design is necessary in many situations where the paying client is not the user client and where the user client cannot fight his or her own battles.

Client Taxonomy   Lacking the benefit of massive psychometric studies, the scheme below may not be absolutely accurate, but the continuum of user clients who need the most design advocacy might start with mental patients and mental retardates followed by seriously ill, general hospital patients and perhaps rehabilitation subjects. The list would then include (in order of need) residents of convalescent homes and other forms of housing for the elderly, prisons, and public housing; students in kindergartens, grade schools, junior high schools, high schools, boarding schools, colleges, and universities; workers in factories, offices, and laboratories; and finally executives and wealthy clients who need no design advocacy at all.

This need does not depend solely on the distance between the user client and the paying client but also on the user client's ability to cope. The issue of ability is determined by two factors: can the user client conceptualize and express his or her real needs and wants (and be listened to), and how much control is exercised by others on the immediate environment of a particular user client?

Federal Intervention   It is my belief that architectural and interior designers have been slow to understand the needs for design advocacy; indeed, their attitude is diametrically opposed to design advocacy. Architectural and interior designers are too accustomed to telling clients (both paying and using) what they can have; they are not accustomed or even geared to making detailed investigations to determine client needs and wants.

However, pressure from a new direction is creating a situation where designers may be forced to consider design advocacy as a way of life. In a surprisingly wide variety of settings, *interior and architectural design is being decided by federal consent decrees and court orders.*

The Wyatt Case   Perhaps the most important landmark court order and consent decree promulgated to date occurred as the result of a case in a federal district court in Alabama, known progressively as *Wyatt* v. *Stickney, Wyatt* v. *Aderholt,* and *Wyatt* v. *Hardin.* While the case was in progress, a succession of Alabama Mental Health Commissioners changed the name of the defendant in the case. Briefly, what happened was that a patient at Bryce Hospital in Tuscaloosa sued the Alabama Mental Health Commissioner, in what later became a class action, claiming that patients there had not received proper treatment and that Bryce did not have a proper physical environment for patients. The case was later expanded to include patients at Searcy Hospital (another Alabama state mental hospital) and at the Partlow State School and Hospital for the Mentally Retarded. After a protracted series of hearings and orders, the court issued a final order and decree to force improvements in the physical facilities, the number ber and quality of staff, and the patients' treatment programs.

The following are some general excerpts from the decision affecting interior architecture: "The Court found defendants' treatment program was deficient in [that] . . . It failed to provide (1) a humane psychological and physical environment." More specifically, the court found "the absence of any semblance of privacy . . . The physical facilities at Bryce were overcrowded and plagued by fire and other hazards."

Friends of the court appeared to give expert counsel to help set standards for improving Bryce, Searcy, and Partlow. These friends included the United States government, the American Orthopsychiatric Association, the American Psychological Association, the American Civil Liberties Union, and the American Association on Mental Deficiency. The court stated in the order and decree that they "have performed exemplary service for which this Court is indeed grateful." Note that no physical design agents, architects, or interior designers (or their professional associations) were friends of this court in this case.

The Standards Set   Before discussing the specific physical environmental standards set by the court, it should be emphasized that these are just minimums, as the court strongly pointed out, and that court-appointed Human Rights Committees were set up at Bryce and at Searcy to monitor the state's compliance with the order and decree. The state of Alabama was also required by the court to find and fund as a consultant at Bryce a Ph.D. psychologist to assist the Human Rights Committee in its work; this psychologist became a full-time consultant to the committee.

It is also noteworthy that the court did not appoint a master, as it might in a bankruptcy case, to run the affairs of the hospitals, although it stipulated: "Nevertheless, defendants, as well as other parties and amici in this case, are placed on notice that unless defendants do comply satisfactorily with this Order, the Court will be obligated to appoint a Master." (That actually did happen in a similar case in Ohio.)

The implications of this statement are clear and the court further strengthened its position by stating that "a failure by defendants to comply with this decree cannot be justified by a lack of operating funds," emphasizing the obligation of the state of Alabama to provide "suitable treatment for the mentally ill." The court further stressed that "how the

Figure 1.1. Makeshift mental hospital outdoor area. (arc photo)

Legislature and Mental Health Board respond to the revelations of this litigation is the very preservation of human life and dignity. Not only are the lives of the patients currently confined at Bryce and Searcy at stake, but also at issue are the well-being and security of every citizen of Alabama."

Appendix A of the court's order and decree is fourteen legal-sized pages long; the following are excerpts that specifically affect the interior environment and its design:

II. Humane Psychological and Physical Environment

  1. Patients have a right to privacy and dignity.

After mentioning the patients' rights to telephone communication and other matters in sections 2–14 Appendix A continues:

15. Patients have a right to be outdoors at regular and frequent intervals, in the absence of medical considerations. . . .

17. The institution shall provide, with adequate supervision, suitable opportunities for the patient's interaction with members of the opposite sex.

19. Physical Facilities—A patient has a right to a humane psychological and physical environment within the hospital facilities. These facilities shall be designed to afford patients with comfort and safety, promote dignity and assure privacy. The facilities shall be designed to make a positive contribution to the efficient attainment of the treatment goals of the hospital.

    A. Resident Unit—The number of patients in a multi-patient room shall not exceed six persons. There shall be allocated a minimum of 80 square feet of floor space per patient in a multi-patient room. Screens or curtains shall be provided to ensure privacy within the resident unit. Single rooms shall have a minimum of 100 square feet of floor space. Each patient will be furnished with a comfortable bed with adequate changes of linen, a closet or locker for his personal belongings, a chair and a bedside table.

    B. Toilets and Lavatories—There will be one toilet provided for each eight patients and one lavatory for each six patients. A lavatory will be provided with each toilet facility. The toilets will be installed in separate stalls to ensure privacy, will be clean and free of odor, and will be equipped with appropriate safety devices for the physically handicapped.

    C. Showers—There will be one tub or shower for each 15 patients. If a central bathing area is provided, each shower area will be divided by curtains to ensure privacy. Showers and tubs will be equipped with adequate safety accessories.

    D. Day Room—The minimum day room area shall be 40 square feet per patient. Day rooms will be attractive and adequately furnished with reading lamps, chairs, television and other recreational facilities. They will be conveniently located to patients' bedrooms and shall have outside windows. There shall be at least one day room area on each bedroom floor in a multi-story hospital. Areas used for corridor traffic cannot be counted as day room space; nor can a chapel with fixed pews be counted as a day room area.

    E. Dining Facilities—The minimum dining room area shall be ten square feet per patient. The dining room shall be separate from the kitchen and will be furnished with comfortable chairs and tables with hard, washable surfaces. . . .

H. Geriatric and Other Nonambulatory Mental Patients—There must be special facilities for geriatric and other nonambulatory patients to assure their safety and comfort, including special fittings on toilets and wheelchairs.

Other provisions of the order and decree provide for "an established routine maintenance and repair program" so that "the physical plant shall be kept in a continuous state of good repair . . . [as well as] adequate heating, air conditioning and ventilation systems" to remove steam and odors and keep air temperatures between a maximum of 83 degrees and a minimum of 68 degrees F. Required temperatures for hot water are set at 110 degrees at the fixture for patient use and 180 degrees at the equipment for mechanical dishwashing and laundry use. The court also decreed:

The physical facilities must meet all fire and safety standards established by the state and locality. In addition, the hospital shall meet such provisions of the Life Safety Code of the National Fire Protection Association (21st edition, 1967) as are applicable to hospitals. The hospital shall meet all standards established by the state for general hospitals, insofar as they are relevant to psychiatric facilities.

Sources of the Standards

The first obvious question that occurs to the designer as he or she reads these very detailed and specific standards set by the court is: "Where are they derived from (especially the square foot minimums and the temperatures)?" A clue can be found in two sections of the 1974 *Federal Register* containing the regulations of the U.S. Department of Health, Education and Welfare for Intermediate Care Facilities. These two sections contain similar water temperatures as standards. It is possible that the "friends of the court" in the *Wyatt* case incorporated these in their briefs and thus they became part of the court order and decree.

The regulations in the *Federal Register* may have been influenced by the standards of the Joint Commission on the Accreditation of Hospitals. Another source also seems likely—"Standards for Psychiatric Facilities," promulgated in 1969 by the American Psychiatric Association (a friend of the friends of the court?). This document specifies a minimum of 80 square feet of floor space in single rooms and 70 square feet of floor space per patient in multiple-patient rooms, slightly less than the minimums set in the *Wyatt* decision. The prescribed square footage in day rooms and the ratios of toilets, lavatories, and showers to numbers of patients are identical to those in the *Wyatt* decision.

Thus, standards have been set that may be as good as any, but only for a start and as minimums. What is worrisome is that definite square footage standards that are part of a landmark court order tend to become rigidly ensconced in the system, and from then on, their validity is hardly questioned. As an example of how these numbers spread, a set of Ohio regulations for residential care facilities for the mentally retarded and developmentally disabled reads: "Every sleeping room occupied by one person shall have a minimum total of eighty (80) square feet of habitable space."

The continued use of these definite numerical standards became even more disturbing when in 1972 the Joint Commission on the Accreditation of Hospitals issued a set of "Standards for the Accreditation of Psychiatric Facilities" that dropped all numbers and moved to a more open format which zeroed in on the welfare of the patient. Instead of talking about numbers this standard used terms such as "preserving . . . human dignity" and "enhancing a positive self-image for the patient." It called for adequate storage space for patient personal belongings, with some of it locked, and suggested open nursing stations and other means of developing "therapeutic intrapersonal relationships" among staff members and patients. It asked for "perceptual clarity" in the "design, structure and lighting of the facility." Provisions for necessary personal privacy as well as the means to communicate with the world outside the institution, including access to the outdoors, were included in this enlightened standard.

Meanwhile, there are literally more than a dozen similar cases in various stages of progress around the country, and many of them are citing *Wyatt* as a precedent in their pleas to improve conditions in mental hospitals and in sites for the treatment of the mentally retarded. As we shall see, the order and decree in one case copies almost verbatim sections of the order and decree in the *Wyatt* case.

Basis for the Standards

There has been little challenge to these standards in terms of their use in mental institutions, especially in reference to the square foot regulations for patient rooms. However, a recognized architectural authority in the field of facilities for the mentally retarded, Arnold G. Ganges, has criticized as "grossly inadequate" the "Standards for Residential Facilities for the Mentally Retarded" set by the Joint Commission on the Accreditation of Hospitals. In 1975 these standards still retained an 80-square foot minimum requirement for bedrooms occupied by one person and a 60-square foot per person minimum for multiple-patient bedrooms. The most comprehensive search of the literature available does not show any experimental or behavioral basis for these square foot minimums. Obviously, behavioral research is necessary either to validate these standards or to find others. However, now that these very definite standards have become part of the law by regulation, consent decree, and court order, the tendency will be to accept them as a fait accompli

Figure 1.2. Typical mental hospital dormitory—no privacy. (arc photo)

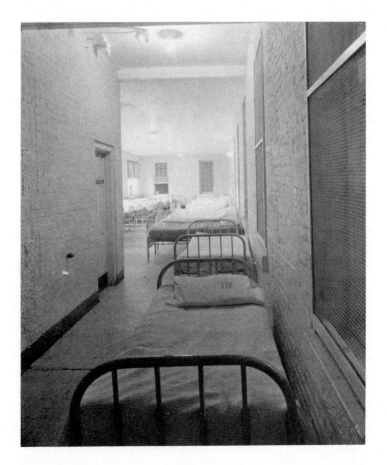

without any attempts at creative interpretation. They will be ignored as the research opportunity that they certainly are; these numerical standards desperately call for an evaluation of their effectiveness on a widespread scale, since their influence seems so pervasive. Incidentally, the British Department of the Environment concurs with this assessment; in a report issued in June 1976, the following statement is made: "Unfortunately, it is all too easy for a standard, simply because it is a standard, to become a formula at which thought stops." That department is recommending "housing environment indices," stating that "the quality of a housing environment depends on much more than can be assessed by reference to quantities."

The Ricci Case   Another landmark case in the field concerns a facility for the mentally retarded where although the standards are not as detailed as in the *Wyatt* order and decree, the meaning for designers is just as clear. The case of *Ricci v. Greenblatt* also became a class action suit, and on November 12, 1973 a consent decree was entered that brought about $2.6 million in capital outlays to improve the Belchertown State School in Belchertown, Massachusetts. This consent decree begins:

For the purpose of providing the mentally retarded residents at the Belchertown State School with their immediate Constitutional rights and further in consideration of their rights to health, safety, and a suitable living environment:

1. Physical Plant—The defendants agree to request of the Legislature an appropriation of $2.6 million in capital outlay funds for the renovation and improvement of various buildings, including furnishings and equipment.

Though *Ricci* v. *Greenblatt* repeats some of the numerical standards found in *Wyatt*, great emphasis is placed on the use of adjectives and nouns to describe the court-ordered environment such as "appropriate," "personalized," "comfortable," "attractive," "homelike," "privacy," and "dignity." One statement in the decree is particularly worth quoting: "The design, repair and renovation of activity rooms shall provide suitable accommodations to promote physical and mental health, and optimal sensory-motor, cognitive, affective and social development, and to encourage movement from dependent to independent and inter-dependent functioning together with provisions for the enjoyable use of leisure time." There are also recurring phrases such as "consistent with their program needs and accepted community standards" and "consistent with those facilities in private residences and accepted by community standards."

There is another statement of interest:

The interior design of living units shall simulate the functional arrangements of a home to encourage a personalized atmosphere for small groups of residents. Space as designed shall be arranged to permit residents to participate in different kinds of activities both in groups and singly. Furniture and furnishings shall be safe, appropriate, comfortable and homelike. Sleeping, living and dining areas in the present dormitories will be divided by partitions, and carpeting shall be installed wherever possible. In addition, wherever possible, lowered ceilings of acoustical material shall be installed.

The $2.6 million was appropriated by the Massachusetts legislature; the consent decree has been implemented.

Other Cases Concerning the Mentally Retarded

There have been several other court cases where court orders and consent decrees have affected the interior architecture of mental health and mental retardation facilities. The following are some of the better known ones:

1. *New York State Association for Retarded Children* v. *Carey* (formerly v. *Rockefeller*): This is known as the Willowbrook case, since it concerns a New York state facility for the mentally retarded, Willowbrook State School. Though a landmark case in many respects, especially in that it directs the reduction of the population at Willowbrook and the moving of patients to intermediate facilities, there seems to be little in the consent decree that directly affects interior architecture except for a provision that "no more than eight residents can live or sleep on a unit" and another ordering "immediate and continuing repair of all inoperable toilets." Some of the Willowbrook residents were to be transferred to the newly built Bronx Development Center; however, *Progressive Architecture* reported that a federal judge had "decided in favor of the Willowbrook Review Panel's recommendation that the class (Willowbrook residents) be placed gradually but directly into the community instead of being transferred first to the Bronx Center. Judge John R. Bartell felt the risks of delaying advancement of the retarded by placing them in another institution outweigh benefits of the improved environment." In this case

and in *Ricci*, there is a clear judicial trend to order the mentally retarded into homes and homelike environments rather than institutional ones.

2. *U.S.* v. *Michael K. Shorter:* The November 13, 1974 decision in this case found that "facilities designed for the treatment of the mentally *ill* are *not* generally *suitable* for the treatment of the mentally *retarded* [italics added]." Though the differences are not specified in the decision, it does indicate a high degree of architectural sensitivity to the specific needs of patients, which unfortunately is not shared by some interior designers and architects.

3. *Welsch* v. *Likins:* This, too, was a class action similar to *Wyatt.* Here the court ordered "extensive alterations to the facility's (mental hospital) physical plant, air conditioning in non-ambulatory units, carpeting in all residential and program areas, removal of bars and limitations on the use of underground tunnels for transporting residents."

4. *Davis* v. *Watkins:* In this Ohio case, the court *did* appoint a special master (as the Alabama court had threatened to do in *Wyatt*) to run Lima State Hospital. Though there are some minor differences between this order and that in the *Wyatt* case, the same square footage figures appear, and this order closely follows the format of the *Wyatt* order and decree, occasionally word for word.

Again in Ohio, a decision affecting both a mental hospital and a facility for the mentally retarded is awaited in *Rone et al.* v. *Fireman et al.,* a class action suit filed against Hawthornden State Hospital (now Western Reserve Psychiatric Center). This case involves the interior architectural environment in a major way.

Cases Concerning the Handicapped

Another type of court order and consent decree is being handed down which fundamentally concerns the rights of handicapped persons to use public buildings and facilities. Such cases include:

1. *Urban League* (also the Paralyzed Veterans of America, the National Paraplegic Foundation, and others) v. *Washington Area Metropolitan Transit Authority:* The plaintiffs wanted to be certain that as handicapped persons, they would be able to use the subway system once it was built and asked for elevators to be available for those who cannot use stairs. The court issued a mandatory injunction on October 9, 1973

stating that the transit authority could not commercially operate the subway until the handicapped were able to use it.

2. *Disabled in Action of Baltimore et al.* v. *Hughes et al.:* This was a class action suit filed on behalf of all elderly and handicapped persons who were being denied access to mass transit vehicles in the Baltimore metropolitan area. The case was settled by a memorandum of understanding which included the agreement that 205 buses would be bought in accordance with specifications that would make them accessible to the elderly and handicapped and that ten buses would be bought for use by people in wheelchairs.

3. *Friedman* v. *County of Cuyahoga:* Friedman, a lawyer confined to a wheelchair by injuries suffered in a car accident, could not enter Cuyahoga county buildings, including the administrative building and the courthouse. He and others sued to be allowed access to these buildings. A consent decree ordered the installation of "ramps, a bell or other signalling device, or other appropriate means to assure ingress and egress by physically handicapped persons to certain public buildings."

Human Behavior reported that "at California State University at San Francisco the new student union building has been closed by a lawsuit since September, 1975 because it is inaccessible to wheelchairs. There are ten accessibility suits pending against the Urban Mass Transportation Administration." Recently, *Civil Liberties* reported that a case filed by the Mountain States Office of the American Civil Liberties Union had resulted in a decision by a federal judge that the University of Nevada must spend $2.7 million "to provide elevators and ramps for easy access to University buildings and classrooms as well as earmarking funds for Braille texts and special tutors."

Cases Concerning Prisons

Another area of legal activity affecting interior architectural design involves interior conditions in jails and prisons, especially as they produce overcrowding. The following are the more important such cases:

1. *Costello* v. *Wainwright:* In its landmark decision, the court stated: "In summary, the overwhelming evidence is that there is a direct and immediate correlation between severe overcrowding, as now exists in the Florida Prison System, and the deprivation of minimally adequate health care. In addition, it appears that severe overcrowding endangers the very

lives of the inmates because of its being a factor in the causation of violence within the prison system."

2. *Baker* v. *Hamilton:* The court further held that "placement of juveniles in county jail constituted cruel and unusual punishment in violation of the Eighth Amendment, in view of cramped quarters, poor illumination, bad circulation of air, broken locks, no outdoor exercise or recreation, and no attempt at rehabilitation."

3. *Osborn* v. *Manson:* In this case, the court held "that conditions of confinement of prisoners, held in administrative segregation in cells which had no running water and only covered buckets which were infrequently emptied by prisoners who had no opportunity for exercise other than to walk up and down two flights of stairs twice a day to wash and empty their buckets, were violative of basic concepts of decency and constituted cruel and unusual punishment."

4. *Johnson* v. *Lark:* Cited in the holding were "three men in tiny two-man cells, absence of recreational facilities and outside exercise areas . . . inadequate ventilation" (from Pa. Cmwlth. ex rel. *Bryant* v. *Hendrick*).

In *Bryant,* the Court also held that "petitioners have been imprisoned in overcrowded, wet, badly ventilated and verminous cells" and that this was evidence of violation of the Eighth Amendment respecting cruel and unusual punishment.

5. *Dillard* v. *Pritchess:* The Court stated: "From the testimony at the trial, it is evident that the punishment imposed upon the pre-trial inmates confined in the jail is not due to the vindictiveness of those in charge of their custody, but stems instead from the antiquated nature of the facility itself."

6. *James* v. *Wallace:* Early in 1976, Federal Judge Frank M. Johnson, Jr. (*New York* magazine called him the "real governor of Alabama"), the author of the *Wyatt* decision, issued another wide-ranging court order, this time affecting the Alabama prison system: "The Court found the prisons wholly unfit for human habitation in terms of public health," and finding that bunks were "packed together so closely that there is no walking space between them," Judge Johnson ruled that "every prisoner must be given at least 60 square feet of living space." He buttressed his order with forty-four major guidelines and also appointed a thirty-nine-

member, blue-ribbon Human Rights Committee for the prison system as he had for the Alabama mental health system in *Wyatt.*

7. *Campbell et al.* v. *McGruder et al.:* Two orders were issued aimed at ending overcrowding in the District of Columbia jail, and at enforcing fire, safety, and building code regulations.

Legislation in Sweden

While the U.S. Congress and state legislatures seem to have been largely waiting for the courts to instruct them on how to make public interior environments habitable and useful, Sweden has taken a significant step toward user participation in the design of some interior environments. According to Ivergard, "Sweden has just introduced a new law on democracy in the workplace that gives all workers the unquestionable right to equal say with the managers about their work, methods, equipment, environment and work policies."

From another source, we learn that changes have been made in Sweden's building laws and worker protection laws that will effect the planning and building process considerably. "To obtain building permission, which is necessary before any building can be started, all drawings and other relevant documents must be examined by the factory inspector. . . ." Then the factory inspector "must contact the employees who will be affected by the building and find out whether they have had a say in, and suitable influence on, the planning of the new workplaces." Even when little changes are being made to existing buildings, the workers' rights to participation in the planning are safeguarded by the new law. Having one's microenvironmental rights guaranteed by law is a bit different from having to sue the government for them.

Canadian Standards

In 1965, the "Canadian Building Standards and Guide Materials for Hospitals and Mental Health Facilities" were issued; they were prepared by Professor Kiyo Izumi, Architect-Planner, and while they are a far cry from the judicial numbers game, they are much more specifically oriented architecturally than the excellent Joint Commission's "Standards for Psychiatric Facilities" of 1972. The Canadian standards make specific suggestions regarding the interior environment for mental health: The following are extracts from Section 10 of the Canadian standards:

Architectural Considerations for Mental Health Facilities

A. Introduction

A-1. There are differences in the architectural and physical requirements of space and details of the various hospital facilities for mental health, depending on the hospital program. These differences may be summarized as follows:

1.1 Regional differences resulting from the assessment of the local situation.

1.2 Fundamental differences in philosophy as to the eventual and existing trend and need for the cure and care of the mentally ill.

A-2. In the drafting of the space and design program the architect is usually confronted with three philosophies. These affect design to a considerable degree depending on which philosophy is advanced by the authority(ies) concerned. The three philosophies could be stated as follows:

2.1 The traditional approach in the care and housing of broad categories of patients, which results in isolated, segregated and monumental architectural solutions, lacking in reasonable amenities.

2.2 The thinking that chemical, biochemical, surgical or some other "physical medicine" advance will solve the problem. This tends to minimize social and related treatment facilities and emphasizes the technological considerations. This approach may be reflected in the architecture.

2.3 The other extreme, as exemplified by C. G. Jung and Karen Horney where, "the search for self-realization without either the false image of an idealized self or without the resigned and dependent clinging to external props like family, social group or church, etc."

A-3. Though existing hospitals in isolated locations imply the latter philosophy, there are many new ones similarly situated with this in mind and provide the minimum of facilities for these "props." The extreme, of course, is when no facilities whatsoever are built.

A-4. It is obvious that the considerations have considerable influence on building standards. It is also obvious that it is not an easy problem to solve and assimilate the desired factors into any standards.

A-5. There appears to be no great difference in opinion that the mentally ill people need to be treated. Among psychiatrists, however, there is considerable difference in emphasis. Unfortunately, in many instances, for the lack of clear directive to the architect, the concept tends to reflect the esoteric considerations of the designer and then both therapist and architect try to justify the concept on extraneous factors. In this way, it seems that existing institutions are perpetuated, alternate use for a new mental hospital is negated, mistakes are repeated, and/or no improvements are made.

A-6. It is hoped that if no "national" philosophy can be established, that at least the architect will be warned by this document, of the more significant trends and criteria.

B-4.2 The degree of physical integration of the facilities for the care of the mentally ill should be considered. For example, the isolated facility, that is, either by distance or by some physical barrier, must provide its own variety store, beauty parlour, places of worship, theatre and other recreational facilities. By contrast in a receptive community, adequately equipped with the above and fairly accessible, the therapeutic milieu may be expanded into the community. This kind of integration permits a much closer design coordination of community, town or city planning facilities.

4.3 Therefore, in addition to those spaces and facilities unique to the requirements of the mentally ill, the list would include to varying degrees facilities social, recreational, spiritual and others which may be considered tributary to the creation of a therapeutic milieu.

B-5. Those stemming from past experience such as can be resolved into figures or other qualitative terms.

B-6. Those stemming from the unique limitations and needs of the mentally ill patients themselves.

6.1 In this respect there is much need for greater research and the major problem is how to extrapolate objective standards from subjective experiences. These can however be reduced to definite design principles or at least to directives, because even though the degree of perceptual distortion experienced is different among individuals, the direction of the distortions is fairly consistent. For example, the consistent tendency for paranoids, psychotics and schizophrenics is to perceive things and spaces to be larger than actuality.

C. Design Considerations

C-1. There are not enough definitive studies of this nature to permit rigid conclusions, but based on the observation of psychologists, nurses, psychiatrists in existing mental hospitals and some architects, and research projects among mentally ill patients, assisted by experience simulated through drugs such as Lysergic Acid Diethylamide, the following is a suggested list of design considerations to keep in mind:

C-2. To avoid certain types of architectural design which lead to ambiguity, e. g.,

2.1 The design of doorways where the size, proportion and treatment of the sidelight is indistinguishable from the door itself.

2.2 Use of panelling in proportion and pattern in such a fashion to make doors, cupboards and other closing panels indistinguishable from the adjacent wall.

2.3   Use of trim, paint lines, hardware and other elements placed to simulate adjacent shelf, drawer, when in fact these do not exist.

2.4   Built-in closets and other features, particularly in patients' private rooms which give the illusion of hidden spaces behind.

2.5   Base board design, e. g. hospital base and its color and material that tends to make the junction of wall and floor disappear. This kind of design where two surfaces melt should be avoided in other places such as at the wall and ceiling, two walls abutting each other, etc.

C-3.   To avoid qualities of finish that tend to heighten illusions.

3.1   Placing of mirrors directly opposite to each other.

3.2   Highly glazed ceramic tile in toilets and other areas which reflect light, one's face in multiplicity, particularly in distorted fashion.

3.3   Highly polished floors or reflective dados, such as terrazo, enamelled walls which not only reflect distorted images under certain light conditions but can also make the plane of the surface disappear.

C-4.   Proportion and scale of spaces and form should be commensurate with the human body. Monumental entrances, lobbies and other features should be avoided. The texture of materials, color, and other architectural elements should be carefully considered so that they complement or are subordinate to the human element. Nothing is so disturbing as to be overwhelmed by the visual and physical environment.

C-5.   There are various kinds of privacy required for purposes of personal activity: acoustical, physical, visual and the difficult space-time privacies. Some of the more obvious ones are:

5.1   Private toilets, that is toilet rooms should be as private as they would be in the normal home. To a psychiatric patient it may be disturbing to see and hear somebody else using a water closet in the adjacent stall.

5.2   The above is found to be true for many patients even when brushing teeth, shaving and other personal toilet functions.

5.3   Noise and other sounds coming from an adjacent room or space are more disturbing that those coming from a corridor. In other words, construction and plan layout should minimize sounds coming from unexpected or hidden areas. Plumbing noises, motor hums, fans, clicking of switches, may be irritating but not unduly disturbing if it is easy to ascertain as to where and why. (A difficulty encountered in very cold climates such as on the prairies, are building noises resulting from expansion and contraction. Certain kinds of steel and even wood construction give sharp gun shot like sounds.)

5.4   The location of treatment rooms, interview rooms, and others from which there may be noise and sounds of patients under treatment, etc., needs to be given greater consideration, while keeping in mind convenience to bedrooms and other patient areas. Soundproofing does not necessarily overcome this problem as the disturbing aspect is not only noise but the visual accessibility of a room that becomes known for experiences that may cause anxiety to the patients.

5.5 Provision of sufficient "personal" storage space.

C-6. On furniture arrangement and design:

6.1 Permit beds to be placed parallel and against walls (contrary to conventional hospital nursing practice).

6.2 Permit the head of the bed to be placed toward corridor or window wall as desired by the patient.

6.3 Use of hospital type beds only for patients requiring nursing care.

Figure 1.3. Typical mental hospital waiting area. (arc photo)

6.4 Avoid arranging chairs and other "sitting" furniture in a manner which suggests a waiting room. The lounge or for that matter any room should be easy to enter and any arrangement of chairs and hence people already in them, that places the subsequent people entering the room to be more or less placed on view is very undesirable.

6.5 Combined seating, that is the sofa type, should be sparingly used and preferably not at all. Chairs should be individual and preferably with relatively high backs and arms to give a sense of enclosure; in addition if these are not light enough in weight to permit the patient to move them to face the direction he wants, they should be provided with swivels.

6.6 Plastic or other materials that are not porous to body heat should be avoided.

We shall refer to these standards again in Chapter 9, "Toward Mental Health."

References

Maurica Anderson, "Power to the Crips!" *Human Behavior* 6, no. 7 (July 1977), p. 48. Citations are not available for these cases.

Baker v. Hamilton, 345 F. Supp. 345 (1972).

"A Bibliography of Materials Useful for Changes in Mental Hospitals: Architecture, Institutional Settings and Health," Exchange Bibliographies #463, 464, 465, 533, and 534 by arc/Architecture/Research/Construction, ARC Research Division, Cleveland State Hospital. Published by the Council of Planning Librarians, PO Box 229, Monticello, Ill. 61856 (1973, 1974). The author was a member of the team that researched and annotated the above 544 pages of bibliography.

Campbell et al. v. McGruder et al., Civil Action 1462-71, U.S. Dist. Ct., D.C. (1975).

"Canadian Building Standards and Guide Materials for Hospitals and Mental Health Facilities," Extracts from Section 10, Part II, Facilities for Mental Health Services, Department of National Health and Welfare, Canada (1965). This section was prepared by Professor Kiyo Izumi, Architect-Planner.

Civil Liberties 311, (April 1976), pp. 1 and 7. A citation is not available for this case.

Costello v. Wainwright, 397 F. Supp. 20 (1975).

Davis v. Watkins, 384 F. Supp. 1196 (1974).

Dillard v. Pritchess, 399 F. Supp. 1225 (1975).

Disabled in Action of Baltimore et al. v. Hughes et al., Civil Action 74-1069-HM, U.S. Dist. Ct., Md. (1974).

Federal Register, vol. 39, no. 12, pt. II (January 17, 1974), Department of Health, Education and Welfare, Social and Rehabilitation Service, Medical Assistance Program, Intermediate Care Facility Services, 249.12, "Standards for Intermediate Care Facilities," and 249.13, "Standards for Intermediate Care Facilities in Institutions for the Mentally Retarded or Persons with Related Conditions," pp. 2224-2229. Same as above except pt. III, Social Security Administration, 405.1134, "Skilled Nursing Facilities," pp. 2247-2248.

Friedman v. County of Cuyahoga, Case 895961, Court of Common Pleas, Cuyahoga County, Ohio (1972).

Arnold G. Ganges, "Planning and Designing Group Homes," in Michael J. Bednar, ed., *Barrier-Free Environments* (Stroudsburg: Dowden, Hutchinson & Ross, 1977), p. 248.

Gates v. Collier, 548 F. 2nd 1241 (1977).

Paul Harrison, "Humanizing Factories," *Human Behavior* 5, no. 8 (August 1976), p. 40.

T. Ivergard, "Ergonomics for the Workers in Sweden," *Applied Ergonomics* 6, no. 4 (December 1975), p. 225.

Johnson v. Lark, 359 F. Supp. 289 (1973).

Jones v. Diamond, 594 F. 2nd 997 (1979).

Newman v. State of Alabama, 349 F. Supp. 278 (1972).

New York State Association for Retarded Children v. Carey, 357 F. Supp. 752 (1975).

Osborn v. Manson, 359 F. Supp. 1107 (1973).

Pa. Cmwlth. ex rel. Bryant v. Hendrick, 444 Pa. 83, 280 A 2d 110. See also Hendrick v. Jackson, 10 Pa. Cmwlth. 392, 309 A 2d 187.

Progressive Architecture (July 1977), pp. 30 and 34.

Pugh v. Lock, 406 F. Supp. 318 (1976).

"Regulations (Ohio) for Licensure of Residential Care Facilities for the Mentally Retarded and Developmentally Disabled" (Columbus: Department of Mental Health and Mental Retardation, July 1, 1976).

Ricci v. Greenblatt, Civil Action 72-496-T, U.S. Dist. Ct., Mass. (1973).

Rone et al. v. Fireman et al., Civil Action 75-355A, U.S. Dist. Ct., Northeast, Ohio (1975).

Mary Saylin, "Disabled Demand Their Rights," *Civil Liberties* 331 (February 1980), p. 4. A citation is not available for this case.

"Standards for Accreditation of Psychiatric Facilities" (Chicago: Joint Commission on the Accreditation of Hospitals, 1972).

Urban League et al. v. WMATA, Civil Action 776-72, U.S. Dist. Ct., D.C. (1973).

U.S. v. Michael K. Shorter, Crim. 67724-23, Superior Court, D.C. (1974).

Welsch v. Likins, 373 F. Supp. 485 (1974).

George Woodford, Kristine Williams, and Nancy Hill, "The value of standards for the external residential environment" (South Ruislip: British Department of the Environment, 1976), as reported in *The Architects' Journal* (June 16, 1976), p. 1166.

Wyatt, 325 F. Supp. 373 (1971).

2 *Designing for All of Us*

Today we hear a great deal about "barrier-free" design. Admirable though that concept is, it does not include every feature of design necessary for all of us to use an interior and its furnishings to our utmost potential of living and working. In addition to "barrier-free" design, we need interior spaces and artifacts that provide options and choices so that we can engage in a variety of behaviors.

Who Are the Handicapped?

We will first take a look at who is handicapped, in order to provide a design service so that everyone, handicapped or not, can fully use interior spaces and furnishings. The special provisions for the handicapped that follow will not hinder the use of space by the able-bodied. Unfortunately, there are no definite figures that tell us the exact numbers of people who are handicapped in the many ways that prevent them from the full use of facilities. According to one federal publication, 10 percent of the total population is handicapped; a well-known expert in the field cited in a second federal publication from the same agency claims that roughly 20 percent of the total population is handicapped.

From *Industrial Design* we learn that "in 1971, an estimated 30 per cent of the population suffered an activity-restricting injury. 62 million Americans had an accident that prevented them from functioning in a normal manner." The same article also states: "Others contend that there are actually 160 million Americans who are not normal according to current design specifications." According to the National Center for Health Statistics, "At least 67,900,000 Americans suffer from limiting physical conditions and would benefit from a more accessible environment. An additional 20 million or more Americans over the age of 65 and limited in mobility as a result of the aging process are not included in this figure."

The use of age 65 as the age for retirement and as the cut-off point for figures of this kind is certainly debatable, widespread through it is, since there are wide differences in ability, disability, and capability among those who reach this age; the arbitrary use of age 65 is being questioned. It should be remembered, however, that the designer for the handicapped is also designing for the aging.

Figures from the second federal publication, "Design Criteria New Public Building Accessibility" are shown in Table 2-1.

Table 2–1. Populations at Risk

Disabling Causes	Total Number	No. per 1000
Chronic: Aging	20,000,000	99.7
Hearing Impairments	8,000,000	39.7
Arthritic Conditions	6,000,000	30.0
Arthritis and Rheumatism		(8.6)
(2,201,000)[1]		
Overweight	4,000,000	20.4
Heart Trouble	4,000,000	19.4
Visual Impairments	2,500,000	12.3
Vascular Conditions	1,500,000	8.0
Cardio-Vascular (800,000)		(4.0)
Varicose Veins (400,000)[2]		(2.0)
Cerebral Vascular (200,000)		(1.0)
Hemorrhoids (200,000)[2]		(1.0)
High Blood Pressure and Strokes	1,000,000[2]	6.0
Asthma	500,000[2]	3.3
Respiratory	500,000	3.0
Poliomyletis	500,000	3.0
Parkinson's	500,000	2.8
Stomach Ulcer	500,000[2]	2.5
Multiple Sclerosis	500,000[3]	2.5
Diabetes	500,000[2]	2.4
Urinary	500,000	2.2
Chronic Bronchitis and Emphysema	500,000[2]	1.8
Hernia	500,000[2]	1.7
Muscular Dystrophy	500,000[4]	1.6
Amputation	200,000	1.1
Ataxia	200,000	1.1
Athetosis	200,000	1.0
Total Deafness	200,000[2]	0.9
Paraplegia	200,000	0.9
Epilepsy	200,000[2]	0.8
Quadriplegia	100,000	0.6

Disabling Causes	Total Number	No. per 1000
Hemiplegia	50,000	0.3
Acute:		
Pregnancy	8,000,000	39.4
Dislocations, Fractures	20,000	0.1

NOTES FOR POPULATIONS AT RISK

1. Specific disease prevalence verified for Rheumatoid Arthritis (1,265,000), Osteo Arthritis (520,000), Arthritis Foundation.
2. These figures reflect the reported disability from the diseased condition of people 18-64. They must be adjusted upward to include those people 65 and over.
3. Multiple Schlerosis Society, *1968 Multiple Schlerosis - Facts*, NYC, 1972.
4. National Institute for Neurological Disease and Blindness.

Additional Sources:

5. Chronic Conditions and Limitations of Activity and Mobility, U.S., Spring, 1966.
6. Current Estimates from Health Interview Survey, U.S., 1970.
7. Prevalence of Selected Impairments, U.S., 1970
8. National Center for Health Statistics, *Incidence of Acute Disabilities*, 1972.
9. U.S. Census, 1970.
10. Lawrence Haber, Epidemiological Factors in Disability: I. Major Disabling Conditions, Soc. Sec. Admin. Report No. 6, Feb., 1969, Table V.

If one adds all the figures in Table 2-1, the result is almost 62 million people who are physically handicapped in some major way; that is roughly 30 percent of the U.S. population. Obviously, this 30 percent figure is too high since some of the individuals included in this estimate have two or more of the disabling conditions named above.

There is, however, another way of looking at disabilities in our population, and that is as activity limitations. Table 2-2 shows a different compilation from the same federal publication.

Table 2–2. Physical Disabilities

Activity Limitations	Millions
Visual (severe, total)	1.5
Visual Impairment (all other)	4.0
Hearing (severe, total)	0.5
Hearing Impairment (all other)	8.0
Difficulty in Interpreting Information	35.0
Limited Movement Ability	20.0

Activity Limitations	Millions
Slow Reaction Time	10.0*
Dizziness	14.0*
Balance	7.0*
Coordination	11.0*
Stamina & Strength	34.0*
Reduced or Irregular Walking Speed	13.0*
Turning Head/ Torso	2.5
Reduced Joint Flexibility	11.0
Kneeling/Stooping	14.0*
Standing from Sitting	8.0*
Sitting from Standing	8.0*
Standing for Long	15.0*
Sitting for Long	10.0*
Clutching & Gripping	15.0
Fine Finger Manipulation	15.0
Reaching Up	15.0
Reaching Down	15.0
Lifting	15.0*
Carrying	22.0*
Reaching Forward	15.0
Pressure/Temperature Sensation Impairment	9.0
Frequency of Urination or Thirst	10.0*

NOTE: The starred (*) figures do not include disabilities occurring in pregnant women. To these
figures should be added a portion of the 8 million noted above.

The total number of disabilities included in Table 2-2 is 357.5 million,
an average of 1.75 disabilities for each of us in the U.S. population;
among other things, this means that many Americans have more than
one of the disabilities listed, and as research has shown, this concentration of disabilities occurs especially in the elderly portion of our population. Note that Table 2-1 shows that aging is a chronic disabling cause
for 20,000,000 people. Perhaps the "160 million" estimate has some
substance after all. At any rate, a significant portion of our population
can benefit from design for handicapped persons, and this compilation
gives us a different view of who is handicapped than that usually presented.

No matter what the statistics, there are individuals in each community
who are handicapped, and they must have the same rights of access to
buildings and the same rights of use of buildings as the able-bodied do.

Figure 2.1. Wheelchair dimensions. (Courtesy of General Services Administration)
Figure 2.2. Dimensions for dining areas. (Courtesy of General Services Administration)

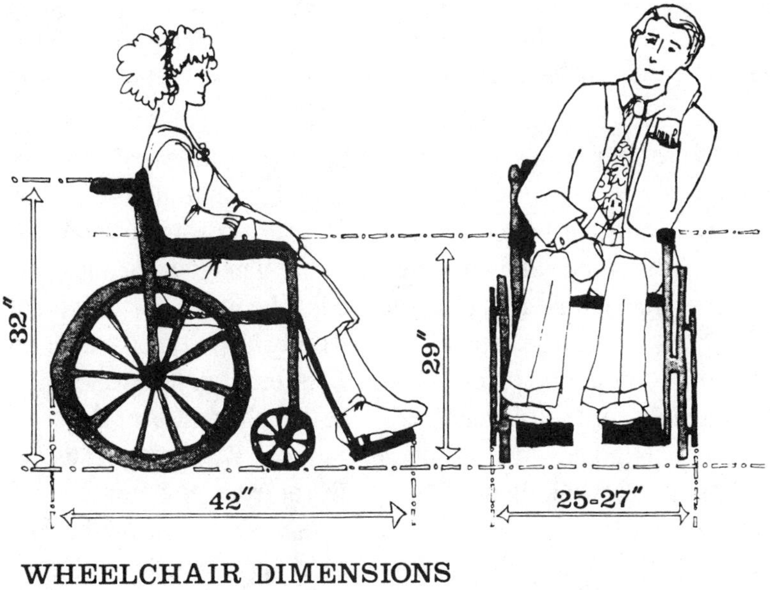

WHEELCHAIR DIMENSIONS

2.1

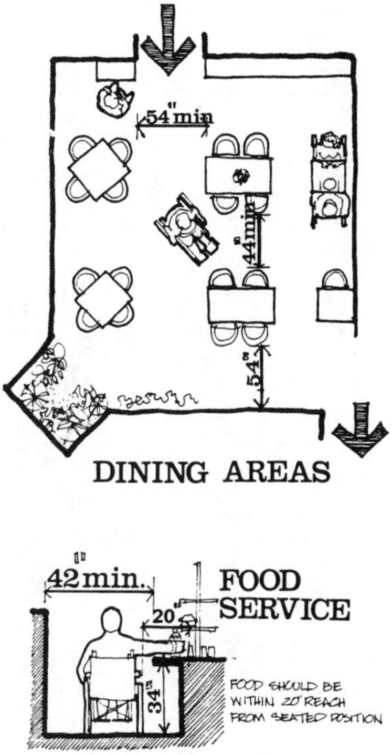

DINING AREAS

FOOD SERVICE

FOOD SHOULD BE WITHIN 20" REACH FROM SEATED POSITION

2.2

The Designer's Response

A designer can respond to these statistics by spending a week or a month or even a day in a wheelchair, as some General Services Administration (GSA) architectural trainees did in the course of their regular work, to experience the plight of the wheelchair-bound, physically disabled. After a day in a wheelchair, one of these trainees wrote:

The first type of inconvenience to persons confined to wheelchairs is the result of the wheelchair's low, wide design. This in turn lowers the person's eye level to approximately four feet from the floor, though this may vary with the individual. Because of the lower sight line, formerly visible areas can no longer be seen, such as some cafeteria and vending machine shelves and upper drawers of filing cabinets. (Glass shelving in the cafeteria permits views of the bottom side of plates, but not of food; they are designed to permit looking down through the shelf, not up.) New designs utilizing both eye levels might require a loss of space (such as not using the upper drawer of a filing cabinet) or a loss economically, but where necessary, could accommodate the handicapped and able people equally.

The low seat also causes a lower total height, which in turn limits the reach of the handicapped person. Elevator buttons, drinking fountains, public telephones and top filing cabinet drawers become inaccessible. Lowering by just a few inches in most cases will alleviate these problems.

It should be noted that height is not the only factor involved here. Horizontal direction and location also affect accessibility, for it is easier for the handicapped person to reach up a wall parallel to the wheels than perpendicular to them.

If this GSA architectural trainee's example were followed, the designer would know how to design from an eye height of about 48 inches from the floor instead of his customary and typical 66-inch height. It should be noted that these and all dimensions for wheelchairs and their accommodation throughout this chapter are based on the use of typical small wheelchairs; the larger ones are mostly geriatric types which do not usually appear in public places. (Where larger chairs are used, the designer must allow for their larger size in the design of interior spaces.)

What about the blind or visually impaired person? What about the deaf or hearing impaired? What about the mentally retarded and mentally ill? Should the designer take a tranquilizer or wear earmuffs or a blindfold while working in a wheelchair? Perhaps. Perhaps then the designer would also experience the sense of frustration and indignity that a handicapped person feels. Michael J. Bednar says, "The built environment as it exists today communicates to the disabled messages of deviancy, incompetence and inferiority." Following suit, Wolf Wolfensberger criticizes the myths and stereotyping that surround the handicapped, calling them "devalued" in our society. The able-bodied also contribute to this attitude with their own demeaning messages to the disabled.

The Case of Dr. Richards

Dr. Van Richards is a well man who was suddenly installed in a cast from hip to foot as a result of a leg injury and who had to travel extensively while so encased. One of Dr. Richards's most poignant experiences took place (repeatedly) as he was being pushed around airports in wheelchairs by porters. Airline ticket agents would ask the porters for Richards's ticket; and he would reply, "I have my own goddamned ticket," mumbling under his breath, "and I'm not brain-damaged."

Because an individual has a physical disability that prevents normal movement does not mean that he or she has lost the capacity to think and reason. This is part of the frustration of being physically handicapped. Another is not being able to conduct ordinary activities because the designer did not make it possible when it could have been done with a little more thought and very little extra cost.

Figure 2.3.
International symbol on airport washroom.

Dr. Richards points out other difficulties he encountered in a cast and on crutches:

1. Public restrooms are frequently located so that a flight of stairs has to be negotiated in order to reach them; only half-humorously he writes that "92.7 per cent of the bathrooms are either up a flight or down a flight."

2. Dr. Richards lived in a fifth-floor walkup apartment in San Francisco which was not easily accessible in his condition. How accessible would the average home be for a person with a hip-to-foot cast and a crutch or two?

Travel and the Handicapped

An article in *Travel Weekly* claims that 40 million Americans are classified as physically handicapped and that the travel industry "is slowly finding that (they) are a huge and long ignored market." The article also notes the publication of a booklet, "Air Travel for the Handicapped," by one of the world's largest airlines; one large hotel chain with some facilities for the handicapped in each of its inns; another large hotel chain with Braille menus in each of its worldwide restaurants; a worldwide car rental agency that is buying lever control units to fit any car in its fleet; and a nationwide bus system that offers "free travel for any fit person accompanying another who is disabled." A few travel agencies have begun to organize tours for the handicapped, and there is even a Society for the Advancement of Travel for the Handicapped. And if they travel to Atlantic City, the handicapped will find at least a dozen and a half slot machines in the casino at the Boardwalk Regency Hotel low enough so that those confined to wheelchairs can play. There are even placards in Braille. Finally, the handicapped are being recognized as a market.

What We Are
Dealing With

What we are dealing with is not simply physical and sensory difficulties; but the total handicapped human condition. We are also dealing with the need for every human being, including the handicapped, to be able to cope with the environment with a sense of independence, competence, and dignity.

We must have an organized way of examining the problem. One method is to divide all disabilities into two categories:

1. physical (movement limited), and
2. sensory (difficulty receiving and interpreting signals).

Another way is to divide them thus:

1. permanent (difficulties that frequently increase with time), and
2. temporary (difficulties that disappear or decrease with time).

Understanding limits to physical movement is not difficult, but handling sensory problems is, often because the designer, having developed high sensory abilities through training, aptitude, and experience, tends to overestimate the sensory abilities of others, especially the handicapped. It is also hard to realize that many handicaps, both physical and sensory, are serious but not visible to others. Yet another look at Table 2-2 reveals that 35 million Americans have difficulty in interpreting information. This fact demonstrates the incidence of sight and hearing impairments as well as faulty communications devices. What does this mean to the designer?

It means that the designer must make certain that information in any designed space must be clear to everyone.

It means that signage and some signals must be comprehensible in three languages: that for the deaf, that for the blind, and that for others, who may have small measures of these handicaps.

It means extra care in design so that all of us will know where we stand and what direction we wish to take in interior spaces.

We must remember, for instance, that the mean eye level of a seated person in a wheelchair is 48 inches from the floor, and that signs at a 54-inch level are optimal for both handicapped and able users. It is probable

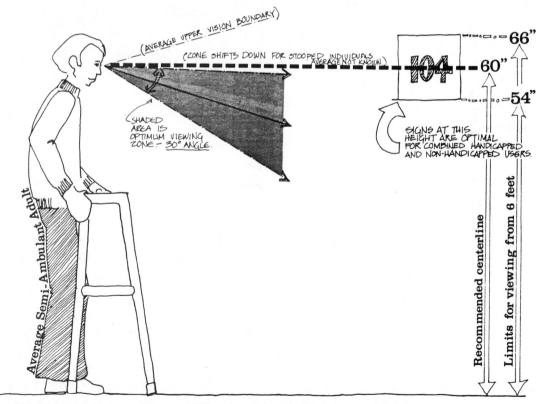

Figure 2.4. Sight lines for the handicapped. (Courtesy of General Services Administration)

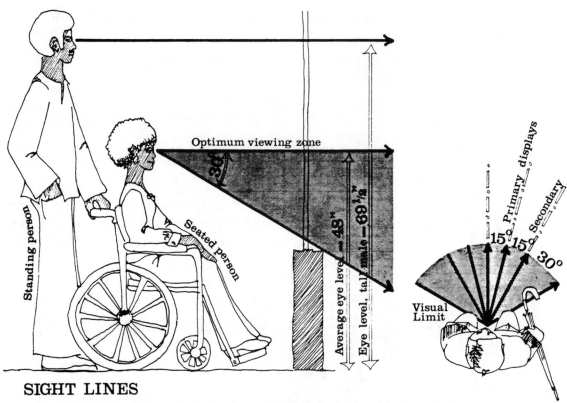

SIGHT LINES

Figure 2.5. Placement of signage for the handicapped. (Courtesy of General Services Administration)

that if we "use black or dark color background with while or light color figures or lettering" we will get "maximum visibility and legibility," especially if the reflectances of the two colors used show at least a 20-percent differential. Further, if a sign is at a height where people can touch it, the letters should be raised for the blind to feel them, since most blind people do not read Braille. Because the prevalence of partial and total color blindness in the population is unknown, it might be better to place white lettering on a black background for the greatest difference in reflectance and therefore the greatest visibility for all. Room numbers and names should also be designed in this way.

More Specifics for the Designer

The following are specific features to consider in interior design for handicapped persons. It should be pointed out that the following material does not necessarily agree with ANSI A117.1-1980, the American National Standard Specifications for Making Buildings and Facilites Accessible to and Usable by Physically Handicapped People. If a designer has a project where that standard must be met, he or she should consult it.

Stairs

There is great disagreement among several authorities about the correct dimensions of stairs. Because agreement has not been reached regarding the correct dimensions for several other elements of interior design, all dimensions given in the text are the author's choice as the most relevant available. Most of them, including those for stairs, await more research before values can be determined with any certainty.

Depending on the authority cited, riser height is correct at 4¾–7½ inches; the safest height is probably from 6 to 7½ inches. Tread depth is estimated from 10 to 12 inches, a narrower range. Stair width should be no less than 5 feet for two-way traffic and no less than 42 inches for one-way traffic. There is also disagreement on tread projection, but the probable best choice is a rounded projection of about ¾–1 inch. Treads and risers should be in contrasting colors for greater visibility, and must not be slippery.

Because stairs will not work for most people in wheelchairs (nor will escalators), ramps are used. Ramps should have a slope of 8.33 degrees or less (1-foot rise in 12 feet of length); they should be textured and nonslip, perhaps with transverse cleats at the edges with a clear pathway for wheelchairs through the center, especially at entrances.

Ramps and stairs should have graspable handrails with a 1½-inch round or oval diameter at a height of 34–36 inches, and they should be installed at least 1½ inches away from the wall to prevent scraped knuckles and fingers. These handrails should extend 18 inches beyond the ends of the ramp or stairs on at least one side. All handrails mentioned throughout this chapter should be able to support at least 250 pounds.

For stairs and ramps, the designer might consider two sets of handrails, especially if both handicapped children and adults are to use them. The second set of handrails should be at 16–18 inches from the surface of the stair or ramp, with the proper height depending "on the age group being served."

For full two-way passage, ramps should be at least 5 feet wide and should have curbs on each side at least 2 inches high to keep wheelchair users from running off the ramps; for one-way passage, the minimum is 36 inches wide. Every 30 feet, a ramp must have level rest areas of a minimum of 60 by 60 inches to accommodate wheelchairs; areas of this same dimension should be provided at the top and bottom of a ramp where it adjoins landings. There should also be a change in the color of the floor covering or a contrasting colored stripe as a visual cue to a change in level or slope; in fact, visual cues of this sort should be provided wherever there is a change in floor level.

Of course, stairs and ramps should be well illuminated.

Doors

To be really negotiable for people in wheelchairs or on crutches, doors, especially entrance and corridor doors, should be automatically operated and preferably sliding. They should open with an exerted pressure of no more than 8 pounds (preferably 5 pounds), and "the closing mechanism should provide a 4 to 6 second time delay." If the door is rotating on hinges, the actuating switch should be far enough away not to open on the wheelchair footrest. As a rule, automatic door closers are particularly difficult for the handicapped person to work against.

Door thresholds must be flush with the floor on both sides; raised thresholds are a formidable obstacle to the handicapped person in a wheelchair or on crutches. Revolving doors are impossible for the handicapped person to operate without assistance.

Although most standard references give smaller minimum widths for doors, the GSA architectural trainee's "scraped fingers" suggest that the minimum width for any door should be 36 inches if a wheelchair is to pass through it without injury to the hands propelling it. The lower edges of vision panels should start at 36 inches from the floor and probably no higher; they should, of course, be made of safety glass.

Horizontal lever-latch door handles 42 inches high or less are preferable to ordinary rotating knobs.

If there are two sets of doors in sequence, as in a lobby or corridor entrance, there must be room for a wheelchair to maneuver between the two. Depending on the reference used, this can be from 42 to 78 inches minimum, and it may depend on how the sets of doors swing. Because the typical wheelchair is 42 inches long, and some may be even longer, 78 inches is a safe minimum. In the North Carolina building code, we find that "the floor on the inside and outside of each doorway shall be level

2.6

Figure 2.6. Comparative passage between vertical points. (Courtesy of General Services Administration)
Figure 2.7. Turning requirements for person in wheelchair. (Courtesy of General Services Administration)

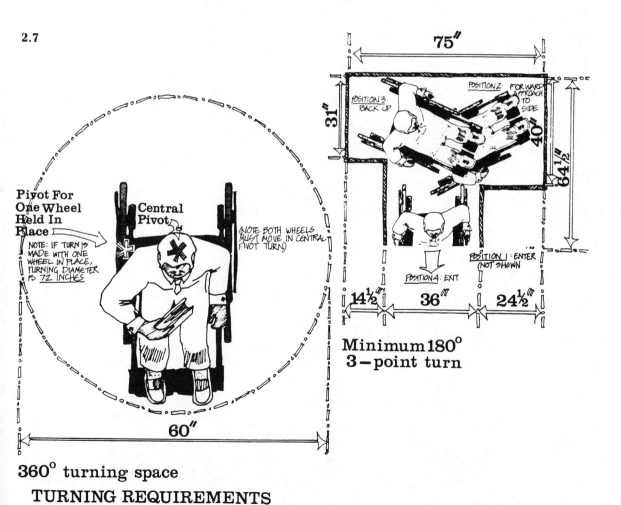

2.7

Pivot For One Wheel Held In Place

NOTE: IF TURN IS MADE WITH ONE WHEEL IN PLACE, TURNING DIAMETER IS 72 INCHES

Central Pivot

(NOTE BOTH WHEELS MUST MOVE IN CENTRAL PIVOT TURN)

60"

360° turning space

TURNING REQUIREMENTS

75"
31"
40"
64½"

POSITION 3: BACK UP
POSITION 2: FORWARD APPROACH TO SIDE
POSITION 4: EXIT
POSITION 1: ENTER (NOT SHOWN)

14½"   36"   24½"

Minimum 180°
3–point turn

32"   22"   28"   26½"

and clear for a distance of 5 feet from the door and shall extend 1 foot 6 inches beyond the side from which the door opens."

Several authorities recommend that the door hardware on "dangerous" doors be knurled (making the surface where the fingers touch abrasive or of a different texture from the normal smooth surface hardware) to indicate that the door should not be opened by the blind or disabled. Examples would be doors leading to loading docks, boiler rooms, fire escapes, and so on.

Doors should have kickplates extending all the way across the bottom part of the door surfaces, and they should be made of materials strong enough to withstand the onslaught of wheelchairs and crutches; the most successful ones seem to be made of steel. They should be at least 16 inches high.

The North Carolina building code also stipulates:

Where possible doors (for general use) shall be:
1. Held in open position, or
2. double-egress, or
3. push-pull, non-latching, or
4. automatically operated, or
5. eliminated.

For any power-operated doors, the designer should consult ANSI A156.10-1979, the American National Standard for Power-Operated Pedestrian Doors.

Windows

Since a person seated in a wheelchair cannot rise to look out a window, placing the sill at a height of no more than 2 feet will allow the seated wheelchair user to get an excellent view. Accessibility of window controls as well as drapery, curtain, and shade controls is also essential.

Edward Steinfeld suggests the installation of easily movable sliding windows. A British authority recommends that not only draperies, curtains, and shades be operated by cords, but also sash windows.

Floors

Any change in floor level without a ramp is a potential hazard to the handicapped. For instance, floor mats should be fitted into the floor so that their surfaces are level with the rest of the floor. Gratings and vents should not be located in a floor surface where people on crutches and in wheelchairs are to pass. The floor surface should be nonslip for crutches and easily transversed by wheelchairs. It should be nonglare for all.

Carpet is being used more frequently, and it should have a dense, level loop pile—of a pile height of no more than ½ inch—(which wears well in any case) with a dense underlayment or be directly glued to the floor with no underlayment at all; this is especially necessary for stairs. Travertine, polished stone, and terrazzo as floor surfaces are particularly hazardous to handicapped people on crutches.

Elevators

We will start by approaching the elevators: The buttons to press should not be too high—not over 48 inches from the floor, preferably about 42 inches. An ashtray should not be positioned under the buttons in consideration of the handicapped person in a wheelchair. To be safe, a Braille "up" and a Braille "down" (or raised letters) beside the buttons on the wall will help the blind, as will a loud bell to indicate "up" and a louder buzzer to indicate "down" (or vice versa, but standard signals are obviously necessary). The usual visual signals work for the deaf. One source suggests that a bell or buzzer should sound once for an elevator "going up and twice for the down direction." Another possibility might be a high-pitched sound for "up" and a low-pitched sound for "down."

Now the elevator doors open: If they close too quickly, the person in a wheelchair cannot pass through them in time. Elevator doors should have two sets of photoelectric door sensors, one low and one in the middle of the door edge, in order to be useful and safe for both the able-bodied and the handicapped.

An elevator must be the correct size for the person in a wheelchair to get into and out of it easily. The inside must be at least 60 by 60 inches, although 75 by 75 inches is better to accommodate a 24 by 72-inch standard stretcher.

Once inside the elevator, there are other features to check. Optimally, there should be Braille or raised numbers beside the visual ones, and an automatic voice device should call out the floors as the elevator approaches them. The highest call button inside the cab should be no more than 48 inches from the floor, although 44 inches is better. This level is also correct for the emergency telephone (which must be operable with a single hand) so that the person in a wheelchair can reach it. Of course, the floor of the elevator should be nonslip.

There should be handrails around the perimeter of the elevator, again with a 1½-inch round or oval diameter at least 1½ inches away from the elevator wall at a height of 34–36 inches. Incidentally, elevators should stop exactly at each floor level so that wheelchairs can travel easily.

The number of each floor should be identified on the jamb of each elevator opening (not on the cab); the floor number should also appear on the wall opposite each elevator opening so that people inside the elevator can see at which floor the elevator has stopped. The floor numbers should also be visible (typically over the doors) as the elevator travels to each floor. The previous recommendations for easily readable signage should be followed.

For elevators, the designer should consult the American National Standard Safety Code for Elevators, Dumbwaiters, Escalators, and Moving Walks, ANSI A17.1-1978 and A17.1a-1979.

Water Fountains

The top rim of water fountains should fall into the 30–34-inch-high range. They should be operable by both palm and foot, with lever-type control for the palm. Whether wall-hung, free-standing, or in an alcove, the fountain should have a clear space in front of it at least 29 inches from the floor, 30 inches deep, and 48 inches wide for wheelchairs to approach. A step on the wall for children (for wall-hung fountains) is helpful, or a separate fountain at a lower height might be furnished. There should be a minimum of one such fountain per floor of a multistory building. So that a cup or glass may be used, the minimum height for the stream of water should be at least 4 inches.

Telephones

The coin slots and/or controls should be no more than 48 inches from the floor, and there should be a clear, unobstructed space 60 by 60 inches in front of wall-mounted or free-standing telephones. Typical telephone booths cannot be used by wheelchair occupants; push-button phones are easier for the handicapped to operate than regular dials. Volume controls should be provided for the hearing-impaired, and the cord on the moveable receiver-transmitter should be at least 36 inches long.

Directories should be mounted on a shelf at a 30–34-inch height in such a way that wheelchair users can reach them; if they project from a wall, there should be a 29-inch-high clear space under them. There should be a minimum of one accessible telephone with volume control per bank of phones.

Figure 2.8. Telephone and fountain placement dimensions. (Courtesy of General Services Administration)

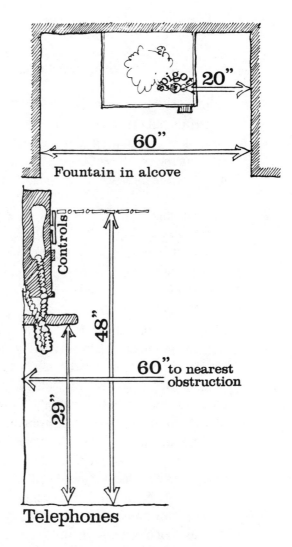

Fountain in alcove

Telephones

Letter Drops

To be accessible to the handicapped, letter drops must be placed 40 inches from the floor or an inch or two lower, but certainly no higher.

Electric Fixtures

Light switches can be located between 36 and 48 inches from the floor, but 42 inches seems to be the preferred height. Electric outlets should probably be between 18 and 24 inches from the floor as a minimum, but a 30–36-inch range of heights would probably be more convenient for all users. Extension cords are hazardous for the handicapped, especially when carelessly placed; they are easy to trip over and get entangled in wheelchairs and crutches. If extension cords are absolutely necessary, they should be placed under metal protectors or enclosed in conduits. Flat cables used under carpet squares are an even better solution.

Lighting Levels

Some authorities recommend lighting levels as low as 5–10 foot-candles in certain public areas of buildings; the setting of these levels requires a great deal of research. The suggested values seem low, especially considering the number of people who have visual difficulties and those who have trouble interpreting information (see Tables 2–1 and 2–2).

Fire Alarms and Thermostats

Because fire alarms and thermostats must be reached by wheelchair users, they cannot be more than 48 inches from the floor; 44 inches is better. Visual fire alarms might be provided for the deaf and audible ones for the blind. All reachable signs should be duplicated in Braille or raised letters and numbers for the blind.

Corners

Richard G. Coss discusses collisions that occur at corners where corridors meet and suggests several methods for dealing with this problem, which is very serious for the handicapped. He recommends bevelled corners, convex mirrors, Swiss-highway style, or perhaps corners made of clear glass for greater visibility. Coss also suggests low planters, perhaps containing plants with spreading leaves, or a change of wall or floor surface, along with deflection graphics (decorations that would draw attention to the corner and thus force people to use a larger cornering radius) as warnings to avoid collisions.

It should be noted that low signs, clocks, and other projections from walls in any area that the handicapped use are a hazard unless there is a clear space beneath them at least 7 feet from the floor. Nothing should project more than 4 inches from the wall in a pathway to be used by wheelchairs. All corners in corridors and other areas where wheelchairs and crutches are used should be reinforced.

Dining Areas

In cafeterias, restaurants, and other eating areas, tables must not have aprons to impede wheelchairs and there must be a clear distance from the table top to the floor of 29 inches. Table bases must also be carefully chosen so that they do not block wheelchairs or keep them from the tables.

The cafeteria's food must be accessible by both sight and reach so that the handicapped can easily place their selections on trays; it would be helpful if trays could be attached to wheelchairs for transport to the tables.

Restrooms

One prime requirement for restrooms is a wide, 36-inch door and wide clearances everywhere. There should be a 60 by 60-inch turnabout space for wheelchairs inside the room clear of all toilet stalls, wash basins, and screens.

The toilet stall for the use of the handicapped should optimally be 72 by 72 inches, with the toilet set off to one side at the back (for side transfer from a wheelchair), with a horizontal grab bar beside it and accessible to it 33 inches from the floor, extending 1 foot 6 inches beyond the front of the water closet. A short vertical grab bar toward the front of

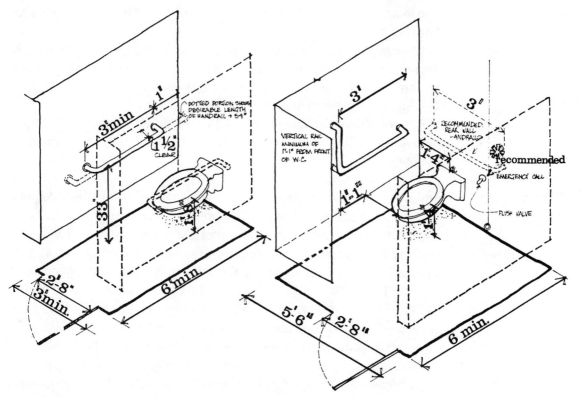

Figure 2.9. Restroom stall dimensions. (Courtesy of General Services Administration)

the water closet should also be available, as well as a horizontal grab bar over the tank.

Wash basins should have 29 inches of clearance under them so that they can be used from wheelchairs; rim height, however, should be 34 inches, and there should be a 30-inch by 48-inch clear space for approach including 19 of the 48 inches underneath the basin. For use by the handicapped, easily operable lever-type faucet handles are best. Pipes under wash basins should be insulated or boxed off to protect the legs of the wheelchair user who may have no feeling in his or her legs.

Water closets should be between 17 and 19 inches high; most authorities recommend a 19-inch height and suggest a seat adapter to bring existing lower water closets to that seating height for easier transfers from wheelchairs.

Urinals can be either wall- or floor-mounted, although floor-mounted urinals are best, especially for small boys. If they are wall-mounted, the maximum hieght for the lower part of the basin is 17 inches. Vertical grab bars are recommended for urinals.

Mirrors should have a maximum bottom height from the floor of 38 inches, and 36 inches is preferred; this is also true for usable shelves. Soap and towel dispensers can be located between 18 and 48 inches from the floor, as can trash disposal devices.

Restroom floors should be level with corridor floors, and there should be one accessible restroom for each sex on each floor of a multistory building.

Offices and Office Furniture

Any office that is to be used by the handicapped must provide adequate clearance for wheelchair users. The minimum is a 36-inch, one-way passage between furniture, partitions, and work stations, and 42 inches is preferred. For major access pathways and aisles where two-way passage is necessary, 54 inches is the minimum width and 60 inches is preferred, though one key government agency requires 66-inch aisle widths. If level passages are 50 feet or more long, 60 by 60-inch wheelchair turning spaces should be provided, at least every 50 feet.

Regarding office furnishings, it is very important that there be no protruding legs or supports on furniture or screens for the handicapped to trip over; nor should the furniture have sharp edges. The GSA's Federal Supply Service (GSA-FSS) has required that all furniture edges and cor-

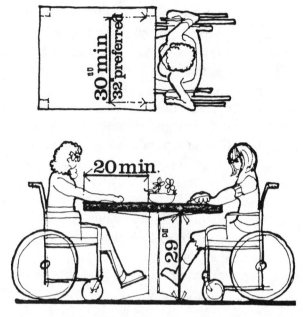

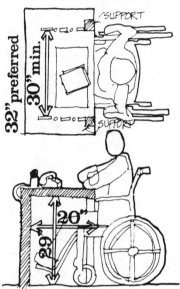

Minimum Clearance

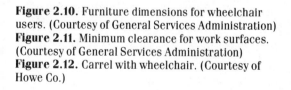

FURNITURE

2.10

Work Surfaces

2.11

2.12

Figure 2.10. Furniture dimensions for wheelchair users. (Courtesy of General Services Administration)
Figure 2.11. Minimum clearance for work surfaces. (Courtesy of General Services Administration)
Figure 2.12. Carrel with wheelchair. (Courtesy of Howe Co.)

ners be rounded and have a minimum 1/8-inch radius. Office furniture should also be strong enough for the handicapped to lean on without mishap; GSA-FSS has therefore required that all horizontal office furniture surfaces be able to support 200 pounds of pressure without tipping or displacing, and with a maximum deflection of 1/16th inch.

From another source we learn: "A group of University of Michigan industrial design students has created a worktable designed specifically for handicapped workers. . . . Features include adjustable heights and cutout portions in the table top, allowing workers in wheelchairs to sit close and stabilize themselves with their arms." Widespread use of such features could increase work opportunities for the handicapped.

Work surfaces, tables, and desks should be so adaptable that the removal of drawers and aprons provides a 25–29-inch clear distance (25 inches is the minimum) from the floor enabling people in wheelchairs to use them; a minimum knee space width of 32 inches is also necessary. This means that furniture must be demountable in parts, and that U-shaped desks should be considered.

Drawer pull forces must not exceed 8 pounds; GSA-FSS has required that drawers be operable with one hand, and that the operating force required not exceed 3 3/4 pounds for some applications. Drawer hardware should be strong, since the handicapped sometimes use it for support; it should be flush or recessed, and trim should not protrude beyond 1/8 inch.

Most desks are 30 inches deep; however, GSA-FSS is now requiring a 25-inch maximum depth for work surfaces where overhead storage is in use so that the limited arm reach of a wheelchair user will still be effective; for the same purpose, units without a work surface take a 20-inch depth maximum.

Regarding personal storage, hanger bars and hooks inside wardrobes and closets must be adjustable between 66 inches and 48 inches in height above the floor.

The General Services Administration has made the following statement about working chairs:

The perfect chair does not exist. People of extremely small or large size, for example, do not benefit from a standard seat size or width. Many disabled people have seating needs that conflict with other disabled or average users.

The ranges of chair adjustability are therefore important to the handi-capped (see Chapter 5, "Sitting Down"). In fact custom-made chairs, especially wheelchairs, are occasionally necessary for disabled people to work comfortably. An unforgettable memory is the work of two devoted members of the staff at Apple Creek Institute in Ohio making custom wheelchairs for mentally retarded children with physical handicaps and deformities. Without specially made chairs to fit their deformities and reduced physical capacities, these children could not be active at all.

Kitchens

It is useful to compare the American kitchen with a Swedish system, Fokus, which seems better able to solve the problems of handicapped people. The typical kitchen shown in the most advanced American source is a Pullman type with a refrigerator, base cabinet, and range on one side, and a sink and work space on the other; there is an aisle between the two. This aisle is preferably at least 66 inches wide to allow a wheel-chair to turn in it, and it should be 72 inches wide. The Swedes advocate an L-shaped configuration, or an "angle kitchen" as they call it; the whole kitchen then becomes a wheelchair turning space.

Both the American and Swedish systems agree that the controls for the cooking range should be at the front of the range so that they are readily accessible to wheelchair users. This placement also obviates the hazard of burns inherent in having to stretch over the burners to reach controls placed at the back of the range.

While both systems stress the necessity for knee room under any hor-izontal surface where a handicapped person works in the kitchen (and this knee clearance varies from 26 to 32½ inches, depending on the source), the Swedish Fokus system introduces *adjustable height* burner surfaces, ovens, work surfaces, and sinks. Each item is securely mounted on a double track fastened to the wall, with flexible pipes where necessary, so that Fokus kitchen components can be adjusted to the various sizes and needs of handicapped people.

There are other items to keep in mind. Cabinet knobs should be at least 18 inches from the floor. The requirements for reachable shelves in restrooms also apply to kitchen shelves and cabinets; they should be no more than 40 inches from the floor, and 36 inches is preferred. American cabinets and counters are easier to use if they have a toe space 6 inches deep by 8 3/4 inches high.

Bathrooms

"Inward opening doors are a safety hazard," according to Edward Steinfeld. Clearances under the wash basin and around the bathroom are identical to those recommended for restrooms; water closet grab bars should also be the same and positioned in the same way.

Most American sources recommend a 19-inch height for the water closet seating surface, but as pointed out by Alexander Kira in *The Bathroom*, for most elderly people this height causes difficulties in defecation. The Swedish Fokus system has solved this problem brilliantly by developing a water closet that is adjustable in height.

A fixture in most American bathroom is the tub-shower combination, and a vertical grab bar at one end of the tub together with a horizontal grab bar over the controls is recommended. The controls are preferably inset and placed midway between the ends of the tub on the wall. It is necessary that *both* upper parts of the sides of the tub have surfaces that are easy to grip, and there should be a fold-away seat for tub or shower use about 18 inches from the tub bottom. Both the tub bottom and the separate shower floor should be nonslip. "A shower is the safest and most convenient means of bathing for a person with severe disabilities," writes Edward Steinfeld.

The Swedish Fokus system has an adjustable-height shower with an adjustable-height seat; it also contains an adjustable-height wash basin for the bathroom. Of course, the whole bathroom should have a nonslip floor.

Bedrooms

Care should be taken in planning bedrooms for use by the handicapped to allow for wheelchair movement and turning as well as access to closets. The height of the bed should be coordinated with the height of the wheelchair seat for convenient transfer from one to the other. One authority recommends that "the mattress top be approximately 22 inches above the floor." Electrically operated beds, for both hospital and domestic use, are available. An excellent review of devices developed for the use of handicapped people in the bedroom appeared in 1976 in *The Architects' Journal*.

Seating for Assembly

The North Carolina state building code requires that "identified spaces for the wheelchair handicapped shall be provided" and that wider seats with extra leg space be installed for handicapped people using leg braces, crutches, and/or walkers. The ratio is 1 percent, or a minimum of one such seat for any place of assembly witn fixed-type seating for 75 persons or more. The code also gives detailed standards for table heights, table spacing, food service rails, and fixed station seating for instructional facilities, dining halls, libraries, and laboratories.

Federal Laws and Regulations

Through its Public Buildings Service, the General Services Administration will soon make some of the above recommendations mandatory for new public buildings. In addition, the U.S. Department of Education has issued its long-awaited regulations on "Non-Discrimination on the Basis of Handicap." This publication incorporates the American National Standards Institute's Specifications for Making Buildings and Facilities Accessible and affects all buildings where U.S. government-funded programs are housed. In addition, the DE has issued its own *Technical Handbook* for the design of barrier-free facilities.

Incidentally, issuance of the DE's regulations was probably hastened by a sit-in of handicapped people in DE facilities. The handicapped are also suing various government agencies for access to public buildings and winning.

Compliance

How does one determine whether or not buildings and facilities comply with the U.S. Department of Education's regulations (or the regulations of any other governmental agency that may affect the execution of a project) that they be accessible to the handicapped? The following list concentrates on USDE because that agency's regulations are issued and in force.

There are three documents to have at hand:

1. ANSI A117.1-1961 (R1971) *American National Standard Specifications for Making Buildings and Facilities Accessible to and Usable by the Physically Handicapped.* New York: American National Standard Institute, 1961, revised 1971, reprinted 1977. This standard is incorporated by specific reference into HEW's regulations for accessibility.
2. ANSI A117.1-1980, the revised and greatly expanded version of the above; as this is being written the U.S. Department of Education has not changed its inclusion by reference in its rules to the older version from 1971. The new version may be included at some future date, however.

3. *Technical Handbook for Facilities Engineering & Construction Manual, Part 4: Facilities Design and Construction - 4.00 Architectural - Section 4.12: Design of Barrier-Free Facilities.* Washington: Office of the Secretary, Department of Health Education and Welfare, January 1975, Rev. August 1978. This was the latest version available at this writing; check with DE for the most current version at the time reference to the *Handbook* becomes necessary.

If, of course, a project is being accomplished under the rules of another government agency, whether it be federal or state, get a copy of that agency's rules.

The DE's *Technical Handbook* is particularly helpful because it has separate chapters on:

1. Criteria for full accessibility to HEW-owned facilities (for new construction and alteration projects after January 1, 1975),
2. Minimum mandatory requirements for accessibility (for federally assisted projects, including new construction and alteration projects),
3. Accessibility requirements for leased facilities, including:

   a. new leases, including new, succeeding, superseding, extension, or renewal type actions after January 1, 1977, and
   b. guidelines for retrofitting of leased facilities (whose remaining term is in excess of four years as of July 17, 1977).

As stated in the *Technical Handbook*: "Each of the three chapters is organized to be used as a checklist for assessing the compliance of a specific project or an existing facility covered by the particular chapter."

The DE has made its *Technical Handbook* understandable; its appendices provide information about wheelchairs (the ANSI *Standard* does so also), as well as sections of the applicable laws and regulations that explain the law, its exceptions and waivers, and the machinery of administration. Another big advantage to having the *Technical Handbook* is being able to ensure that the person in charge of a project is aware of the applicable regulations.

There are some things to watch for in using the *Technical Handbook*. To quote from it: "The use of the words 'shall' and 'must' in the text indicates that the item is a mandatory requirement. The word 'should' indicates that the item is recommended as a means of making the environment accessible." In other words, there are requirements and there are recommendations. Common sense will, of course, dictate which recommendations should be used.

As examples of items that fall into the mandatory and suggested categories, one of the chapters has a section on "Identification and Warning." The DE recommends that fully accessible buildings *should* display the International Symbol of Access, *should* use knurled-finish handles on doors leading to dangerous areas, and *should* provide abrasive strips or textured flooring material on floors at the head of open stairs, ramps, or curbs. The same section makes it mandatory that plaques with very specific dimensions be used to identify rooms and offices; that warning signals *shall* be both visible and audible; that low-hanging signs, light fixtures, door closers, or similar objects *shall* not protrude into regular traffic ways at a height of less than 84 inches; and that hazardous areas of a temporary nature *shall* be separated on all open sides by barricades placed at least 96 inches from the hazard and equipped with both visible and audible warning devices.

The *Technical Handbook* leaves some questions unanswered. For example, "nonslip materials" are required in several instances. It would be well to find out exactly what materials are needed for each application and, further, how they are to be cleaned and maintained to meet the DE's requirements. It should not be assumed that a particular material or procedure will meet its requirements unless the DE says so. (If your own checklist and evaluation procedure turns up something you don't fully understand, don't hesitate to ask DE. Their people have been very helpful in writing this chapter, especially Mike Lopez and Kurt Vragel of the Denver Regional DE Office.)

In addition to asking questions, the designer should use a common sense approach to the *Technical Handbook*. For instance, there are two definitions of "handrails," one for ramps (exterior and interior) and one for stairs (exterior and interior). Both definitions should be combined to obtain the relevant information. Although both specify that handrails must be 32 inches off the walking or climbing surfaces, one definition holds that "rails must be smooth, at least 1 1/2 inches clear of walls," and the other that "rails should be circular or oval in section, 1 1/2 inches in diameter and have a non-slip finish."

The designer should also realize that these regulations are not permanent and that there may be changes in the future. One candidate for change is the recommendation for minimum adequate lighting on ramps and stairs—5 foot-candles. At some point, it will be realized that there are at least 5 million Americans who have severe visual difficulties and at least 25 million more who do not see well. When this happens, the minimum will have a good chance of being raised.

A change might also come about in the requirement that doors have a clear opening of at least 32 inches when open. According to the *Technical Handbook*, although the typical wheelchair is 26 inches wide when open, there are standard wheelchairs on the market that are 32 1/2 inches wide. But even with the 26-inch chair, the present requirement leaves a bare 3 inches on each side for pushing hands and knuckles. A clear opening of 36 inches would ensure the comfort of those in wheelchairs.

There is something else that can be done in the planning stages: a person in a wheelchair can be asked to tour the proposed facility or review the plans. He or she will help the designer to understand what will or will not work and why.

Compliance and Cost-Effectiveness

Under the regulations issued by the U.S. Department of Education to implement Section 504 of the Rehabilitation Act of 1973 (which prohibits discrimination against qualified handicapped persons in DE-assisted programs), schools, colleges, and health facilities are required to make buildings or parts of buildings accessible for the handicapped to participate in the activities being supported there by agency funds.

According to David S. Tatel, Director of the Office for Civil Rights, DHEW: "Specifically, the notion that these institutions must eliminate all architectural barriers . . . has gained widespread belief. This is erroneous. The regulations do not require the elimination of all architectural barriers." He continues: "While a part or percentage of an institution's facilities must be accessible, there is no prescribed number or percentage that is required. The object is to make the programs of an institution accessible, not every classroom or dormitory room." For health care institutions, this means that every service must be accessible to handicapped people, not that every part of the institution be accessible. Tatel adds:

Institutions that overestimate what is required and elect to do nothing at all because of this misunderstanding will do a disservice to themselves as well as to handicapped persons.

There will be some costs and burdens on the institutions, fully anticipated by Congress in the enactment of the law and the legitimate costs will pose a serious enough problem without the additional headaches caused to administrators by unfounded fears. A recent report by Mainstream, Inc., a private nonprofit organization that encourages compliance with the Rehabilitation Act, indicates that the cost of making 34 facilities accessible—in a survey they conducted—totaled one cent per square foot. These same facilities spend 13 cents a square foot to clean and polish their floors.

It is obvious from Tatel's statement that he believes that people and institutions have many illusions about the difficulties of complying with the standards of Section 504. There are some facts that will make it easier and less costly to satisfy the rules. For new construction, the architects can simply be instructed to comply with the regulations, which can be done with minimal additional cost; however, where old constructions are being used that were not designed to meet today's accessibility standards, several considerations will help to keep costs down. First, as Tatel stated, the DHEW is interested in making an institution's *programs* accessible, not whole hospitals, buildings, or campuses.

Second, the regulations apply to *qualified* handicapped people, patients, medical personnel, students, and faculty. According to DE rules: "With respect to employment, a handicapped person is one who, with reasonable accommodation, can perform the essential function of the job in question." Further, a qualified student is one who can meet the entrance requirements of the institution he or she wants to enter. For health care providers who receive DE financial assistance (including Medicare payments), a handicapped patient is one "who meets the essential eligibility requirements" to be a patient, and they must take steps to accommodate those who have "a physical or mental impairment which substantially limits one or more major life activities." These major impairments are not always obvious or visible. Heart disease, epilepsy, mental illness, and rheumatoid arthritis are examples of serious, nonvisible handicaps.

Third, there is an exemption for institutions employing fourteen persons or fewer: they are permitted to refer handicapped people to larger institutions.

Fourth, although the regulations of Section 504 supersede state codes and rules on accessibility, certain states that have been leaders in breaking down the barriers, especially North Carolina, have different requirements. It would be wise to consult state authorities before planning any changes, and since some cities have different rules, it would be wise to check with them also. One clear message comes through in all this: The designer should be certain of the requirements *before* beginning a project, since additional changes will cost more money.

There is another possible complication that should be mentioned. The designer may be receiving federal financial assistance for a program from agencies other than the DE; all federal agencies are required to issue their own "504" regulations on accessibility, and while none have issued them at this writing, it is possible that each one might be a little different, so it would be wise to consult them, too.

Fifth, it should be kept in mind that help *is* available. Each DE regional office has a facilities engineering and construction unit with architects and professional engineers who can help to plan renovations of facilities. Lawyers in each regional DE office are also available to answer questions. There is further the possibility (not yet a reality) that the DE might institute a grant program to assist needy institutions in meeting accessibility requirements.

Sixth, the DE warns against making any building accessible for any one particular person because this is not cost-effective. If changes are made, they should be planned so that the building is accessible to all kinds of handicapped people, as the rules stipulate.

Seventh, there are numerous examples where common sense and ingenuity have made facilities accessible at minimum cost. Some of them follow. Rather than requiring recessed water fountains that are costly to install, the DE has permitted some facilities to use a paper cup dispenser hung on the wall by the fountain. In a few facilities, this alternative has obviated the necessity of changing the height of the fountain. In one building, it was less expensive to construct an outside elevator than a complex series of ramps. In certain circumstances, common toilets for both men and women that were modified for handicapped use have been permitted.

In its own Hubert Humphrey Building (formerly called South Portal), the DE experimented with demountable, changeable furniture systems, and one of the specfications was that these systems accommodate handicapped workers. In the original installation, *every* work station and *all* the aisles were designed to provide access for people in wheelchairs.

Although this is not the official opinion of the DE, there are knowledge-able officials in the agency who feel that this solution used up too many square feet, since every work station had space for wheelchairs. They found that although extra space should be planned for wheelchair users, this was not necessary in every office.

It would be wise, however, to consider furniture systems that are changeable and demountable, especially those with height-adjustable work surfaces, to accommodate wheelchair users and persons whose disabilities permit them to work only at certain heights. These features also make it possible to change configurations so that there is enough space in a work station to allow wheelchair access and use. Adjustable-height seating is, of course, also necessary.

Another way of meeting accessibility requirements without structural changes is to bring a particular service to the handicapped. One univer-sity provided a room on the first (accessible) floor of an older building where its financial aid people could come from their offices on the sec-ond floor to render service to handicapped students unable to travel to the second floor. More than one university has moved courses to acces-sible floors to make possible the participation of handicapped students. Using this method, a large midwestern university that has made approx-imately one-third of its buildings accessible is able to accommodate the needs of all its handicapped students. The DE also suggests the use of aides in libraries to bring books to handicapped people who cannot reach stacks accessible only by stairways; this makes unnecessary the addition of extra elevators or lifts.

Another suggestion that the DE has offered to reduce costs is the use, by some county or even state agencies, of vocational school educational programs in the planning and construction of ramps, widening of doors, and revamping of toilet facilities. These projects can be made into class assignments.

In summary, the designer should use common sense and ingenuity and take advantage of all opportunities for consultation.

The University of Denver's Approach

The University of Denver's program to accommodate the needs of the handicapped is two-pronged: satisfying accessibility standards in new buildings under construction and renovating existing buildings for con-tinued use. The new buildings are, of course, being designed from scratch and the architects can ensure that federal requirements are met in the typical architectural design process, according to the director of Facilities Planning and Management for the university, Jerry L. Schillinger. Making older buildings accessible is not that simple however, even though the university was involved with accessibility long before the introduction of any legal requirements and long before the DHEW issued its *Technical Handbook* on the subject in 1975. In the intervening years, new buildings have been built and old ones have been renovated with accessibility goals being satisfied.

At the University of Denver, these goals take several forms. For instance, though a single ramp can cost up to $12,000, eleven ramps have been finished. Although it is difficult to construct ramps at the front entrance of all old buildings that are being renovated, the university prefers the front location. In all new buildings, the ramps are in front because the university does not want to force handicapped faculty and students to use the back entrance, which would in effect make them second-class citizens.

When older buildings are recycled, the interiors are completely gutted if funds are available, making accessibility an easier goal to reach. For instance, several years ago, the University of Denver relocated its Graduate School of Social Work into an existing building that was gutted, and then totally redesigned and remodeled. At that time, a grant from the Kresge Foundation provided basic funds, and the university was able to obtain an additional grant from the Colorado State Division of Vocational Rehabilitation for the express purpose of providing ramps and elevators for necessary accessibility.

The University of Denver, however, is a private school and has the same financial problems that all private institutions of higher learning face today. To meet these problems in terms of its physical plant, the university is in the midst of a $50 million fund drive that has passed the halfway mark. Most of the $50 million is earmarked for new buildings, but the fund drive will also raise significant amounts for the renovation of several existing structures on the campus.

As an example, a building from the 1890s now scheduled for renovation represented a typical planning problem: Should UD renovate it or replace it with a new structure? Detailed analysis showed that it could be gutted, leaving the walls and foundation. What will be left is worth $15 per square foot and well worth saving, according to Schillinger, who added that $3.5 million will be spent to gut the interior and replace it. Ramps and elevators will be added so that every student and member of the faculty can use all of the areas within the building.

This particular renovation is a part of a 3½–4-year phased plan that the university has begun; each element of the plan for accessibility is put under contract as funds become available for use.

In the operation of this plan, the same kind of analysis that was used for the 1890s building is used in deciding whether to renovate or replacing each structure on the campus. Generally, the buildings that the university is replacing with new construction were built during World War II. The plan has as its first objective to make classrooms, offices, and residences accessible. However, with the mix of old and new buildings on the campus, it is obviously impossible to make all buildings and all areas of all buildings accessible.

According to Schillinger, each building must be analyzed separately and thoroughly; common sense plays a vital role in each analysis. For instance, the university is making *some* of every type of living unit accessible according to the number of handicapped people expected to use any particular type. With the large number of existing living units, for example, money is not available to renovate them all, and thus, just one of the married student housing units is being made accessible.

Where renovation or relocation into new facilities is not feasible, other solutions are sometimes implemented. For example, the university's financial aid office is on an upper floor and it would be too costly to move its machinery and files (in addition to electrical connections) to a lower floor. Thus, for those who are not able to reach the financial aid office, the office will serve them in a first-floor room reserved for this purpose.

In order for every student to have access to every program in the various curricula that the university offers, it is sometimes necessary to move a particular class to a lower-floor classroom. Other common sense measures are also taken to ensure accessibility.

The problem is not, however, merely one of making offices, classrooms, and buildings accessible; the University is also tackling the problem of cross-connections. Some of every type of campus buildings must be connected to each other by pathways that the handicapped can use, and a large part of the University of Denver campus is already linked in this way.

A Bill of Rights

The following guidelines may be considered a Bill of Rights for human beings who use interior spaces. *Any* user of an interior space should have the right to:

1. Enough dimensional space to comfortably engage in the intended activity in that space, with no crowding permitted.
2. The necessary artifacts for that activity.
3. Barrier-free space so that any user, handicapped or hale, can use the space.
4. Adjustable artifacts so that they can fit any user.
5. Flexibility of artifacts so that they can be moved or changed to fit the needs of the user and the activity.
6. Adjustable and changeable light, heat, sound, and humidity to fit the needs and wants of the user.
7. Interior environments which offer the user options of behavior in that environment.
8. Interior environments that do not harm the user, especially those where the user is being treated for some form of ill health.

References

"Affirmative Action Obligations of Contractors and Subcontractors for Disabled Veterans and Veterans of the Vietnam Era," *Federal Register*, vol. 41, no. 124 (June 25, 1976), pp. #26386-26393. Also vol. 42, no. 70 (April 12, 1977), p. 19145.

ANSI A117.1-1980 American National Standard Specifications for Making Buildings and Facilities Accessible to and Usable by the Physically Handicapped, (New York: American National Standards Institute, 1980).

Michael J. Bednar, ed., *Barrier-Free Environments* (Stroudsburg: Dowden, Hutchinson & Ross, 1977).

Sven-Olof Brattgard, "The Fokus Housing System," in Bednar, *Barrier-Free Environments*.

Jerry Brown, "Travel for the Handicapped Client," *Travel Weekly* (March 31, 1977), pp. 13, 16, 17.

Richard G. Coss, "The Cut-Off Hypothesis: Its Relevance to the Design of Public Places," *Man-Environment Systems* 3, no. 6, 1973, 427.

"Day on Wheels," GSA DC 75-7013 Washington, D.C.: General Services Administration, Public Buildings Service, January 1975.

"Design Criteria New Public Building Accessibility," PBS(PCD): DG5 Washington, D.C.: General Services Administration, Public Buildings Service, May 1977.

Selwyn Goldsmith, *Designing for the Disabled* (London: Royal Institute of British Architects, 1976 and New York: McGraw-Hill Book Co., 1976).

"The Handicapped Majority," *Industrial Design* (May 1974), p. 25.

"HEW Furniture Systems Study—South Portal Building," mimeographed, Washington, D.C.: Department of Health, Education and Welfare and General Services Administration, Public Buildings Service and Federal Supply Service, July 1977.

"Implementation of Executive Order #11914 - Non-Discrimination on the Basis of Handicap in Federally Assisted Programs," *Federal Register*, vol. 43, no. 9 (January 13, 1978), pp. 2132-2139.

Industrial Design 24, no. 2 (March-April, 1977), p. 14.

Alexander Kira, *The Bathroom* (New York: Viking Press, 1976).

Joseph A. Koncelik, *Designing the Open Nursing Home* (Stroudsburg: Dowden, Hutchinson & Ross, 1976).

Ronald L. Mace, (Betty Laslett, ed.), *An Illustrated Handbook of the North Carolina State Building Code*, Handicapped Section (Raleigh: North Carolina Department of Insurance, 1974). Also amendment of September 14, 1976 [11x 3.2 (c)] and amendment of March 8, 1977 (11X 4.3.1).

P. J. R. Nichols, "Aids for Daily Living: The Problems of the Severely Disabled," *Applied Ergonomics* 7, no. 3 (September 1976), pp. 126-132.

"Non-Discrimination on the Basis of Handicap," *Federal Register*, vol. 42, no. 86 (May 4, 1977), pp. 22676-22702.

"Part 60-741—Affirmative Action Obligations of Contractors and Subcontractors for Handicapped Workers," *Federal Register*, vol. 41, no. 75 (April 16, 1976), pp. 16147-16155. Also vol. 42, no. 12 (January 18, 1977), p. 3307.

Van Richards, *Cast for a Character* (Boston: Massachusetts Arts for the Handicapped Week, 1977).

Gary O. Robinette, "Site Planning and Design to Accommodate the Disabled," *The Construction Specifier* 28, no. 11 (November 1975), p. 27.

Edward J. Steinfeld, *Barrier-Free Design for the Elderly and Disabled* (Syracuse, N.Y.: Syracuse University, 1976).

Technical Handbook for Facilities Engineering and Construction Manual, Part 4: Facilities Design and Construction - 4.00 Architectural, Section 4.12: Design of Barrier-Free Facilities (Washington, D. C.: Office of the Secretary, Department of Health and Welfare, January 1975), revised August 1978.

"Three Wheelchair Units," *The Architects' Journal* (April 20, 1977), pp. 745-753.

Harold P. Van Cott and Robert G. Kinkade, eds., *Human Engineering Guide to Equipment Design*, rev. ed. (Washington, D.C.: U.S. Government Printing Office, 1972).

Alan G. Winslow, "Access to the Environment," in Bednar, *Barrier-Free Environments*.

Wolf Wolfensberger, "The Normalization Principle, and Some Major Implications to Architectural-Environmental Design," in Bednar, *Barrier-Free Environments*.

Note: At the present writing, the two most useful publications are:

"Design Criteria New Public Building Accessibility," as noted above. Available at regional GSA-PBS offices.

Technical Handbook for Facilities Engineering and Construction Manual, as noted above.

3 *Light, Color, Texture, Complexity, and Health*

This chapter is a tribute to the work of the late Darell Boyd Harmon, optical theorist and biomechanics authority; the author had the good fortune to study with Harmon and this chapter is the result.

Harmon's Physiological Approach to Color and Light

Harmon was dissatisfied with psychological explanations of how we use color to see. He felt that these psychological explanations contain too much subjective material and, in addition, are not really measurable. His approach was a physiological one, starting with the entrance of light into the eye.

As a single-ray bundle of light enters your eye, the light is distributed along the central axis of the ray bundle with the yellow-green part of the spectrum falling to focus on the retina. Blue and green portions come to focus in front of the retina; orange and red come to focus behind the retina. These facts account for blue and green being called "receding" colors since because they come to focus in front of the retina, we must in effect pull them back in order to see the details of patterns and colors. Conversely, red and orange are called "advancing" colors since we must pull reds and oranges forward to bring them into focus.

These shifts of focus change the apparent position of the background color: if the background color is blue, blue will seem to be moving away from the viewer, and conversely, if the background color is red, red will seem to move toward the viewer. It is therefore possible to make a room seem larger with the use of blue and smaller with the use of red; the magnitude of the effect will, of course, depend on the saturation of the colors involved—the stronger the saturation, the larger the effect. Harmon conducted an experiment in which a wall was painted pure, primary red at 50 percent reflectance; an object placed against it appeared to be one-third larger at a six-meter distance from the viewer, as measured with a retinascope. However, people interpret spacial shifts differently; some interpret them as size changes in objects while others interpret them as differences in distances from whatever they are looking at. In this situation the wall appeared to be two-thirds of a meter closer than it really was as measured with a retinascope.

Harmon also conducted an experiment using a three-color wall. At the top was a band of pure white two feet down the wall. The next band down was raw umber gray at 70 percent reflectance for seven and one-half feet, and below that was a thirty-inch band of primary blue at 55 percent reflectance. In this situation, at a distance of six meters from the viewer, the blue apparently moved five-sixths of a meter away from the viewer as measured with a retinascope. Pure black and pure white also apparently move in a similar fashion; black seems to move toward the viewer, while white seems to recede from the viewer.

People with eye problems may see these color displacements in an opposite way from the reactions described. For instance, some near-sighted people in a contrast situation may see blue as approaching rather than as the expected recession.

From Harmon's experiments it is possible to predict these types of color reactions to a limited extent. Three factors are to be considered here:

1. The degree of saturation of the color involved; the stronger the saturation, the stronger the reaction.
2. The percentage of reflectance of the surface; the higher the reflectance, the stronger the reaction.
3. The source and quality of light.

Much research needs to be performed in connection with these phenomena.

In the course of his work, Harmon also found that people are quite sensitive to very small light changes and adverse reactions can result from these small changes. As an example, in a Texas segregated school for black students (some years ago) the usual specification for lighting was used, 55 foot-lamberts illumination on the desks, 37 foot-lamberts reflected at the eye. However, after some months in the new school, the black children were found not to be achieving as well as white children in an architecturally almost identical school in the same area. Harmon found that their black skin absorbed too much light—so that the effective foot-lamberts were reduced substantially below the desired levels. Also the natural birch finish on the desks, which worked well with white children, did not work at the black school because the children's dark arms on their desks contrasted too much with the task. When these conditions were corrected by slightly darkening the natural birch finish surface of the desk with a stain, and by raising the incident light level about 20 percent to maintain the needed 37 foot-lamberts reflected at the eye, the black children achieved as well as the white children in the area according to standard achievement tests administered to a small sample of those involved.

As this example shows, the designer's code of ethics must satisfy biologic needs; we must design so that our building structures are equivalent to our biological structures. Another example would be the selection of colors in areas frequented by older people. An older person has a deteriorated eye medium that approaches yellow as he grows older. The interior designer therefore cannot use strong yellows in these areas, because its effect will intensify in the presence of the yellow eye medium and produce a very strong reaction that may even go beyond avoidance and approach psychosis. Note also that the use of blue in these same areas will likely be ineffective, since it will be seen as gray in the presence of a yellow eye medium.

These are biological and physiological reactions to color and are consonant with studies performed by and for the National Aeronautics and Space Administration to determine the color and light data needed for producing the optimum environments in spacecraft and space stations; NASA's spacecraft designers fully realize the critical need for such data.

NASA's definitive *Habitability Data Handbook* makes a statement that should be put in neon lights in the front of every interior design textbook (p. 3-74):

The association of colors with definite mental conditions and moods is general, and much has been written on the *psychology* of color. *No absolute relationships have been established* and the subject is open to individual interpretation. However, research has shown that certain general reactions are common to most people. [italics mine]

Exactly what this last paragraph means can be illustrated by the results of a research effort headed by Bennett and Rey with the provocative title "What's So Hot About Red?" They tried to find out whether or not the "hue-heat" hypothesis really works or not—the idea is that if you paint a room red (a so-called "warm" color) the room will seem warmer to those who enter it.

After reviewing the failure of this idea under widely varying conditions Bennett and Rey concluded that the "hue-heat" hypothesis is widely held intellectually, but there are no hard data to back it up, including their own experiments. A later study by Fanger, Breum, and Jerking "on the possible effect of color on the preferred ambient temperature" found that "the effect of colour on man's comfort is so small that it has hardly any practical significance. There was found no effect of noise on thermal comfort. None of the physiological measurements were influenced by colour or noise." Harmon also tested this hue-heat hypothesis and found that definite changes of body *surface* temperature occurred on exposure to color; other physiological changes were found as well.

These changes in temperature are partly a function of apparent distance from an object occupying the center of our attention, whatever its color may be, and are associated with changes in blood supply and changes in muscular tension. For example, when blood rushes to the surface of the skin, the skin's temperature rises because this increased blood supply comes from interior blood pools, which are warmer than the blood at the surface of the skin. This has been confirmed by thermocouples placed directly in subjects in experiments supervised by Harmon; this is sometimes referred to as *adjacency* or *avoidance phenomena* and may occur because of the closeness of an object or person without reference to color.

Intellectual Folklore

With this background in mind the following material is presented as abstracted from NASA's *Habitability Data Handbook*, volume 2, Architecture and Environment and from Baratono et al. While the material on light and lighting represents hard experimental data, the material on color does *not*—it is simply a summary of the commonly accepted "intellectual folklore" about color, its use and effects. Here is an example from NASA's *Habitability Data Handbook*:

Spatial Perception

Color affects the apparent size of objects and their position in space. Warm colors (reds, oranges, yellows) are advancing colors, and cool colors (blues, greens, purples) seem to recede in space. As these hues are muted their effects upon position diminish.

When a small colored area is surrounded by other colors, intense red is the most advancing color and dark blue and black are the most receding.

When color is applied to a large area such as the walls of a room, black and dark red are the most advancing colors.

White and light blue are the most receding colors. Intense colors mixed with black tend to advance, making rooms seem smaller; intense colors mixed with white tend to recede making a room seem larger. (MSC-03909, p. 3-3)

Recommending that glare be wholly eliminated from the "total seeing environment" of spacecraft, the *Handbook* goes on to say that "a high brightness of the work surface with a comparatively low brightness of the surroundings is undesirable, since it forces continual adjustments of the eyes from one brightness level to the other. Brightness in the peripheral field higher than the brightness of the task tends to attract the eye away from the task." These investigators recommend a "comfortable balance" of brightnesses to "prevent eye fatigue." Table 3–1 shows the NASA *Handbook* calculations of maximum brightness ratios.

Table 3–1. Maximum Brightness Ratios

Condition Between Task and Surfaces/Surroundings	Maximum Brightness Ratio for Optimum Seeing Conditions
Adjacent darker surroundings	3 to 1
Adjacent lighter surroundings	1 to 3
Remote darker surfaces	10 to 1
Remote lighter surfaces	1 to 10
Luminaires and surfaces adjacent	20 to 1
Within normal field of view	40 to 1

NASA, *Habitability Data Handbook*, volume 2, *Architecture and Environment*, MSC-03909, p. 3-4.

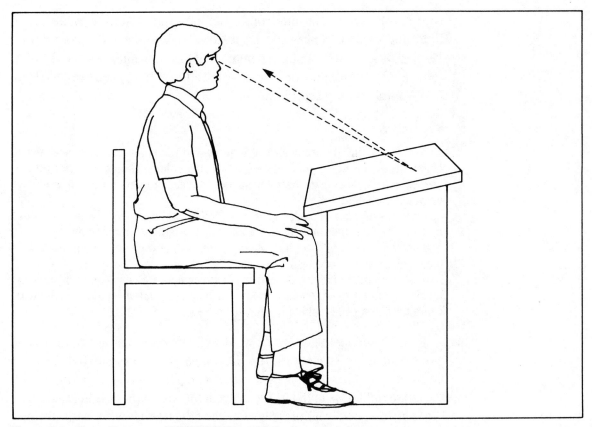

Figure 3.1. Glare. (Courtesy of *CONTRACT* Magazine)

Table 3–2 gives NASA's description of effective glare reduction methods.

Table 3–2. Glare
Reduction Methods

Type of Glare	Reduction Methods
Direct	Avoid bright light sources within 60 degrees of the center of the visual field. Use indirect lighting. Use several low-intensity sources rather than one high-intensity source. Lights placed high and directly above task area. Use shields, hoods, and visors to keep direct light from source out of viewers' eyes.
Indirect	Use diffuse light. Use dull, unpolished surfaces. Place direct light source so that viewing of task area is not equal to the angle of incident.

NASA, *Habitability Data Handbook*, MSC-03909, p.3-5.

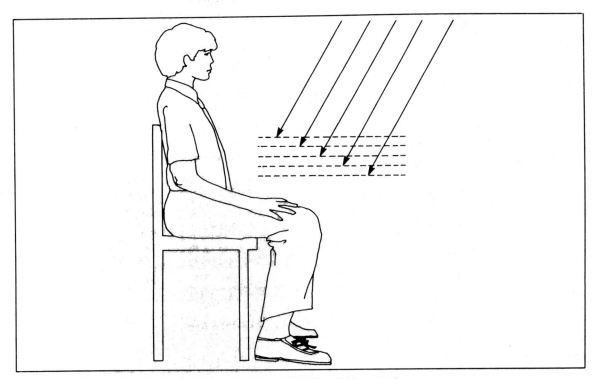

Figure 3.2. Glare again at several levels. (Courtesy of *CONTRACT* Magazine)

Table 3–3 shows NASA's figures on acceptable ranges of reflectance for interior surfaces.

Table 3–3. Reflectance Ranges for Interior Surfaces

Interior Surface	Reflectance Range
Ceilings	60 to 85 percent (white or pale tint)*
Walls	35 to 60 percent**
Window or glass wall	Fabric treatment: Wide expanse or backgrounds = 45 to 85 percent. Limited areas of decorative design on light background or side draperies = 15 to 45 percent.
Floors	15 to 35 percent (25 to 35 percent preferred)*** (Values of high end of range recommended for use in rooms where lighting efficiency is a major consideration: kitchen, bathrooms, utility rooms)

*70 percent or more is required for effective performance of indirect lighting methods.
**Appreciably higher than 50 percent creates brightness problems when portable luminaires are placed near walls and when extensive wall lighting methods are used. According to paint manufacturers, the public prefers 45 percent.
***Middle to high values preferred because of their predominance within the 60-degree cone of vision when performing many visual activities.

NASA, *Habitability Data Handbook*, MSC-03909, p. 4-38.

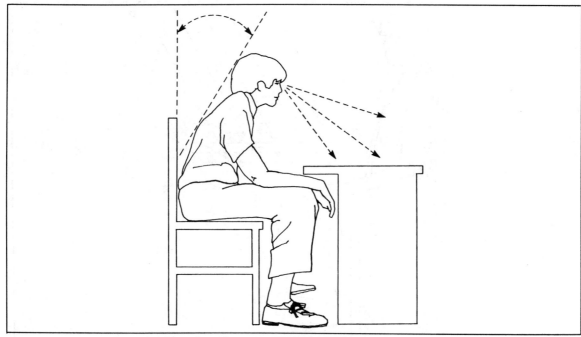

Figure 3.3. Back angles and sight angles. (Courtesy of *CONTRACT* Magazine)

In Table 3–4, the NASA figures are given for the maximum to minimum ranges of illumination needed for various kinds of seeing tasks.

Table 3–4. General Illumination Levels for Various Tasks

Task (Seeing)	Description	Illumination (fc) Maximum	Desirable Range	Minimum
General	General lighting requirements for proper identification of items and general maintenance	10	5–10	1
Casual	Suitable for relaxing or reading, detailed maintenance, and movement of people	30	20–30	10
Functional	Emphasis placed on efficiency and functional aspects used for investigation and observation of experiments and animals	70	50–70	20
Medium Detail	Detail inspection and reading small markings	100	50–100	30
Fine Detail	Fine detail on intricate tasks examining human patients—generally short duration	1000	500–1000	100

NASA, *Habitability Data Handbook*, MSC-03909, p. 3-4.

Table 3–5.
Psychological Moods in
Lighting

Mood	Lighting
Gaiety	Higher levels of illumination with color and movement. Changing effects of color and changes in illumination should not be sudden, but should be smooth and stimulating.
Solemnity	Subdued patterns of light with emphasis at dramatic points. Color should be used sparingly and with atmospheric effect. Changes of illumination should be imperceptible.
Restfulness	Low brightness patterns, no visible light sources, subdued color, dark upper ceiling, and a low wall brightness, decreasing upward to the ceiling.
Activity	Higher levels of illumination, with proper local lighting for the more difficult visual tasks.
Warmth	Colors at the red end of spectrum: red, red-orange, orange, yellow, amber, gold, and pink.
Coolness	Colors at cool end of spectrum, such as blue, blue-green, green, magenta, and violet. These colors mixed with white produces various cool tints.
Human Complexion	Light tints of red, such as pink and rose, improve human complexion and produce pleasant effects. Blue, blue-green, purple, and green detract from the human complexion, and produce ghastly effects.
Dramatize Color of Object	Spotlight by a beam of light of same color.
Prevent Fatigue	Avoid use of intense red, blue, or purple light.

NASA, *Habitability Data Handbook*, MSC-03909, p. 3-18.

Table 3–6.
Psychological
Architectural Emphasis
and Lighting

Emphasis on Increasing	Lighting Pattern
Height	Vertical lighting patterns from floor to ceiling.
Width	Accentuate lines of light across room, on both walls and ceilings.
Length	Use lighting lines that give perspective such as parallel, longitudinal lines.

NASA, *Habitability Data Handbook*, MSC-03909, p. 3-18.

From the MSC-03909 *Handbook,* p. 3-72:

Hue

Most good color schemes consist of no more than three hues. Whether warm or cool hues should be used is determined by the function of the room involved. Warm hues are associated with extroverted responses and feelings. Where it would be beneficial to emphasize feelings of extroversion, an area in which social contact is implicit to the function of the area, usage of warm hues will maximize these feelings, usage of cool hues will minimize them. Warm hues generally should be used if the temperature of the room is cool, the noise element is low, the room size is too large, texture is smooth, physical exertion is light, time exposure is short, a stimulating atmosphere is desired and lamps are fluorescent (cool). The introverted response is associated with cool hues. Where a contemplative atmosphere is dictated by the function of the area cool hues will add emphasis; warm hues will dilute this type of atmosphere. Cool hues should generally be used when the temperature is warm, the noise element is high, room size is too small, texture is rough, physical exertion is heavy, time exposure is long, a restful atmosphere desired and lamps are incandescent or fluorescent (warm).

Intensity

Color intensity induces two basic mental sets which may be described as centrifugal and centripetal. A centrifugal mental set is one in which an individual's attention is directed outward. High color intensity and high levels of illumination as well as warm hues evoke this set to its highest degree.

Conversely, the centripetal mental set directs an individual's attention, inward. Low color intensity and low illumination as well as cool hues maximize the centripetal mental set.

Intense colors will be used primarily as accent colors. Intense colors should be used if time exposure is short, responsibility low, noise level is low and stimulating atmosphere is desired. (MSC-03909, p. 3-72, 3-73)

Table 3–7.
Psychological Effects of Hue

Psychological Effect	Hue	Contrast
Exciting	Bright Red	High
	Bright Orange	
Stimulating	Red	Moderate
	Orange	
Cheering	Light Orange	Moderate
	Yellow	
	Warm Gray	
Neutralizing	Gray	Low
	White/Off-White	
Retiring	Cool Gray	Low
	Light Green	
	Light Blue	
Relaxing	Blue	Low
	Green	
Subduing	Purple	Moderate
Depressing	Black	Low

NASA, *Habitability Data Handbook*, MSC-03909, p. 3-77.

Table 3–8. Color Effects on Perceptions of Time, Size, Weight, and Volume

Color	Perception of Time	Size	Weight	Volume*
Warm: red yellow pink ivory cream peach lemon coral rose wine	Time is over-estimated; use warm colors for areas where time in apparent "slow motion" might be more pleasureable (eating, recreation).	Things seem longer and bigger	Weights seem heavier	Decreases apparent size of room
Cool: green violet blue bluish-green turquoise lilac lime jade aqua	Time is under-estimated; use cool colors for areas where routine or monotonous tasks as performed.	Things seem shorter and smaller	Weights seem lighter (Use on boxes & containers which must be carried about.)	Increases apparent size of rooms

*The conditions of brightness, color saturation, and level of illumination required to either enlarge or close-in a living area are presented elsewhere.

Source: NASA, *Habitability Data Handbook,* MSC-03909, p. 4-34.

Table 3–9. Brightness, Color Saturation, and Illumination Level Effects on Perception of Volume

Volume (Roominess)	Brightness	Color Saturation	Illumination Level
Enlarge*	Areas will be enlarged by lightness and small paper patterns. (Use to alleviate feelings of oppression or "closed-in".)	Pale or desaturated colors "recede." In situations where equipment projects into a room and tends to make it appear smaller than it actually is, paint the projections the same color as the ceiling or wall—a very light shade—to make them appear to recede into ceiling or wall.	High

*In establishing space relationships in interiors, there is a natural sequence of perspective where white, black, pure hues, and deep shades will appear near the eye. In what is called aerial perspectives, as colors shift or fall back into the distance, that which is dark increases in value; that which is light softens in value, and all colors eventually fade into medium gray. Color schemes can be planned to feature this phenomenon by using strong contrasts for near elements and grayish or weak contrast for far elements.

Table 3–9 *(cont.)*

Volume (Roominess)	Brightness	Color Saturation	Illumination Level
Close-in	Areas will be closed-in by darkness and large paper patterns.	Dark or saturated hues "protrude."	Low

NASA, *Habitability Data Handbook*, MSC-03909, p. 4-35.

Table 3–10. Effects of Color on Habitable Areas in Spacecraft

	Exciting	Stimulating	Cheering	Neutralizing	Retiring	Relaxing	Subduing	Depressing
Private								
Crew Compartments			X	O		X	O	O
Public								
Dining room			X			X	O	O
Lounge			X			X		O
Recreation	X	X						O
Library	O	O		X		X	X	O
Study	O			X	X			O
Conference		X						O
Passageways				X			O	O
Chapel	O	O			X	X	X	O
Gym	X	X			O	O	O	O
Locker room			X		O	O	O	O
Theater		X					O	O
Briefing room		X					O	O
Service								
Galley			X					O
Snack Bar			X	O				O
Bathroom		X	X	X		X		O
Dispensary			X			X		O
Laundry				X				O
Barbershop			X			X		O
Work								
Equipment				X				O
Maintenance				X				O
Power				X				O
Storage, food				X				O
Supply				X				O
Control room	O	O		X				O
Communications	O	O		X				O
Computer	O	O		X				O
Shop	O	O		X				O
Offices	O			X				O

	Exciting	Stimulating	Cheering	Neutralizing	Retiring	Relaxing	Subduing	Depressing
Laboratories	O			X				O
Dock	O			X				O
Photographic support				X				O
Animal housing				X				O
Agri. study area				X				O
Air locks				X				O

Legend: X = Desirable effect; O = Undesirable effect

NASA, *Habitability Data Handbook*, MSC-03909, 3-76.

Interrelationships in Living Areas

Interrelationships among colors, temperature, sound, and overall subjective impression in living areas are presented in Table 3–11.

Table 3–11. Living Area Interrelationships

Color	Sound	Temperature	Subjective Impression in Living Area
Warm: red yellow lemon pink ivory cream peach coral rose wine	Noise induces a hazier perception of warm colors. Brightness, loudness stimulation of senses in general are associated with the most active effect of warm colors.	Warmness Use to soften up chilly or vaulty spaces.	Centrifugal action—with high levels of illumination, warm & luminous colors, the person tends to direct attention outward. There is an increase in alertness, outward orientation, and activation. Such an environment is conducive to muscular effort, action, and cheerfulness.
Cool: green blue violet lilac bluish-green turquoise lime jade aqua	Noise increases sensitivity for cool colors. Dimness, quietness and sedation of the senses in general are associated with the most active effect of cool colors.	Coolness Use where working conditions expose person to warm temperatures.	Centripetal action—with softer surroundings, color hues, and lower levels of illumination, there is less distraction & a person's ability to concentrate on difficult visual and mental tasks is enhanced. Good inward orientation is furthered.

NASA, *Habitability Data Handbook*, MSC-03909, p. 4-39.

TEXTURE AND PATTERN

Introduction

Texture produces the most common yet the least acknowledged sensory experience, that of tactile response. Textures produce such a common source of stimuli to us that we tend to take them for granted. Hence, very little objective data are available on the subject. Textures provide a very valuable means of replacing some of the stimuli which man may be deprived of in the extraterrestrial environment.

Virtually every part of the body is affected by one texture or another throughout the course of a day. The clothes we wear, the surfaces which surround us, every aspect of the environment has one or another quality of surface. Texture is appraised and appreciated almost entirely by touch, even when it is visually presented. With few exceptions it is the memory of tactile experiences that enables us to appreciate texture.

Patterns

A pattern may be described as a two-dimensional or three-dimensional design put together in a particular arrangement of motifs. Motifs used for patterns may be natural, conventional, abstract or imaginary.

There is close correlation between pattern and texture; in fact, the difference is almost indiscernible, since every pattern creates a texture of some sort. Frequently this texture is only visual, since it does not have a tactile quality. We tend to think of pattern as basically visual and texture as something essentially tactile. The two are thus highly interrelated, and too clear a definition between the two may be misleading. (Baratono, et al., p. 2-127).

Let us now turn from the intellectual folklore (with some hard data thrown in) about light and color to speculation.

No Rules for the Designer

How does a designer use this mass of material to design environments for people? Well, there are not any hard and fast rules. At this stage of the art, it is only possible to speculate.

For those who are interested in people's reactions, there is a study by Amos Rapoport and Robert E. Kantor that gives us a few clues. First, the study questions too much extreme simplicity and clarity in environmental design, which may perturb the afficionados of the Bauhaus and the International School that stemmed from the Bauhaus. Rapoport and Kantor's review of psychological research up to the date of their study leads them to believe that people "prefer ambiguous, complex patterns in their visual fields." They also found a surprising number of architectural commentators and analysts who agreed with them. For instance, Mayer Spivack commented that "we know a few important basic things about our behavior when confronted with stimuli of varying complexity. The most important of these is that we choose complexity over simplicity from earliest infancy onward. We are a stimulus-seeking species."

However, Rapoport and Kantor frankly admit that they do not know how much or what kind of complexity and ambiguity people prefer and there just does not seem to be any data available to tell us; if complexity, for instance, is increased to the point of distraction and disorientation, certainly no useful purpose would be served. (The author has proposed the development of a distraction index to give designers cues as to the amount of complexity needed in a given environment, from a point of view of finding out how much complexity is too much.)

Color Contrasts

Harmon had some strong feelings about distraction. He felt that in a classroom, for instance, where contrasts commonly reach a level of as much as 20 to 25 to 1, memory retention of lecture material may reach a low of as little as approximately 20 percent because of the distraction produced by the high contrast ratio; for us to retain lecture material we must be relaxed and undistracted.

Because the contrast between direct sunlight hitting a piece of white paper and the shadow imposed by the window sill is between 50 and 60 to 1, and because classrooms exposed to direct sunlight can have contrasts as high as 500 to 1, the importance of light control in the learning environment is emphasized. In other words, high contrasts prevent the pupils from completing their work or even being interested in it, as well as making it more difficult to remember what they hear and see.

The school cafeteria is one place where strong colors and strong light contrasts may be desirable, however, if you want to move the students through quickly. You can use contrasts of about 10 to 1; the students will organize for big muscle activity and not stay very long.

In an expensive restaurant, though, you would use dim lighting with almost no contrast; you would perhaps just use a small spot over the table to make the silver and china sparkle. This would keep you there for quite a while and lead you to say that the conversation was beautiful and that the $50 check was worth it; the conflicts have been removed from the surroundings by concealing them with dimness.

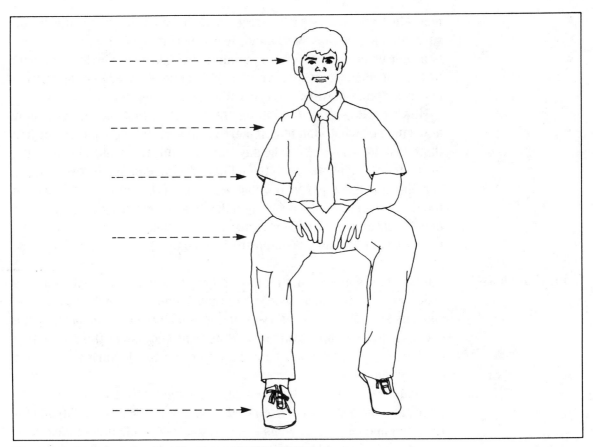

Figure 3.4. Light from the side. (Courtesy of *CONTRACT* Magazine)

To get back to the school cafeteria, many of these are multipurpose rooms. If you have used windows for strong contrasts, you must then have a system of blinds that when closed will hide the windows and have a reflectance equaling the reflectance of the walls so that you can use the cafeteria for lectures, conferences, or other purposes without distracting contrasts.

In the cafeteria display area around the steam tables the color should not be sanitary white because the after-image of white is gray—which makes all of the food look unpalatable. A highly reflecting complementary color to the food should be used. For example, if you want to sell hamburger, use turquoise because the after-image of turquoise is the color of nice, fresh, palatable meat, especially beef. For the same reason turquoise green should be used in hospital operating rooms since the complement of turquoise green is the color of the flesh that the surgeon cuts through; this will enable him or her to see better.

To return to the subject of contrasts, time is also involved in adaptation to contrast levels or changes in them; it takes from one-half to three-fourths of an hour to adapt from an integrated brightness of 125 foot-candles to twilight at 5 foot-candles, although it only takes about five minutes to adapt from 125 foot-candles to 50 foot-candles.

High contrast ratios produce conflicts between high and low light levels as well as between specularity and resolution; if they are too high for the activity going on in the surroundings in which they exist, they become destructive to the receptors and produce an attitude of avoidance, thus preventing human adaptation to the environment.

The process of adaptation to contrasts should affect, for instance, the choice of movie screens. For the usual aluminum screen it is necessary to darken the room (heighten the contrast) in order to see the movie, one reason being that an aluminum screen only reflects 35 percent of the light. In addition to this disadvantage, the screen also shifts what it shows into the blue sector of the spectrum.

It is possible, however, to use a screen that reflects 55 percent of the light and that color-corrects to the sensitivity of the human eye—a gold screen. With a gold screen you may not have to darken the room, since it can be used with as much as 30 foot-candles of illumination. This of course reduces the contrast in the room in which you are showing movies, making it easier for the human eye to resolve what it sees on the screen and reducing the adaptation time.

The general use of aluminum screens is one small aspect of the situation that exists in the United States; lighting is planned with too much emphasis on visibility alone. While it is true that, as you increase the intensity of light up to a certain point, you increase visual acuity; beyond that point, acuity becomes such that you recognize details of a construct rather than the totality. You see the flyspecks, not the table.

This emphasis on visibility alone is a result of confusion between inspection visibility and communication visibility. Inspection visibility requires 100 foot-candles or more at the point of inspection, while communication visibility requires only 55 foot-candles, which is the optimum for reading. Above 55 foot-candles, the reader will see letters instead of words. Since skilled readers derive meaning from minimum clues, that is, they recognize a sort of construct phenomena, if you force them to see letters, they will slow down.

The Cut-Off Hypothesis

We should mention here one seminal scientist-designer, Richard G. Coss, who has tentatively proposed certain uses of complexity to satisfy human needs, which he has identified in "The Cut-off Hypothesis: Its Relevance to the Design of Public Places." Coss thinks that modern urban environments are causing great stress among human beings because of the huge increases in the "intense exposure to strangers" occasioned by city life.

Human beings are exposed to many more strangers in today's cities than they ever were, even in the recent past. Coss says that "Constant exposure to strangers as one walks, drives, stands in elevators, and waits in public lounges may shock the nervous system with possible debilitating results." He feels that the resulting stimuli are so strong and frequent as to overload human receptors to the point where people cut off further sensory intrusions.

Distraction Graphics

To relieve this kind of sensory overload, Coss proposes the consideration of "distraction-graphics" as a tentative possible solution to the problem to increase the comfort of human beings in certain public situations where they are confronted with strangers. Distraction-graphics would simply consist of prints or paintings strategically placed so that people could focus their attention on the graphics instead of on other people with the resulting stress of eye contact with strangers.

After careful observation of situations and sites where people seemingly experience sensory discomfort from this kind of stress, Coss suggests elevators, waiting rooms, restaurants, subways, airports, corridors, stairways, conference rooms, offices, and even playrooms as possible sites for carefully considered distraction-graphics. Coss offers his proposals tentatively indeed, and is quite cognizant that certain designs might produce the opposite of the wanted effects. However, he feels quite strongly that "the designer should be concerned with the comfort of people in the designed environment" and suggests several existing methods for doing the immense amount of research he thinks is needed in this new area.

Health Hazards and Design Considerations

Light and Health

We know that we have to provide artificial light indoors so that we can see; we light the indoors for visibility. Logan calls this "visi-lighting," and suggests that we should now be conscious of the growing evidence of light's effect on our body processes and that we should design lighting to promote our physical health; he calls this latter process "bio-lighting."

He and others feel that natural sunlight, the visible portion and its accompanying sidebands of invisible electromagnetic radiation, has long been the most important environmental input for man, after food, in controlling bodily function; man seems to have evolved in natural sunlight and it is probable that his body processes are tuned to the radiations of the sun that reach the earth. However, over the centuries of man's existence on earth, human beings have come to live increasingly indoors and in cities—more and more under artificial light and less outdoors under natural light. Yet, much artificial lighting does not contain the full range of visible and nonvisible radiation contained in natural sunlight, and recent research is beginning to indicate that this full range of natural radiation is necessary for full human vitality.

Until recently, artificial light had never been developed for biological purposes, though quite sophisticated lighting technology has matured for many other purposes: Spurred by the belief that we must change the character of our artificial lighting so that man's life span can be increased, researchers are developing artificial light sources that nearly duplicate the full range of visible and invisible radiation contained in the rays of the sun. They are doing this also because they believe that increasing air and light pollution are creating conditions that may limit man's life span.

Logan believes that periodically we may be starved for natural solar radiation, especially during winter in urban areas, and points to the peaking of urban death rates in March, the end of the solar radiation deprivation season, as a possible indication of the importance of full solar radiation of man's health. He theorizes that as man evolved on earth, his biological functions became attuned to natural sunlight in the rhythm of the seasons. As spring and summer progressed, man tanned, which reduces the amount of radiation entering the body to an acceptable level; then during fall and winter his skin became more translucent as he lost his tan, admitting more of the decreased amount of solar radiation available as the weather worsened and the angle of the sun's rays became less direct.

Now, though, we live more and more indoors and in the polluted cities and this natural process has been drastically altered; Logan and others believe that we must take steps to see that the character of artificial lighting sources is changed so that they more nearly duplicate the full range of solar radiation to make up for the losses incurred by these changes. Their belief is partially based on experimental evidence; while some of it is fairly rudimentary, further research may indicate an even more important role for light in human biological process. Some of these studies are:

1. Neer, Davis, and Thorington who found that older people living indoors in the winter absorbed almost twice as much calcium into their bloodstreams while living under a light source closely resembling sunlight than did a control group living under cool-white fluorescent light. Calcium absorption is most important to the elderly to keep their bones from becoming more brittle.

2. Even though rickets is still widely believed by many to be a disease due to dietary deficiencies, Loomis marshalls the evidence that it is caused fundamentally by lack of sunlight. He relates the original appearance of rickets in England and northern Europe to the beginnings of industrial smog; it may have been the first air pollution disease in the sooty cities.

3. Wurtman and Weisel experimented with rats who were born and raised under a light source closely resembling sunlight and a control group who were born and raised under cool-white fluorescent light. Both sexes raised under the cool-white illumination developed smaller gonads and larger spleens than the rats under the light source closely resembling sunlight.

4. Zamkova and Krivitskaya found that increased ultraviolet irradiation of school children in their classes improved their working capabili-

ties by enhancing their stability of clear vision, producing a shorter reaction time to light and sound, and increasing their resistance to fatigue.

5. Volkova noted a cut in working days lost due to catarrhal affections and cold among machine shop workers who were given increased ultraviolet irradiation while at work. The irradiated workers lost about half the number of days that an unirradiated group did.

6. Hyperbilirubinemia is a condition especially found in newborn, premature infants which can lead to neonatal jaundice, and if unchecked, to motor and mental retardation. There are a number of studies describing the successful treatment of this condition by using a light therapy: Hodr, Land, Zarkowsky, and Vietti; Karon, Imach, and Schwartz, and Gorodischer; and Levey, Krasner, and Yaffe. Hospitals now buy special lighting equipment for the treatment of this condition, and in 1974 about 25,000 babies were treated in this manner.

7. Himmelfarb, Scott, and Thayer indicate that a light source with a spectrum closely resembling that of natural sunlight may be a help in the widespread campaign to reduce the incidence of the scourge of staphylococcus aureus in hospitals.

8. Wurtman, a leading investigator of the physiological effects of light, describes the effects of light on the production of hormones in the human system.

9. Wurtman reports on the work of John A. Parrish and Thomas B. Fitzpatrick at the Massachusetts General Hospital in developing a successful treatment for psoriasis involving the use of special lighting equipment, and summarizes much recent work in photobiology.

10. Arehart-Treichel discusses experimental work that indicates that ordinary fluorescent lighting may be a causal factor in hyperactivity and other behavioral problems with children, work on the effects of different light spectra on the growth and development of plants, fish and animals, and experimental work that shows the possibility of controlling dental caries with the use of full-spectrum fluorescent lighting. She closes her article with "perhaps, as MIT photobiologist Richard Wurtman predicts, some day we will make use of different wave-lengths and exposure—since light is as potent as any drug."

At this point the situation seems to be that while it is known that light has biologic effects on the human physical system, with the exception of the few studies available, these effects are largely unknown in specific terms. The most informed researchers in the field recommend that we design lighting to produce a spectrum as close as possible to that of natural sunlight—until more data are available. Fluorescent tubes superior in this respect to anything heretofore available are on the market now (Vita-Lite).

Visual Ambiguities

What we can do is to design as many hazards out of the interior as possible. Izumi exposes visual ambiguities as a frequent cause of injuries and death. The first target of his criticism is glass doors that are placed next to sidelights were you cannot tell one from the other; they are identical in appearance. Izumi mentions more than twenty fatalities in one city due to glass-door accidents, and emphasizes that more than 100,000 of these mishaps have been recorded in New York City alone, which means that there were many more that were not recorded.

Another hazard is the erroneous placement of the door knob in the center of the door; if this placement is combined with hidden hinges, it is impossible to tell which way the door swings. When this uncertainty is combined with the loss of leverage involved in the placement of the knob in the center, doors can become dangerous, especially to those who have even minor visual or physical infirmities.

The most dangerous door by far, though, is the camouflaged exit door. If an exit door is made to look exactly like the rest of the wall by painting, papering, or paneling, the resultant visual illusion can result in panic, injury, or death. Even though there may be exit lights and signs over them, these are, in effect, concealed doors. In a crisis, such as a fire, explosion, or other emergency, the great stress produced often reduces acuteness of perception and makes the door impossible to find. The more clues we have visually to lead us to the exit, the greater chance we have to avoid the danger.

Another hazard is the incorrect placement of mirrors. They must be placed very carefully. Though mirrors are quite necessary and useful, functionally and decoratively, as Izumi points out, placing a "large, one piece floor to ceiling mirror" on a stair landing can lead to all sorts of accidents.

References

Joan Arehart-Treichel, "The Good, Healthy Shining Light," *Human Behavior* 4, no. 1 (January 1975), pp. 16–22.

John R. Baratono, Bill F. Fowler, Edward W. Karnes, Arthur A. Rosener, and Melvin L. Stephenson, "Architectural/Environmental Handbook for Extraterrestrial Design," Springfield, Virginia: National Technical Information Service, 1970. Accession Number N71-17560.

Corwin A. Bennett and Paule Rey, "What's So Hot About Red?" *Human Factors* 14, no. 2 (1972), pp. 149–154.

Richard G. Coss, "The Cut-Off Hypothesis: Its Relevance to the Design of Public Places," *Man-Environment Systems* 3, no. 6 (November 1973), pp. 417–440.

P. O. Fanger, N. O. Breum, and E. Jerking, "Can Colour and Noise Influence Man's Thermal Comfort?" *Ergonomics* 20, no. 1 (1977), pp. 11–18.

Rafael Gorodischer, Gerhard Levey, Joseph Krasner, and Sumner J. Yaffe, "Phototherapy for Jaundice," *New England Journal of Medicine* 282, no. 7 (February 12, 1970), pp. 375–377.

"Habitability Data Handbook, Volume 2, Architecture and Environment," Houston: Habitability Technology Section, Spacecraft Design Division, Manned Spacecraft Center, National Aeronautics and Space Administration, July 31, 1971. MSC-03909.

Philip Himmelfarb, Arthur Scott, and Philip S. Thayer, "Bacterial Activity of a Broad-Spectrum Illumination Source," *Applied Microbiology* 19, no. 6 (June 1970), pp. 1013-1014.

R. Hodr, "Phototherapy of Hyperbilirubinemia in Premature Infants," (original in Czechoslovakian, translation courtesy of Duro-Test Corp.) *Ceskoslovenska Pediatie* 26 (February 1971), pp. 80–82.

Kiyo Izumi, "Psychosocial Considerations of Environmental Design," New York: National Society of Interior Designers, 1968.

Myron Karon, Daniel Imach, and Allen Schwartz, "Effective Phototherapy in Congenital Nonobstructive, Nonhemolytic Jaundice," *New England Journal of Medicine* 282, no. 7 (February 12, 1970), pp. 377–380.

Vita J. Land, Harold S. Zarkowsky, Teresa J. Vietti, "Phototherapy for Jaundice," *New England Journal of Medicine* 282, no. 7 (February 12, 1970), p. 397.

Henry L. Logan, "Vision," Environmental Design Seminar, University of Wisconsin–Madison, May 1-2, 1969. (mimeo)

W. F. Loomis, "Rickets," *Scientific American* 223, no. 6 (December 1970), pp. 77–91.

R. Neer, T. Davis, and L. Thorington, "Use of Environmental Lighting to Stimulate Calcium Absorption in Healthy Men," *Clinical Research* 18, no. 4, December 1970.

Amos Rapoport and Robert E. Kantor, "Complexity and Ambiguity in Environmental Design," *American Institute of Planners Journal* 33, no. 4, 1967, pp. 210–221.

Mayer Spivack, "Hospitalization - Time Without Purpose," *Ekistics* 245 (April 1976), pp. 200–204.

N. V. Volkova, "Experience in the Use of Erythemic Ultraviolet Radiation in the General Lighting of a Machine Shop," (original in Russian, translation courtesy of the Duro-Test Corp., North Bergen, N.J.) *Gig. i Sanit.* 32 (October 1967), pp. 109–111.

Richard J. Wurtman, "The Pineal and Endocrine Function," *Hospital Practice* 4, no. 1 (January 1969), pp. 32–37.

Richard J. Wurtman, "The Effects of Light on the Human Body," *Scientific American* 233, no. 1 (July 1975), pp. 68–77, bibliography on p. 132. This is an excellent review of photobiology in relation to the human body up to 1975.

Richard J. Wurtman and Jeffrey Weisel, "Environmental Lighting and Neuroendocrine Function: Relationship Between Spectrum of Light Source and Gonadal Growth," *Endocrinology* 84, no. 6 (December 1969), pp. 1218–1221.

M. A. Zamkova and E. I. Krivitskaya, "Effect of Irradiation by Ultraviolet Erythema Lamps on the Working Ability of School Children," (original in Russian, translation courtesy of the Duro-Test Corp., North Bergen, N.J.) *Gig. i. Sanit.* 31 (April 1966), pp. 41–44. See also Goromosov, M.S., "The Physiological Basis of Health Standards for Dwellings," Geneva: World Health Organization, 1968, which details long-term Russian interest in the biological effects of light. In Chapter 3, "Illumination and Insolation—Biologic Effects of Radiant Energy and Their Importance to Health," Goromosov mentions "light starvation" in the biologic sense and states that "indoor illumination should approach the qualities of natural outdoor light as closely as possible, both quantitatively and qualitatively." In this chapter there is also a section on "Physiological standards of visual comfort," which, among other things, calls for "optimum biological activity of the light," (in dwellings) and later on asks for "improvement of the spectrum of light emitted by flourescent lamps destined for homes" (pp. 48–67). At the time the book was written, M. S. Goromosov was Assistant Director and Head, Department of the Health Aspects of the Microclimate and of Radiant Energy, Institute of Sciences, A. N. Sysin Institute of Individual and Communal Hygiene, USSR Academy of Medical Sciences, Moscow, USSR.

4 *Communication Distance*

Communications among us are all-important, and the quality of the face-to-face interchanges is a major factor in the success or failure of human relationships, especially in the office. How can interior designers affect the quality of these relationships? The answer may be that they are affecting it now without being aware of their influence.

One crucial factor may be the distance at which people interact; the interior designer, by the very nature of the work, sets that distance. Diverse evidence from studies in several distinctly different areas of research tends to show that it may not be possible to hold a fully involved, completely perceptive personal exchange between two or more persons at a physical distance of more than 66 inches face to face (or perhaps more accurately, mouth to mouth).

In one study, Robert Sommer experimented with the distance for comfortable conversation for subjects seated on couches. He used two sofas, 50 inches wide, facing each other and placed at various distances from one another in a segregated section of a nicely furnished lounge 46 feet by 48 feet. Two subjects were studied at a given time, as they talked to each other. When the sofas were from one to three feet apart, the subjects sat opposite one another, but when the sofas were three and one-half to six feet apart, they shifted to a side-by-side position. Since on the type of sofas used, the actual head to head distance was two feet longer than the distance between the sofas, Sommer observes that five and one-half feet is the limit for comfortable conversation. This is roughly borne out by the observations of Edward T. Hall and others, which are discussed more fully in following paragraphs. To put it another way, in this and previous experiments Sommer found that his subjects would sit across from each other, even at an angle, until increasing distance made them feel uncomfortable or less engaged. Then they would shift to the only possible closer position in this situation, side by side.

In another series of experiments Sommer went further with his observations. Instead of two couches, he used four chairs, so that he could introduce the further variable of side-by-side distance. The chairs were placed in different combinations of side-by-side and cross distances. The distances varied from one to five feet across and from one to five feet side by side. Here again, although there were other furniture and furnishings in the room, the four chairs used in his experiments were in a segregated area, separated from the rest of the room and the rest of the furnishings.

People in this setting preferred to sit across from one another, rather than side by side, except when the distance between them got too far for comfortable conversation—in excess of five and one-half feet, head to head—except when the distance across became greater than the side-by-side distance. Easily movable chairs were used in this study. Slightly more than one-quarter of the observations showed that one of the chairs was moved; most of the moving occurred when the chairs were farthest across from one another.

Fovea Controls Comprehension

Part of the explanation of Sommer's results in these studies may lie in the ability of the human eye to fully comprehend facial expressions and facial muscle movements up to about a 66-inch distance, and the possible inability of the human eye to comprehend them beyond that distance.

If we examine the structure and functioning of the human eye, as Hall did, we find there is a very small area in the center of the retina, the most light sensitive portion of the eye called the fovea. The fovea is closely packed with cones, which are the major cells that distinguish color. Cones exist only in the fovea, which is so small that we see less than one degree with it, less than 1/360th of a circle; it is about one-seventh the size of the head of a pin, or 0.7 millimeter across.

Yet, the fovea is the only part of the retina with which we see directly and sharply. The visual impressions we get from other parts of the retina are not nearly as sharp and direct. We can refer to vision other than foveal as peripheral.

We probably need the sharp foveal vision to fully comprehend movements of facial muscles, and body attitudes as well. This most distinct portion of our vision tells us with great accuracy whether the persons we are conversing with are frowning, laughing, approving, disapproving, tense, relaxed, loving, hating, and so on through the whole range of human reactions. In short, in order to completely grasp the subtleties of the reactions of the persons we are communicating with, we must be able to accurately see their facial movements and expressions, as well as any changes in them.

Acuteness of foveal vision is reflected in material from the *Applied Ergonomics Handbook* relating to product inspection procedures in industry. The general rule given there is that if what you are looking at is more than five degrees outside the center of your vision (foveal field), visual acuity—the ability to discriminate and see fine detail—is reduced by about one-half. The reason that we are able to see more than five degrees distinctly within a short period of time is that the eye scans in jumps at very high speed, but it is the fovea which is scanning comprehensively.

Social Distance Midpoint

Although foveal vision is theoretically unlimited as to distance, it is obvious that the amounts and kinds of detail that we can see varies with the distance away from whatever we are looking at. In other words, there are limits, largely unknown, on the usefulness of foveal vision for various purposes. The 66-inch distance observed by Sommer falls exactly at the midpoint of "social distance" as defined by Hall, and Hall emphasizes that persons who work together tend to use "close social distance." It is possible that foveal visual abilities are just one factor that influences conversational distances. Ostrander and Schroeder (1971) report that a special type of photography named Kirlian after its Czech discoverer has revealed that human beings, animals, and plants are surrounded by an aura or force field which leaves its imprint on special film when the subject is placed in an electromagnetic field. The nature of the aura or force field is unknown, but the discovery of its origin and composition is the objective of several Soviet researchers.

Since this aura or force field has already been detected at distances up to about 16 feet according to Ostrander and Schroeder, the possibility that there exists some form of energy hitherto unknown must be considered in the study of conversational distance. Perhaps good and bad "vibes" can be detected and measured; there certainly are unknown factors in how people communicate with each other, and at what distances.

It is, of course, quite possible that 66 inches is not even a good approximation of the limit on fully perceptive, involved conversation for all portions of the population; the studies cited here do not have definite age parameters, for instance. For the elderly, whose perceptions are impaired, the limit might be less than 66 inches. High noise levels in an interior space might also reduce the distance, as would various types of perception difficulties in any portion of the population.

Let us suppose that we accept the possibility that the 66-inch distance is a limiting factor in face to face communication, and let us further suppose that we want to find the maximum number of persons who can fully communicate with one another at one place and at one time.

Geographically, we find that the uppermost limit for good communication is nine persons in a circle, whether sitting or standing. This allots about 23 inches to each person in a circle 66 inches in diameter. This limit is, of course, based on the necessity for each person in the group to be able to see every other person in the group. Otherwise, we theoretically could cram quite a few more people into the center of the circle.

Another strong indication of an uppermost limit of nine persons is garnered from a study by George A. Miller, "The Magical Number Seven, Plus or Minus Two: Some Limits on Our Capacity for Processing Information." Miller traces studies of human abilities to discriminate among and identify pitch, loudness, taste, points on a line, points in a square, colors, random dots, binary digits, decimal digits, letters, letters and digits, words and phrases. He traces the human ability to increase the amount of information and increase the number of information sources we can handle by recoding, and the successive reorganization of bits of information. From his work it would seem possible that seven, plus or minus two, sources of information is the limited number that typical human beings can handle without confusion.

If seven is the typical number, we might then reduce our theoretical uppermost limit to eight, since each person interacting in a group of eight would be processing information from seven other sources, the seven other persons in the group. The 66-inch circle would then be a bit looser in structure, since eight persons in it would leave a bit more room between them.

The relationship of distance and good communication around a table is also underscored by a study by Charles S. Green III, where in studying committees and the way they work, he found that "as a member's participation increased, he began to sit nearer to the committee chairman."

Here we might quote from a design fantasy by Charles W. Rusch: "At last . . . I arrive at . . . some sort of high-level conference. There are, of course, exactly eight people present, the content of our conversation flows easily, and communication is good. Apparently the seats in our Conversation Unit are perfectly spaced, and the lighting level is correct."

Robert F. Bales mentions seven participants in a committee as a crucial number. Participation among committee groups he studied was much more thorough and widespread at seven, six, or five, than in committees of greater size; committees with more than seven members showed much more concentration of communication among fewer members, rather than the mutuality of activity at seven members or slightly less than that number. He even goes so far as to recommend seven as a maximum size for an effective committee, unless it is absolutely necessary for various reasons to appoint a larger one.

There is some empirical evidence that tends to strengthen this idea. The prime example is probably the activities of the Congress of the United States. There is certainly no secret about the importance of the negotiations that take place between and among small groups, the committees and sub-committees; the real interaction occurs there. Full sessions of either House are a rarity, and little really important work occurs on the floor, except for final voting.

Small Groups Are More Productive

The activities of large corporate boards of directors would also tend to confirm these observations. Frequently, where the number of board members exceeds the optimum conversational number of eight or nine, duties often are divided and the real work is done by committees of not more than eight or nine chosen from the whole board. Each committee then performs decisive separate functions or groups of functions.

For example, quite often there are separate finance, executive, pension, and/or marketing committees functioning as working parts of many corporate boards of directors. The meeting of the full board then becomes a reporting session, with the committees apprising the whole board of their activities with aid of microphones, slide projectors, and other audio-visual devices necessary for the larger group.

The literature also indicates that the number of persons in an interacting group is material in setting the quality of that group's interaction. A study by A. Paul Hare tends to support the proposition that, as the sizes of the groups he studied changed from smaller to larger, there was less satisfaction with the participation and less consensus.

Hare's study compared groups of five with groups of twelve. One interesting reaction was that the groups of five felt that there was enough time for discussion and that everybody in the groups had sufficient chance to speak; the feeling among the groups of twelve was the opposite of this. In the groups of twelve, he also found a tendency for group members to hesitate to speak, because they probably did not feel important enough in the larger group. He also found a trend toward factionalism in the twelve-member groups, and felt that this would become more apparent in groups larger than twelve. From this study we can suspect that groups of twelve are probably too large for complete and satisfactory interaction.

Perhaps the hostess who separates her large dinner party into smaller groups of four around card tables rather than seating her guests at one large, long table instinctively knows that her friends will have a better time because they will be able to interact more in the smaller groups and at lesser distances from each other, well within the theoretical 66-inch distance. She is also placing her guests in the positions where Sommer's studies show that most interaction takes place at rectangular or square tables—across corners and face to face across the table, rather than side by side. Returning to our theoretical limit of eight or nine persons as a maximum for real interpersonal communication, it is up to the interior designer to allocate the space so that the interaction can come about.

Table Size

To get eight people sitting at a table in the least space, the indicated shape for the table is round, 60 inches in diameter. For comfort, with no other facilities in the room, this would of course take a room approximately 12 feet by 12 feet square. If the designer is confronted with predetermined, permanent walls, as we were on a recent project, this becomes academic, because the architect had already determined the shape of the table to be used with his dimensions for the conference area, 10 feet by 21 feet. A 60-inch round table would look quite peculiar in that space, and it wouldn't seat the twelve people the client said it must.

The fact that a round table is the indicated shape for interaction among the most people, eight or nine, in the least space, has other implications which may be a bit more fundamental. The fact is that most tables in use for conferences, board meetings, seminars, and committee meetings are rectangular, a shape that seems to have certain connotations in the American culture.

According to tradition in this country, the boss sits at the head of the table, usually a rectangular one, with his subordinates in meticulous rank as the seats get farther away from the boss. This is true for the chairman of the board, the seminar head, the committee chairman, the department supervisor, and the jury foreman.

Position Is Power
Most jury rooms in America contain a long table, with five seats on each side, and one at each end. Fred L. Strodtbeck and L. Harmon Hook found that the jury foreman is chosen, more often than you statistically would expect, from those who sit at the ends of the table. While there is no certainty that those who sat in the end seats were leaders outside the jury room, there is some statistical evidence that this is true, and there is the natural and observed tendency of those who are leaders elsewhere to head the procession into the jury room; they thus have the opportunity to select the end seats and do so. Of course, one reason leaders might take the end seat could be that it offers more elbow room and an unobstructed view of the others at the table. Incidentally, the previously mentioned study by Sommer also points to leaders' preference for end positions at tables in groups of four or more.

As Hall has pointed out, in France the leader typically sits in a side-center position at a rectangular table, being conscious, he feels, of the communications advantages of this position. Sommer too mentions less isolation of the other participants in a group, when the leader takes a side-center position in a discussion at a rectangular table.

Conference Table Shapes and Peace
Seidel goes back to the year 1504 to illustrate disputes over seating positions in diplomatic meetings and peace negotiations. He describes instances of this at the end of the Thirty Years War in 1640, the Turkish-Russian War in 1878, World War I in 1919 (the Versailles Treaty), and at

4.1

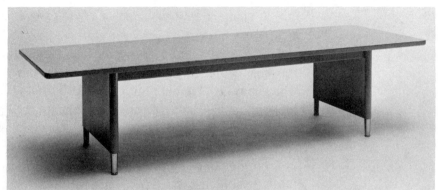

Figure 4.1. This is the standard American hierarchical rectangular table. (Steelcase photo)
Figure 4.2. Several manufacturers make round tables like this one. (Steelcase photo)

4.2

the end of the Korean conflict in 1953. At Panmunjom he felt that the substitution of a round table for the rectangular tables which had been used shortened these truce talks appreciably.

However, the most spectacular and publicized dispute over table shapes was that which took place in the arrangement period preceding the truce talks on the Vietnam war in 1969. The dispute over the table shape and size became so heated that Seidel quotes a *New York Times* writer, E. S. Goldman, as saying, "It is likely that the next winner of the Nobel Peace Prize will be a furniture designer." In view of this discussion of table shapes, it seems significant that in the beginning negotiation skirmishes, both Hanoi and the U. S. proposed tables with right angles, both rectangular and square, but a round table was the final agreed solution.

Seidel also feels that in this study of peace negotiations, small, informal groups of delegates are much more effective in reaching agreement than the rather public large groups necessary so often to represent all factions involved. Round tables might produce more participation and interaction from these small groups so that agreements might be reached sooner and more effectively.

Management Theory and Practice

There are some grounds for belief, however, that the usual American choice of a rectangular conference table may be somewhat tied in with management theory and practice, however unconsciously it may be done. The behavioral management theories of the late Douglas McGregor show how the shape of a table might relate to the way a company is managed.

Theory X, as he labeled it, indicates a hierarchical organization, tightly controlled from the top. This theory of operation assumes that only the boss knows how anything must be done and that workers must be forced to work under threats of harsh disciplinary action. Further, independent thought and action are discouraged, so that nothing will disturb the hierarchy.

Opposite Theory Y, on the other hand, assumes that the worker will respond to challenges by assuming responsibility and by using the freedom to act independently in the best interest of the organization. Under the operation of Theory Y, instead of being ordered to perform a task, the worker is stimulated to accomplish it on his own. Theory Y is participatory, rather than hierarchical.

Rectangular Implies Hierarchical

It is, perhaps, no accident that the prevailing management theory in America has been predominantly hierarchical until the recent past, and that the conference tables have been rectangular to match. However, when a round table is used, the customary automatic psychological leadership points at the ends are gone; everyone is equal (or at least has an equal position) around a round table, and therefore, a round table is more suited to participatory Theory Y.

It is probable that circular seating patterns are perceived by participants as more informal, less hierarchical, as David V. Canter pointed out in a study of classroom seating. Margaret Mead and Paul Byers also recorded in their exhaustive study of "The Small Conference" that whenever a spontaneous gathering occurred in a setting without furniture, outdoors, or on the floor, it always took the shape of a circle or a semi-circle. It is therefore possible that the choice of the shape and size of tables may affect the way a business operates, or vice versa; the shape of the dining table may be a similar factor in family life. Certainly there is enough evidence in this area that further research efforts might be quite fruitful and revealing.

Design Checkpoints

1. Think about the kind of activity or activities planned for the space you are designing and relate it to the shape and sizes of tables you specify. If you want a table for a round table discussion, specify a round table.

2. Relate the shapes and sizes of tables to the shape and size of each room with nonmovable walls.

3. Consider folding tables that can be stored when not in use, perhaps several different sizes and shapes, for different activities.

4. Remember that most chairs are moveable for interaction; most sofas are not.

5. The 66-inch distance is roughly head-to-head; allow for this in calculating distances; this distance does hold if, for instance, you use chairs with arms that do not fit under the top of a 60-inch diameter round table.

6. If you are designing for a business or a governmental agency, relate table shape and size to size of the group and whether or not the client operates on McGregor's Theory X or Theory Y.

References

Applied Ergonomics 1, no. 5 (1970), pp. 290–291.

Robert F. Bales, "In Conference," *Harvard Business Review* 32, no. 2 (1954), pp. 44–50.

David V. Canter, "Architectural Psychology," London: RIBA Publications, 1970.

Charles S. Green, III, "The Ecology of Committees," *Environment and Behavior* 7, no. 4, December 1975, pp. 411–427.

Edward T. Hall, "The Hidden Dimension," Garden City, N.J.: Doubleday & Co., 1966, pp. 13–14, 66–69, 114–116.

Paul A. Hare, "A Study of Interaction and Consensus in Different Sized Groups," *American Psychological Review* 17, no. 3, pp. 261–267, 1952.

Douglas McGregor, "The Human Side of Enterprise," New York: McGraw-Hill, 1960.

Margaret Mead and Paul Byers, "The Small Conference," Paris: Mouton & Co., 1968. New York: Humanities Press, 1968.

George A. Miller, "The Magical Number Seven, Plus or Minus Two: Some Limits on Our Ability to Process Information," *Psychological Review* 63, no. 2, 1956, pp. 81–96.

Sheila Ostrander and Lynn Schroeder, "Psychic Discoveries Behind the Iron Curtain," New York: Bantam Books, 1971.

Charles W. Rusch, "On the Relation of Form to Behavior," in Moore, Gary T., ed., "Emerging Methods in Environmental Design and Planning," Cambridge and London: MIT Press, 1970, p. 279.

Andrew D. Seidel, "The Use of the Physical Environment in Peace Negotiations," *Journal of Architectural Education* 32, no. 2, November 1978, pp. 19–22.

Robert Sommer, "Leadership and Group Geography," *Sociometry* 24, 1961, pp. 99-110.

Robert Sommer, "The Distance for Comfortable Conversation: A Further Study," *Sociometry* 25, 1962, pp. 111–116.

Robert Sommer, "Personal Space: The Behavioral Basis of Design," Englewood Cliffs, N.J.: Prentice-Hall, 1969, p. 62.

Fred L. Strodtbeck, and Harmon L. Hook, "The Social Dimensions of a Twelve-Man Jury Table," *Sociometry* 24 (1961), pp. 397–415.

5 *Sitting Down*

The act of sitting down is certainly a commonplace in the interior, but unfortunately, it is not always done in comfort. As an extreme example, we bought a chair from one of the world's most prestigious and well-revered—as well as largest—architectural furnishings sources. It had been designed in Europe by a famous designer, and it is good looking enough and innovative enough in construction that it has been specified by some of our best known interior designers and architects. We bought samples for our showroom; we liked it too, and it is a chair extremely reasonable in price to be so well made and well designed (as to form).

One of my long-term clients, a woman who happens to appreciate good modern design, needed a stenographic chair (which this is) for her workplace at home, and when I told her about this chair, she said, "Send it out." We did, and it came right back. Why?

This woman is only four feet and eleven inches tall, and the chair did not fit her. But, you say, any good stenographic chair is adjustable. You are right, and this one is, too, but its lower adjustment limit is too high—it will not go below 18 inches in seat height. In other words you cannot get the chair seat below 18 inches no matter what you do.

Our client, being four feet and eleven inches tall, must have a seating height of less than 18 inches or she will not be comfortable; actually, when she sat on this chair, her feet did not even touch the floor. According to Kroemer and Robinette, "the height of the seat should be adjusted so that both feet can be placed firmly on the floor while the thighs are horizontal." However, this distance varies among persons of different heights, and even to a measurable extent among persons of the same height, and our diminutive client probably hits the bottom of the range of heights among her female contemporaries who are the chief users of this type of chair.

The important thing here is that the chair be adjustable in height; adjustable, that is, within the range of heights that will fit most users.

According to Kroemer and Robinette, a secretarial chair (also called an operator chair in most factories and shops) should, at a minimum,

Figure 5.1. This chair has one of the widest ranges of seat height adjustability on the market, 14⅝″ to 20⅝″; it comes close to the desired 13⅔″ to 20⅔″ range. (Steelcase photo)

have an adjustability range from a lower limit of 13⅔ inches to 20⅔ inches as the upper limit for the seat height. Kroemer and Robinette's figures are based on twenty-nine separate studies made between 1948 and 1967 by eminent and recognized European and American orthopedists, physiologists, and engineering anthropologists in five countries. Such data provide an international basis for arriving at this adjustability range for this type of chair and this range is confirmed by popliteal height data from NASA's worldwide compilation of anthropometric data. However, one authoritative American source, Damon, Stoudt, and McFarland, presents evidence for a needed adjustability range of 9½ inches for this chair rather than the 7 inches called for by Kroemer and Robinette. According to Floyd and Roberts the chair with a lower limit of 18 inches for its seat height is too high for about 60 percent of both the male and female population of Great Britain, for instance.

When Your Legs Dangle

Kohara and others have done studies of what happens when you sit on a stool that is too high and lets your legs dangle. As pressure increases on the bottom of your thighs, the temperature of your toes goes down enough so that the drop can easily be measured (due to partial cutoff of blood circulation and perhaps to nerve pressure) and the calves of your legs increase measurably in size; hence if you like the present shape and size of your legs, do not sit for long periods of time with your legs and feet dangling. Poorly designed chairs can cause discomfort, and though it may not be very severe or very noticeable, this discomfort can affect your health and efficiency. Sometimes, even though you may not be conscious of the discomfort, you make small postural changes to counteract it.

Alton Ochsner, a surgeon who specializes in correcting blood clot problems, believes that blood clots are an occupational hazard for seated office workers, as many as 400,000 of them today. The same seems true of truck drivers. As one example, in too-high seating, pressure is usually felt under the more sensitive forward parts of the thighs, (popliteal areas). This usually results in movements forward toward the front of the seat. At first this new position may be an upright one; then after a short time the back and abdominal muscles become fatigued, and the result is a slumped position which makes it quite difficult to pay attention to what is going on, or even to work at all.

In preventing excessive pressure on any part of the underside of the thighs, it is necessary that the front of the seat itself have no sharp or hard edges; and while this is especially true for the front of the seat, it is also required for other edges so that users will not hurt themselves.

A too-low seat height can also cause problems; the sharper angle between the thighs and the pelvis that results from an excessively low seat causes pressure on the abdominal organs, and even pain if continued for extended periods of time. Older people find it quite difficult to get up from a too-low seat, also.

Think for a moment what wrong height seating can do to a conference or to a sales meeting; it can ruin one. Think what it can do to the efficiency of an office worker, or to a student who just wants to study, or to the working ability of a seated craftsperson or assembly-line worker.

Before discussing the other measurements and characteristics of comfortable seating, it might be well to look into what constitutes seating comfort. Hertzberg says:

Although we tend to speak of comfort and discomfort as if they were two states of consciousness, for testing purposes it is more realistic to consider that there is only one, discomfort, and that "comfort" is only the absence of discomfort, just as cold is the absence of heat. It is the neutral sensory condition. Thus, one cannot "provide comfort" in a seat design; one can only eliminate sources of discomfort. In this sense of comfort, the implication of euphoria or active pleasure is ignored.

Hertzberg also points out that there have been two principal approaches to the comfort problem by the leading investigators in the human engineering or engineering anthropology field. Akerblom has espoused the theoretical approach by studying human anatomy in relation to seating, while Hertzberg and others have taken the approach of "comfort testing" by getting actual responses from groups of human subjects to actual samples of various types of seating.

A difference of opinion is apparent in this field between the testing group, led by Hertzberg, and the smaller theoretical group, led by Akerblom. They differ first on the shape of the seat itself. While Akerblom leads those who feel that a flat, hard surface is the best seat, Hertzberg heads a larger group who believe that "a properly contoured surface with some cushioning produces the least discomfort among conventional types of seating over relatively long periods of time." Hertzberg stresses that "the expected duration of occupancy" is a most important factor; "what is 'good' for two hours may be 'bad' for four hours and so on," he said.

Without going into the details of measurements of types of seating used in the many U.S. Air Force tests conducted by Hertzberg and others, and without giving the specifics of the reaction measurements obtained, it was found that the flat uncushioned U.S. Air Force seat "made test subjects uncomfortable in about 1½ to 2 hours, the contoured seat with a one-inch rubber pad in about 4 to 5 hours. The contoured seat pan with a contoured rubber cushion (USAF type MC-1) was used by every pilot in a flight of F-84's from the United States to England—a 15-hour trip—and the pilots were enthusiastic about it."

Hertzberg, on the basis of this particular series of tests and many others he has run and been involved with, feels strongly "that the adequately cushioned, contoured seat is superior to a flat surface for persons who cannot frequently leave the seat."

Protagonists of the flat, uncushioned seat argue that it is possible to shift weight easier from buttock to buttock on a flat surface to relieve pressure; Hertzberg has found that though brief relief is obtained, recovery is not fast enough, and increasing discomfort ensues even though constant shifting occurs on a flat surface, because alternately one buttock carries a double load. Since one of the prime requirements of good seating is that it permits the occupant to change postures frequently, as often as once every six to eight minutes, in comfort, this goes to the heart of the matter.

In another series of tests Hertzberg, using ingeniously contrived external visual methods (not needles or probes that would have distorted the results), found that for large but slender subjects "individual loads may rise as high as 70 pounds per square inch on the ischial tuberosities [points of the bones on which you sit]." He also points out that "on a flat surface the load is concentrated with little or no support from the surrounding tissues; whereas on a contoured surface, especially with a cushion, the surrounding tissues absorb an appreciable portion of the load." Of course, in this way pressure is reduced at the critical buttock points, and "experience with both the static and dynamic cushions (used during 56-hour sitting tests at Wright Field) indicate that if a person's buttock pressures can be kept below a certain critical level, he can sit almost indefinitely without undue discomfort."

It is interesting that Hertzberg's measurements of buttock point pressures as high as 70 pounds per square inch (previously thought by other investigators to be at maximum a little more than one pound per square inch) were replicated independently in Japan by Kohara.

There Is No "Average Man"

To return, however, to the measurement parameters of seating, in the author's opinion, Hertzberg's most important contribution to the design of seating has been his rejection of the "average man" principle and his advocacy of the idea of "design limits." He points out that "no such creature as the 'average man' exists," primarily because variations among different human dimensions are so wide that human bodily proportions are not constant. For example, he stresses, that "if the pure average were used for, say, arm reach from the operator's body position to a control lever, only the larger 50 percent of the population could reach the control adequately." He quotes a survey by Daniels to prove his point. Daniels studied the dimensions of 4,063 U.S. Air Force flying personnel to see how many would be average in ten body measurements related to sizes of clothing procured for the Air Force.

The study, called "The Average Man?" did not use exact averages; it allowed 15 percent on either side of the exact average, thus using the middle 30 percent of the sample for each dimension, and called this middle 30 percent the "approximate average." Here's what happened when

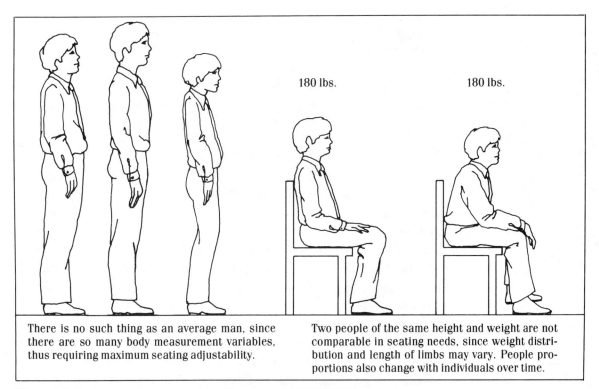

180 lbs.   180 lbs.

There is no such thing as an average man, since there are so many body measurement variables, thus requiring maximum seating adjustability.

Two people of the same height and weight are not comparable in seating needs, since weight distribution and length of limbs may vary. People proportions also change with individuals over time.

Figure 5.2. Body measurement variables. (Courtesy of *CONTRACT* Magazine)

they constructed a theoretical obstacle course using each dimension in sequence:

1. Of the original 4,063 men, 1,055 were of approximately average stature.

2. Of these 1,055 men, 302 were also of approximately average chest circumference.

3. Of these 302 men, 143 were also of approximately average sleeve length.

4. Of these 143 men, 73 were also of approximately average crotch height.

5. Of these 73 men, 28 were also of approximately average torso circumference.

6. Of these 28 men, 12 were also of approximately average hip circumference.

7. Of these 12 men, 6 were also of approximately average neck circumference.

8. Of these 6 men, 3 were also of approximately average waist circumference.

9. Of these 3 men, 2 were also of approximately average thigh circumference.

10. Of these 2 men, 0 were also of approximately average crotch length.

By the time the fourth step had been reached in this elimination process, as Hertzberg points out, less than 2 percent of the 4,063 men remained, and the correlation, for all practical purposes, had nearly disappeared.

Therefore, not only is there no such animal as the "average man," but—and this becomes most important in the design of not only seating but workplaces as well—the categories of height and weight in which interior designers and seating designers tend to place the total population are basically meaningless—in exact terms.

As the Daniels study demonstrates, just because two men are six feet in height and also equally weigh 180 pounds each, that does not mean that the lengths of their legs are same or that their weight is distributed in the same way. These two men would not necessarily therefore be comfortable or work well in chairs of the same height. Since these two men (or two women of equal height and weight) might be the users of a typing chair, this same observation would roughly apply to the data concerning seating height of a typical stenographer's chair. What is needed is enough adjustability that each occupant can adjust for his/her own proportions. In another context Wortz and Nowlis have said, "if you design for the average, you design for nobody."

Ranges of Adjustability

The lower limit of 13⅔ inches and the upper limit of 20⅔ inches as a minimum range of adjustability for the height of the seat of this chair is an example of the sort of range that Hertzberg proposes for many other anthropometric design purposes, and adjustability becomes *the* necessity to achieve the range of proportions needed. This will be emphasized strongly as the other parameters are explored in terms of this and other types of seating.

There are also at least two other important reasons for adjustability in chair design:

1. *The user of a particular chair may change.* The same employee may not be on the same job as long as the chair lasts. In public transportation seating, where the users change with each trip, this has become so important that Henry Dreyfuss Associates has included an additional adjustable portion to the airline seat design for American Airlines 747s—a variable air cushion in the lower back (or lumbar) region. At least one other major airline, Sabena, has also added this adjustment to their 747 seats.

2. *The need for adjustment changes with age.* This has perhaps most strongly been shown in Darell Boyd Harmon's work with school children, but it is also a factor in any long-term use of seating, since the user's adjustment needs will change with age even though his body dimensions may not; for example, his customary body posture is quite likely to change.

The height of the chair and its adjustability are regarded by most competent human factors engineers as the ideal starting point for engineering a work station for human beings. They say strongly that the chair must at the outset be adjusted in floor-to-seat height for the person who uses it. This is the first essential step in fitting the work station to the worker; the other factors should proceed after this first step. Kroemer and Robinette are very explicit: "Chair and desk (or table) should be treated as a unit and the height of the working surface should be derived from the height of the seat surface."

The next logical question is: "Now that you have determined the correct seating-surface height, how much higher should the top of the desk be in order that it is most comfortable for the user?" The consensus of the studies on this point seems to be 10 to 12 inches, depending on the worker's height; this distance is for an ordinary desk surface, not a typing surface. The distance from the seating surface height to the top of a typing surface can vary from 5½ inches to about 7 inches, depending on the typist's height and thigh thickness. One reason for this narrow range is Ellis's finding that, depending on the person, the elbow and forearm are not comfortable while working unless the forearm is within one to three inches of a horizontal position, measured at the tips of the fingers.

The Chair Back   The next most important part of the chair is of course the back. The European and American literatures generally agree that it is absolutely essential that sitters be able to change their posture from time to time in order to reduce the fatigue of staying in one position. This allows us to use different groups of muscles at different times to keep our posture upright in different positions. The back of the chair must be designed so that you can change positions from time to time, especially so that you can lean back now and then. Leaning back temporarily takes the weight off the spinal column and thus keeps the muscles associated with the spinal column from getting tired. According to Akerblom, "a good chair is one which permits as many good postures as possible to be adopted without interfering with the work."

The European and American authorities agree that there is no one good posture—there are several. The important design factor about the back (as well as the seat) of a chair is that it must allow for seating position changes with an acceptable range of postures, not only for these physical reasons, but also for the reason that shifts of mood will also result in posture changes. To allow for these changes, the back of a chair

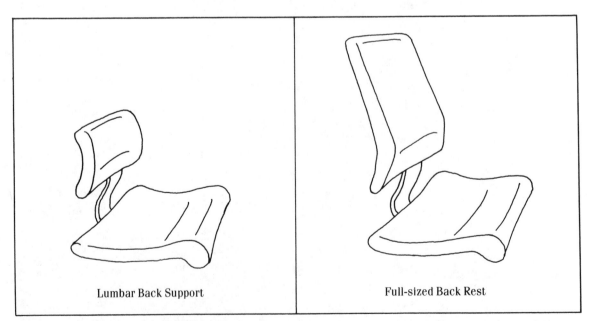

Lumbar Back Support   Full-sized Back Rest

Figure 5.3. Back rests that support either the lumbar area or the entire back. (Courtesy of Kroemer and Robinette, 1968)

must be adjustable, and to some degree at least, it must be automatically adjustable. Probably more research has been done on this and the necessary angles between the seat and the back than on any other factor in seating.

Angles

For a working chair to be comfortable for most people in most tasks it must be capable of assuming an angle of 80 degrees (10 degrees forward from perpendicular to the floor) to 120 degrees (30 degrees backward) with relation to the seat. Usually a good, well-designed working chair has an adjustable tension spring governing the position of the backrest in terms of this angle so that it can fit each person who sits on it in accordance with the individual force exerted on it. Usually the back also is vertically adjustable so that it can be made to fit persons needing different heights.

Some authorities also ask for a seat capable of changing its angle to the floor so that it can slope slightly forward or backward, depending on the need. Such a chair was introduced in Germany according to *MD* (Möbel Interior Design).

Dr. A.C. Mandal, a Dane, has been responsible for the introduction of more than 100,000 chairs into Denmark that allow a forward adjustment of 15 degrees downward, and he makes a very logical case for this design feature in his book. At this time, four companies in the United States are offering chairs with this adjustment.

Up to this point, we have been discussing a working chair without arms. For some workers we can add arm rests. Arm rests on a chair should not be higher than 8½ inches above the seat so that they reduce fatigue by taking some weight off the spinal column and the muscles associated with it; arm rests alone support 12.4 percent of body weight, according to Damon et al. However, arm rests do reduce the mobility of the person using the chair, and may limit the body breadth of the sitter.

Another disadvantage of an arm rest is that usually it connects the seat and back of the chair to make a fixed angle that cannot be changed. This reduces the number of postures that a sitter can have in such a chair, which is not a desirable quality. Of course, in some chairs with arm rests the seat and back can move separately, but these are usually more expensive, which puts pressures on the typical buyer to choose the

5.4

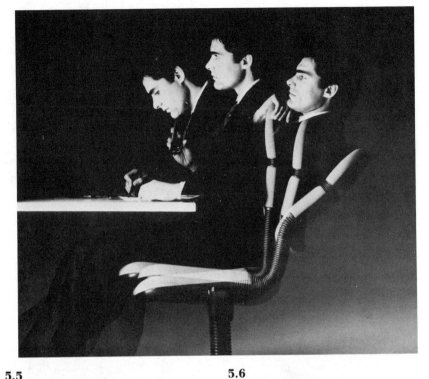

Figure 5.4. You can change the angle of the seat pan to the floor with this chair. (Kreuger photo)

Figure 5.5. Chair with back fixed in place by the arm rests. (Steelcase photo)

Figure 5.6. The back of this chair is not fixed in place by the arm rests. (Steelcase photo)

5.5

5.6

ones with arm rests that in effect fix the position of the seat and back at one posture.

Perhaps arm rests on the working chair are just a status symbol to most people who have them, but properly integrated into the design of a well thought out chair, they can produce some benefits.

The Largest Survey on Seating Comfort

In what is probably the largest survey on seating comfort, the author and Thomas Prunier of the National Furniture Center, Federal Supply Service, General Services Administration, digested material from 1,967 questionnaires with ninety pieces of information on each one. The information came from 1,967 air traffic controllers working for the Federal Aviation Administration:

1. When chairs are hard to adjust, people do not adjust them. The FAA chairs are quite difficult to adjust and only about one out of every eight controllers adjust their chairs. Easier-to-adjust gas cylinder devices are entering the American market and should be considered for working chairs and the comfort of the people who use them.

2. However, you have to tell people how to adjust chairs; more than half of the controllers did not use their back height adjustment because they did not know their chairs had one.

3. The controllers prefer a chair with upholstered arms and a back; a stool would not meet their needs.

4. Woven fabric (not vinyl) was overwhelmingly preferred as the upholstery material.

5. They prefer that the back should tilt and that it should reach shoulder height.

6. A chair's fit/comfort is of first importance to the controllers. Here is the complete ranking from this study:

Rank	Attribute	Percentage agreeing with this ranking or higher
1	Fit/comfort	75.2%
2	Safety	57.3%
3	Adjustability	59.1%
4	Durability (mechanical)	65.3%
5	Durability (of upholstery)	67.7%
6	Repairability	61.9%
6	Appearance	51.9%
6	Interface with other equipment	51.6%

5.7

Figure 5.7. Secretarial posture chair with easy gas cylinder seat height adjustment and five-pronged base. (Steelcase photo)
Figure 5.8. Principal dimensions and adjustments of a chair. (Courtesy of Kroemer and Robinette, 1968)

5.8

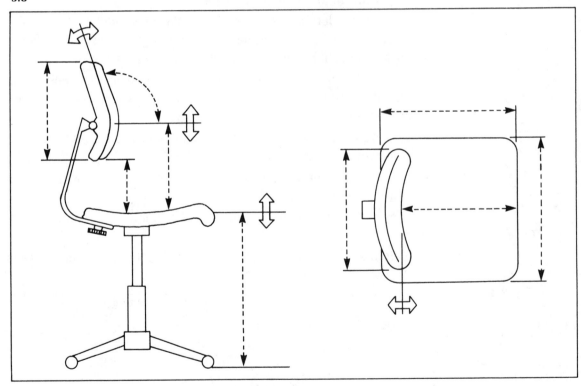

An FAA spokesman says, "We would rank fit/comfort and adjustability as one and the same, or at least equally important. With the number of differently sized people who use these chairs during a 24-hour day, we do not believe that the desired degree of fit/comfort can be obtained without satisfactory adjustability."

7. Seat height adjustment was ranked first among wanted adjustment features. The complete ranking of adjustments is:

Rank	Adjustment	Percentage agreeing with this ranking or higher
1	Seat height	73.3%
2	Back height	59%
3	Back tilt	64.4%
4	Seat depth	63.8%
4	Seat pitch	57.7%
4	Arm height	57.9%
4	Seat width	50%
5	Back width	56.7%
5	Back lateral	51%
6	Arm	63.6%

8. Slightly more than half of the controllers were uncomfortable in their chairs. In looking for causes, we found that the seat height adjustability range of the FAA chair was from 17 to 21 inches compressed seat height (recall Kroemer's recommendation of 13⅔ to 20⅔ inches). We found a lot more discomfort in shorter people, who might be expected to need lower seat height, and we think that seat height adjustability was shown to be very important in seating comfort in this survey; the FAA chairs tested did lack the range of 13⅔ to 17 inches.

9. A not-unexpected finding of this study was that as time spent sitting increased, people were less and less comfortable. A few of the controllers spent almost all their working time on an eight-hour shift sitting.

10. The study provided additional evidence that seating comfort may depend heavily on whether seat height adjustments have enough range to match the diversity of popliteal heights.

11. The study found that some controllers are concerned about the stability of their chairs; a five-pronged base instead of the present four-pronged base might help.

Chairs for the Home

As you may suspect by this time, there just is not much definitive material on nonworking seating—seating for home use or relaxation. Still, there are a few recommendations for working chairs that apply to residential chairs as well.

Upholstery should not be too soft, and cushioning should not be too soft. Most investigators agree that reasonably firm upholstery and firm cushioning are necessary to help spread the area of buttocks pressure, in contrast to a wood or metal surface. If the cushions are too soft, they do not permit the postural changes necessary to prevent fatigue. Too soft upholstery and cushioning also seem to inhibit brain activity, and under some conditions can induce sleep. Damon et al say that "common experience and actual tests show that people prefer and perform more efficiently for longer periods in soft seats—not 'supersoft,' but certainly cushioned—than on hard surfaces."

Because there is not much data for nonworking seating, we had a rule in our organization for years—that we would not specify or buy seating unless we sat in it first. This was an impractical rule, but there just is not any other way to be sure that seating is comfortable. It also had the disadvantage that the members of my organization were not necessarily typical in size and preference in relation to the total population. We would have liked very much to have had detailed information to help us choose proper seating for nonworking use.

There is some evidence that the information that we do have on working seating might apply to residential seating—the sales of the recliner and recliner-rocker for home use. The recliner is the only kind of chair for home use that allows for a change of angle between the seat and the back. Industry sources estimate that more than 15,000 of them are sold every day. Perhaps the fact that many of those sold have heat and vibration attachments should tell us that these consumers are trying to alleviate the lower back pain and other ailments that some investigators tell us have their roots in poor seating where they work or in the other parts of the home. Market surveys by major recliner producers repeatedly have confirmed the continuing consumer interest in these chairs.

Gaps in the Data

The reasons for our seating discomfort may not be the fault of designers; unfortunately—even with the seeming abundance of studies that are available on seating comfort—there are gaps in the basic information designers must have to create seating comfort for the entire population.

Hertzberg has called for the creation of a National Center for Anthropometric Data. Under his plan, the federal government (perhaps within the National Bureau of Standards, U.S. Department of Commerce) would establish a small group whose continuing mission would be (a) to perform periodic anthropometric surveys (perhaps every fifteen years) sampling statistically adequate numbers of the entire civilian population; and (b) to publish the data in comprehensible form, thereby producing an indispensible tool for design of all kinds of furniture, machinery, clothing, and personal equipment; and (c) to provide assistance in the most effective use of that tool to business and all governmental agencies.

One reason Hertzberg has suggested the creation of a National Center for Anthropometric Data is that the limited useful information we have for the general civilian population of the United States is contained in the results of the Health Examination Surveys of 1960–1962 and that material is now more than twenty years old. Another reason is that available studies do not reflect the racial mixture of this country. While NASA's Anthropometric Source Book does give dimensions for many different races, that information is hard to apply to the American population.

Unfortunately, racial differences in anthropometric dimensions can be wide. Hertzberg presents data obtained from studies of military personnel in Turkey, Greece, Italy, Japan, and the Republic of South Korea. Comparing data for ten selected dimensions from those populations with U.S. Air Force data, he concludes that "our Air Force people (and hence, our population at large) are giants to these other populations. Not only is the large majority of the flying personnel among our Mediterranean and Oriental allies below our 50th percentile in most dimensions, showing that their sizes are different from ours, but also their proportions are different."

The Anthro-pometrically Disadvantaged

The information cited by Hertzberg indicates that significant portions of the American population are being inadequately accommodated—on a racial basis. Because there are no usable, representative anthropometric samples of American blacks, Indians, Chicanos, and other racial minorities, their dimensions are not a part of the meager information available to American designers, not only for seating, but for workplaces, clothing, and other consumer products. Yet, we know that the body dimensions of these minorities can vary considerably from those reported in the available studies.

Another reason Hertzberg suggests periodic surveys is the known fact that Americans are getting larger; their body sizes are changing and this must be adequately reflected in the data available to designers on a *continuing* basis so that proper design dimensions can be used. (See Table 5–1.)

Table 5–1.
Changes in Weight and Stature of USAF Flying Personnel

Group	Weight (lb)			Stature (in)		
	Mean	S.D.	Change	Mean	S.D.	Change
Cadets, 1942[1] (N = 2959)	153.1	—		69.0	—	
			10.6			.1
Flyers, 1950[2] (N = 4063)	163.7	±20.9		69.1	±2.44	
			9.9			.7
Flyers, 1967[3] (N = 2420)	173.6	±21.44		69.8	±2.44	
			20.5			.8

[1]Randall et al., 1946; [2]Hertzberg et al., 1950; [3]Unpublished data, Anthropology Branch, AMRL-USAF, 1967

It is important to specify that his recommendation is for a continuing series of studies. This would give designers a consecutive series of bases for their work, a sequence of checkpoints for anthropometric reality.

Still another anthropometrically disadvantaged group in our population must be pointed out—children. Most material that is available is so obsolete that it is almost useless, especially in view of the changes in body sizes that are known to be occurring.

Therefore, so that all of us can be comfortable while sitting down, designers need the necessary information on our anthropometric dimensions, which could be furnished by Hertzberg's proposed National Center for Anthropometric Data.

Design Checkpoints

Stenographic and Operator Chairs

1. Seat height adjustability range should be from 13⅔ inches to 20⅔ inches (minimum range).

2. Pitch of the seat should be level or sloping slightly (3° to 7°) from the front to the rear, preferably adjustable. It might allow for up to 15° slope forward, also.

3. Width of the seat should be no less than 16 inches, preferably 17 inches.

4. Depth of the seat should be no less than 15 inches, preferably 16 inches.

5. A contoured, shaped seat surface is best to support buttocks, but since most chairs now available have flat seating surfaces, actually sitting on the chair for a half hour or more is probably the best method of testing and choosing.

6. Back rest should swivel vertically within a range of 80° (10° forward from 90° or perpendicular to the floor) to 120° (30° backward).

7. Back rest should be adjustable in height so that the bottom of it can be from 8 inches to 13 inches above the seat surface.

8. The tension of the back rest and its support should be adjustable; try it out.

9. Cushioning should be firm and of sufficient thickness so that it does not "bottom out." Have a 200-pound person sit on it.

10. Upholstery material should be durable, cleanable, and textured enough for some ventilation around the buttocks.

Visitors' Chairs

1. Use the same checkpoints as for stenographic or operator chairs, but omit the adjustability points 1, 6, 7, and 8.

2. Seat height must not exceed 17 inches; 16 inches is better.

Executive and Other Armchairs

1. Use the same checkpoints as for stenographic or operator chairs; modify point 6 to the realities of the marketplace.

2. Arm rests should be adjustable in height between 6 and 9 inches, but since most are not, they should be about 8 inches above the surface of the seat.

All Chairs
1. Have the actual user try it out, please!

Desks
1. Match size and shape of desk to needed work surface for the adequate performance of each task.
2. Match the number of drawers and their sizes to the needs of the task.
3. Make sure there is a hook underneath the center of the desk for a purse; provide storage for boots, galoshes, and other personal items away from the immediate workstation.
4. Check top surface of the desk for the matte (nonglare) characteristic.
5. Check the color of the top and sides of the desk so that the percentage of light reflectance falls within 30 to 56 percent (Munsell values 6–8).
6. Total height of desk should be no more than 30 inches (28 or 29 is better); typing surfaces should be no higher than 27 inches (26 is better). Both preferably should be adjustable.
7. Check the acoustical insulation within steel desks.
8. Verify the interchangeability of pedestals and tops for changing tasks and people.

References

B. Akerblom, "Standing and Sitting Posture," Stockholm: AB Nordiska Bokhandeln, 1948.

Ulrich Burandt, "Projekt Arbeitsstuhl," MD (Moebel Interior Design), Stuttgart, April 4, 1970.

Charles E. Clauser, John T. McConville, E. Churchill, Lloyd L. Laubach, and Joan A. Reardon, "Anthropometry of Air Force Women," ARML-TR-70-5, Aerospace Medical Research Laboratory, Wright-Patterson Air Force Base, 1972.

A. Damon, H. W. Stoudt, and R. A. McFarland, "The Human Body in Equipment Design," Cambridge, Mass.: Harvard University Press, 1966.

G. S. Daniels, "The Average Man?", Wright-Patterson Air Force Base: Wright Air Development Center, Report #WCRD-TN-53-7, 1952.

Niels Diffrient, "Design With Backbone," *Industrial Design* 17, no. 8 (1970), pp. 44–47.

Douglas S. Ellis, "Speed of Manipulative Performance as a Function of Work-Surface Height," *Journal of Applied Psychology*, 35 (1951), pp. 289–296.

W. F. Floyd, and D. F. Roberts, "Anatomical and Physiological Principles in Chair and Table Design," *Ergonomics* (1958), pp. 1–16.

Darell Boyd Harmon, "The Co-Ordinated Classroom," Grand Rapids: American Seating Company, 1949.

H. T. E. Hertzberg, "Some Contributions of Applied Physical Anthropometry to Human Engineering," Symposium on Dynamic Anthropometry, Annals of the New York Academy of Sciences, Vol. 63, art. 4, 1955, pp. 616–629.

H.T.E. Hertzberg, ed., "Annotated Bibliography of Applied Physical Anthropology in Human Engineering," Wright-Patterson Air Force Base: Aero Medical Laboratory, 1958.

H. T. E. Hertzberg, "World Diversity in Body Size and Its Meaning in American Aid Programs," *OAR Research Review*, 7, no. 12 (December 1968), pp. 14–17.

H. T. E. Hertzberg, "On the Nation's Need of a National Center for Anthropometric Data," mimeo, Aerospace Medical Research Laboratory, Wright-Patterson Air Force Base, 1971.

H. T. E. Hertzberg, G. S. Daniels, and E. Churchill, "Anthropometry of Flying Personnel—1950," Aero Medical Laboratory, Wright Air Development Center, Wright-Patterson Air Force Base, 1954.

Walter Kleeman, Jr., and Thomas Prunier, "Evaluation of Chairs Used by Air Traffic Controllers of the U.S. Federal Aviation Administration—Implications for Design," Session VI, Applications 1, NATO Symposium on Anthropometrics and Biomechanics, Theory and Application—Proceedings, Queens' College, Cambridge, England, July 1980.

Walter Kleeman, Jr., "The FAA Chair Study," *The Designer* 21, no. 278, (April 1980), pp. 72, 74, 76, 81.

Walter Kleeman, "Some Notes on the Future of Chairs, *"Furniture Manufacturing Management* 25, no. 2 (February 1979), pp. 26–27.

Jiro Kohara, "The Application of Human Engineering to Design - Chair - Bed - Vehicle Seat," Chicago: Institute of Design, Illinois Institute of Technology, 1965.

K.H. Eberhard Kroemer and Joan C. Robinette, "Ergonomics in the Design of Office Furniture - A Review of the European Literature," AMRL -TR-68-80. Wright-Patterson Air Force Base: Aerospace Medical Laboratories, July 1968.

W. E. Lay and L. C. Fisher, "Riding Comfort and Cushions," *SAE Journal* (Transactions) 47, no. 5 (1940), pp. 482–496.

A. C. Mandal, "The Seated Man (Homo Sedens)," (DK) 2930 Klampenborg, Denmark, Taarbaek Strandvej 49, 1979.

F. E. Randall, Albert Damon, Robert S. Benton, and Donald I. Patt, "Human Body Size in Military Aircraft and Personal Equipment," Army Air Forces Technical Report #5501, Air Material Command, Wright-Patterson Air Force Base, 1946.

R. F. Slechta, E. A. Wade, W. K. Carter, and J. Forrest, "Comparative Evaluations of Aircraft Sitting Accommodations," WADC-TR-57-136, Wright Air Development Center, Wright-Patterson Air Force Base, 1957.

H. W. Stoudt, Albert Damon, R. A. McFarland, and June Roberts, "Weight, Height and Selected Body Dimensions of Adults, United States, 1960-1962," Washington: Report #8, Series 11, June 1965, National Center for Health Statistics, U.S. Dept. of Health, Education and Welfare.

Jason Thomas, "A Chair That Takes a Back Seat to No Other One," *Chicago Sun-Times*, 1976.

Unpublished Data, Anthropology Branch, Aerospace Medical Research Laboratories, Wright-Patterson Air Force Base, 1967.

Webb Associates, ed., "Anthropometry Source Book, Volume I, Anthropometry for Designers, Volume II, A Handbook of Anthropometric Data and Volume III, An Annotated Bibliography of Anthropometry," NASA Reference Publication 1024. Washington: National Aeronautics and Space Administration, Scientific and Technical Office, July 1978.

E.C. Wortz, and D.P. Nowlis, "The Design of Habitable Environments," *Man-Environment Systems* 5, no. 5 (September 1975), pp. 280–288.

6 *The Ergonomics of Desks*

What does ergonomics have to do with desks? In the present state of the art of designing desks, not much. That is the trouble. There is plenty of ergonomic research waiting to be used (in fact, begging to be used), but not many designers are using it, judging from the typical desks now on the market. Let's look at some examples of data produced by ergonomic research that could be used for the design of better desks than we have now. These examples show that the designer of conventional desks is being challenged by the findings.

Most of the useful data comes from studies done in Sweden, Germany, Holland, and especially Great Britain, where work in this specialty has been going on for years. Much important work also has been done in the United States, notably by the Aerospace Medical Research Laboratories of the U.S. Air Force as a spinoff of work on cockpit design.

Desks Only Adjust Upward

One of the most obvious facts about any desk—American as well as those from most other parts of the world—is that they are almost invariably 29 to 30 inches high and adjustable only upward. They do not even follow the British Standards Institution recommendation of 28 inches as the correct height for nonadjustable desks. All typing returns or surfaces are 26 or 27 inches high and adjustable only *upward,* too. Yet the consensus of ergonomic opinion and years of experimentation is that different sizes of people need different heights, and they further pinpoint a range of needed desk heights from 26½ inches to 31 inches and needed typing surface heights from 20½ to 26½ inches.

The ergonomists go even further and say that the height of the desk or typing surface is a part of the whole (which is the work station) and that this includes the chair, of course. Therefore, the height of the work surface must depend on the height of the seating, and the heights of both must be adjustable.

The conventional office desk, as we can buy it or specify it in the United States, is not adjustable in height within the proper range of adjustability to match the people who may have to work at it. There is one major exception, a line of desks from a major manufacturer, but with a rather primitive and difficult adjustment mechanism.

Adjustable Chairs and Desks

We adjust the chair to fit the desk, not to fit the person using it, because almost all working chairs are adjustable in height and it is easy to adjust the height of the chair. However, the technology *is* available for an adjustable height desk—as long as you avoid the type in which the lowest drawer in the pedestals almost hits the floor. As a matter of fact, a Jap-

6.1

Figure 6.1. It would be difficult to make this desk adjustable in height. (Steelcase photo)
Figure 6.2. Adjustable height desk with telescoping legs from Sweden. (Facit AB photo)

6.2

anese ergonomist has not only designed one, but he has also had them built and put into successful use in Japan. They also are made in Sweden and are now being imported into this country. However, the desk only adjusts from 26⅜ inches to 29½ inches in height and the typing surface from 23 inches to 26¼ inches in height, about half the needed ranges.

Instead of doing what the Japanese and Swedes have done, other ergonomists recommend the use of adjustable foot rests for short people. For short people the top of the desk does not adjust far enough downward, and if they adjust the chair to the static desk height, their feet are

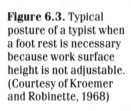

Figure 6.3. Typical posture of a typist when a foot rest is necessary because work surface height is not adjustable. (Courtesy of Kroemer and Robinette, 1968)

off the floor and they experience discomfort at best. (See the discussion in the previous chapter.)

Currently the typical American desk is made for just two types of people: the tall and the very tall. They are not built for the typical American, though the mythical, typical American is growing taller by the year. Perhaps as a people we will eventually grow up to our desks. Meanwhile, what is happening to the people who are not tall enough for their desks? Researchers are just beginning to dig out the answers, but the present indications are that nonadjustable desks (and poorly designed seating, too) are responsible for a host of troubles and pains that seated workers complain of. Ask any general practitioner or industrial plant doctor what the most-difficult-to-diagnose complaint is and you will be told it is lower back pain. Ergonomic studies show not only a definite connection between bad working-surface heights and lower back pain but also a connection between these heights and wrist-forearm problems, too.

Harmon's Studies   Several years ago, Darell Boyd Harmon performed studies of thousands (160,000 for three years in preliminary studies, then 1,774 children for three years in intensive studies) of Texas school children to try to find out what the connections might be between badly designed, non-adjustable-height school desks and various physical problems found among these same school children.

He found a definite correlation in the following way. To begin the chain reaction, Harmon feels that the distortion of the child's vision is the first step. If the distance from the desk (and therefore the child's reading angle) are distorted because the desk is not adjustable in height, eye strain results. The rest of the chain reaction that starts at this point is not so well known.

When a child reads at a distorted angle, his head is not in an upright position; it is cocked to one side. At first this only affects, let's say, the muscles of the neck—but is it so farfetched to say this might affect the way his teeth meet for chewing? Harmon's studies indicate that this is probably true—that dental defects can result from poorly designed desks and seating.

Then, to take the dental defect a bit further, if the teeth do not quite meet correctly, the child cannot chew well and does not digest food properly. Certainly it will not be long before nutritional problems show up because not enough of the needed dietary elements get into the digestive system. The next step to chronic infection and chronic fatigue is obvious; a child who is not getting proper nutrition certainly will have less resistance to infection as well as a lower energy level.

This is one part of the chain reaction, but it can take another path, starting from the child's head cocked to one side. Not only the neck muscles are affected by this. The neck muscles are only one part of the human muscular system, and any part of the system is interrelated with the other parts; if one part is out of kilter, the other parts are affected, too. Harmon shows, through a series of observations of the workings of the human muscular system, how, anatomically, the act of reading affects the total human set of muscles to produce all sorts of posture problems, especially in the back and arms, when the visual angle is distorted and/ or at the wrong distance. His findings coordinate with the lower back and wrist-forearm problems spotlighted by the ergonomists abroad. However, there is more to this.

The child's ability to perform school work is adversely affected by this same set of conditions. Harmon devised a test to show that this is true. He had the children draw free-hand squares on a blank piece of paper. The results of these tests repeatedly showed that the distortions in their reading angles showed up as distortions of the shape of the squares that the children drew.

Perhaps one might think these things happened only to children. But while it is true that no comparable studies are available for adult workers, Harmon's logic has stood up over the years, and the literature contains plenty of indications that these troubles start in school and get worse when the grown-up child becomes an office worker.

The lack of height adjustability in the proper ranges is not the only thing that is wrong, ergonomically speaking, with desks; we seem to have forgotten that the angle of the desk top to the floor must be adjustable, too. Harmon graphically illustrates how nonadjustable desk tops can start the visual-defects–physical-defects process. Harmon's findings are partially supported by Eastman and Kamon's study of posture, back movement, and fatigue of subjects reading and writing at flat and slanted (at 12 degrees and 24 degrees) desks. Their "results indicated more erect posture and less back movement (reduced EMG) at the slanted surfaces, while slanting the desks also reduced fatigue and discomfort."

Mandal also highly recommends a desk top slanted at 10 degrees. Yet, only one standard desk on the market now in the United States has an inclined top, and none has tops that can be adjusted in their angle to the floor, except quasi-desks and tables for draftsmen. Perhaps we should consider an alternative, a reading stand, or book base on a flat desk for reading, which a few scholars use.

Light Reflectance Is Important

Another characteristic of the desk top—the way it reflects light—receives too little attention. The first aspect is the color and pattern of light.

If you choose rosewood or walnut (either real wood or melamine laminate) for a desk top, it may be pretty, but it is wrong, ergonomically speaking. Why? Because your eyes do not do their best work when there is too much contrast between white paper (which is mostly what you look at on a desk top) and the color of the top of the desk. The contrast line captures the attention of your eyes, distracts you, and makes it quite difficult to concentrate on your work.

The workplace designer must be conscious of other possible distractions that may enter the design to distract the sensitive reader, such as colors that are too bright or contrast too sharply, or arresting shapes; these may have to be excluded from the worker's viewing cone. For the same reasons, a wood pattern that is apparent in the desk should be subdued, because a strong pattern, characteristic of some highly figured rosewood species, also provides a strong contrast and distraction point to take your attention away from your work.

Some of the darker woods, including rosewood and walnut, give as little as 9 percent reflectance (the percentage of white light reflected to the eye) and you need between 30 and 50 percent reflectance for proper contrast; too little contrast is just as bad; a white top fatigues the eyes, and also makes it too difficult for your eyes to find the white paper that makes up so much of your work. While you can obtain the exact reflectance percentages for most melamine laminates from their manufacturers, some ergonomically approved tops available are the familiar dull marbleized greens and beiges as well as some oak, maple, cherry, and teak tops, both wood and laminate.

Another factor to watch out for is glare. There is general agreement in the field that a dull, matte surface is best for a desk top; shiny, glossy finishes produce too much glare, which is especially fatiguing to the eyes.

Ergonomics is also concerned with the outer surfaces of a desk (in addition to the top) from the acoustic point of view. For example, some of the early office landscapes were not successful because of poor acoustic control, and one of the factors involved turned out to be the fact that the sides of desk pedestals are great sound reverberators. To make some installations work it has been necessary to put various kinds of acoustically functional cloth on all outer desk surfaces except the top. This reduces the acoustic confusion and reverberation and damps the sound level. On the other hand, the paper and the filing folders in open-sided filing carts also absorb sound, which is another acoustic benefit.

Top of the Desk

For the next ergonomic observation, we return to the top of the desk and mention that the typical desk top is a flat, unbroken surface. Some designers feel that it should not be so, for ergonomic reasons.

Several researchers, especially Humphry Osmond, Robert Sommer, and Robert Propst, have stressed the need for visual triggers, so that the office worker is reminded of tasks, by sight. Sommer was more interested in the purely research environment when he pointed out the need for a visible method of keeping notes and studies so that they are not on the desk top, but still where they can be seen by the researcher. He felt that they would get lost in the hidden recesses of a distant file cabinet. Propst later took this idea a bit further when he put the files in the top of the desk covered with a movable, rolling tambour. He also developed bound note holders and shelves for them that can be installed above the desk; the note holders can then be clearly marked and seen by the person at the desk. The file in the top of the desk has been changed by other designers, notably Douglas Deeds and Barry Rosengrant, from the tambour cover to a partial flip top over the file, but the basic idea is similar: you break the flat top of the desk with a filing system to give the user visual reference points for his or her work.

Another change is coming to the top of the desk. Until recently, the automatic editing and typing machinery of the word processing innovations in offices had been marketed along with furniture sold by the machine makers, most of which seems clumsy and not particularly well designed for the purpose. However, designers may be paying attention

6.4

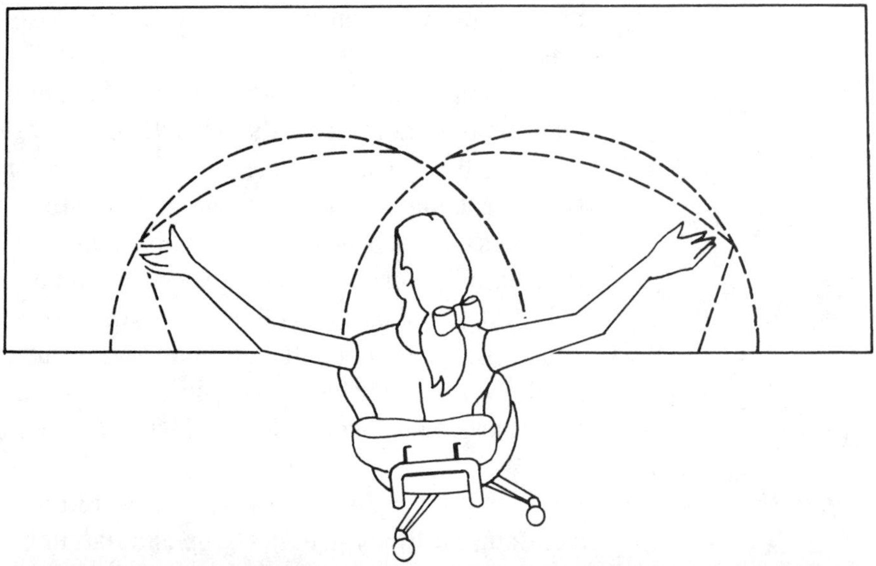

Figure 6.4. This is the way people use the tops of desks while seated. A typical arm reach uses only 24 inches of the desk depth.
Figure 6.5. The Cluster 120 desk. (Oxford Pendaflex photo)

6.5

to this design opportunity; the same Swedish manufacturer who exports the adjustable height desk has recently offered a sound-absorbing word processing desk, with a 26-inch square recessed area. The base of the recessed area is a perforated sheet of steel that sends the sound from the machine down to the carpet where it is absorbed, as opposed to a solid bottom that bounces the sound back at the typist.

The microprocessor revolution, which has miniaturized so many electronic products, has begun to revolutionize desk design. A desk containing a complete computer and printer is on the market for about $3000. Yet, it is the same size as and looks just like a normally well-styled, single-pedestal desk. Other aspects of the electronic revolution are discussed in Chapter 12, "Life in the Office."

In passing it should be noted that Propst advocates a stand-up desk, and for a very good ergonomic reason. An office worker who has both a sit-down and a stand-up desk will spend time at each, and the worker's circulation and muscular activity will increase, which is desirable for relatively sedentary workers. Some of the newer stand-up desks, which are attached to partitions in systems developed for office landscapes, consist basically of tops that are attached to the partition at any desired height; therefore, within limits, they are adjustable in height. It is doubtful that users yet see that adjustability in the ergonomic perspective we have discussed, although Winston Churchill wrote his books standing up, and many people like to work standing up some of the time.

Despite the advent of office landscape, the typical office desk is still 60 inches by 30 inches and its shape is rectangular. One group of desk designers at Oxford Pendaflex has tried to improve the shape of the desk top for two principal reasons:

1. To allow more of the top surface to be used according to characteristics of human reaching ability so that people can reach everything on a desk without getting up.

2. To allow better use of office floor space.

The explanation is apparent from the diagrams shown in Figures 6.6 through 6.11.

A typical 60-inch-by-30-inch desk has a top area of 12½ square feet, but only 8½ square feet can be used (68 percent of the top area) by a seated worker because of reach limitations; the worker typically would have to get out of his chair to reach the unshaded portion of Figure 6.6.

Figure 6.7 is a diagram of Oxford's 120 desk. The shaded portion represents the part of the top surface that can be reached by a sitting worker without getting up. The 120 desk has a total top area of 10¼ square feet, and 95 percent of that area (or 9¾ square feet) is typically accessible to,

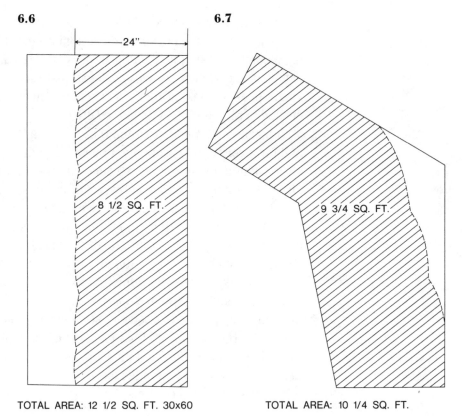

6.6

6.7

Figure 6.6. Useable space on a desk top for a seated person.
Figure 6.7. Useable space on Oxford's desk top for a seated person.

24"

8 1/2 SQ. FT.

9 3/4 SQ. FT.

TOTAL AREA: 12 1/2 SQ. FT. 30x60   TOTAL AREA: 10 1/4 SQ. FT.

and can be reached by, the seated worker, which makes it a much more efficient shape than the typical rectangular 60-inch-by-30-inch desk.

The advantages do not end with the usability of the desk top alone. Because of the way the desks can be clustered together, use of total floor space can be more efficient, as the comparison diagrams show in Figures 6.8 through 6.11.

It is also noteworthy that when these differently shaped desks are clustered, the workers who use them do not face each other directly, thus removing one distraction factor from the work environment.

No Desk Needed   Despite all this discussion of desks, we should emphasize that some offices do not require desks. In fact, when business is done between businesspeople from different cultures, a desk may be a bar to doing any business at all. The reason is that the preferred conversational distance varies greatly from culture to culture around the world. Latin Americans,

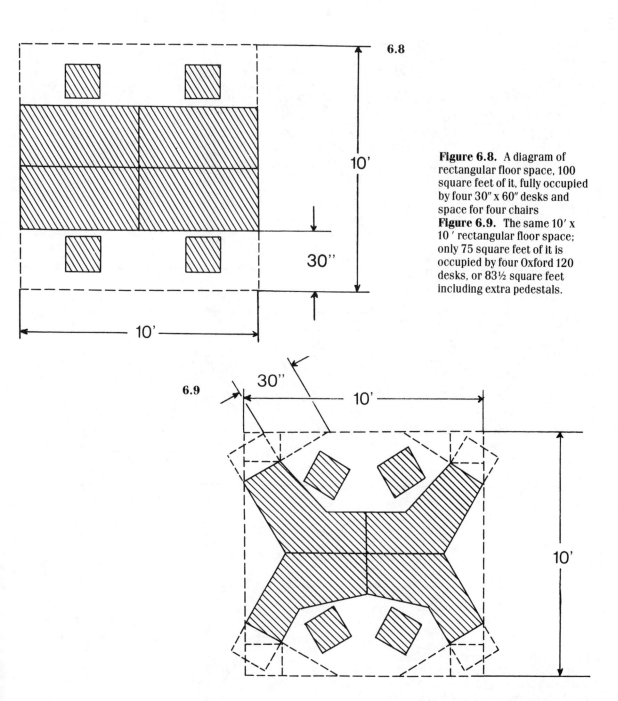

6.8

10'

30''

10'

Figure 6.8. A diagram of rectangular floor space, 100 square feet of it, fully occupied by four 30" x 60" desks and space for four chairs
Figure 6.9. The same 10' x 10' rectangular floor space; only 75 square feet of it is occupied by four Oxford 120 desks, or 83½ square feet including extra pedestals.

6.9

30''

10'

10'

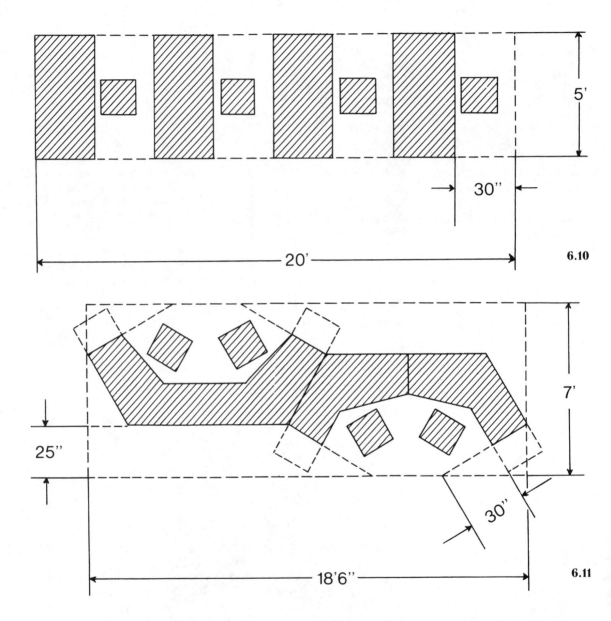

6.10

6.11

Figure 6.10. A configuration of 100 square feet of floor space fully occupied by four 30″ x 60″ desks and their attendant chairs.
Figure 6.11. Only 75 square feet is taken up with four Oxford 120 desks clustered, or 83½ square feet including extra pedestals.

for instance, like to talk to someone of either sex at about half the distance that we North Americans prefer; they also want to be in actual physical contact with the person they are talking to. A desk makes this impossible since it is a barrier to the conversational distance with which a Latin American feels comfortable. Many Middle Eastern cultures produce the same type of reaction. These are called close-contact cultures.

Even in our own culture, in, for example, certain types of interviews and in doctor-patient relationships, the desk can be a barrier to the business at hand. Zweigenhaft's study of "Personal Space in the Faculty Office: Desk Placement and the Student-Faculty Interaction" bears on this concern. His findings indicated "that those faculty who used the desk-between (them and the student) interior design tended to be older and of higher academic rank, were rated less positively on those student evaluation items that concerned the nature of the student-faculty interaction, and in general, were rated less positively as teachers by their students."

So, in certain contexts in our own culture or if you want to negotiate or do business with people from a close-contact culture, you might do well to eliminate desks so that they are not barriers to involved conversation. If the office is big enough, you might set up a separate area around a coffee table where the seating is movable and will permit close contact with no barriers.

There are, however, other cultures in addition to our own where the desk provides the acceptable distance for doing business or negotiation, notably Great Britain, Germany, the Netherlands, and Scandinavian countries.

For a further discussion of conversational distances, see "Communication Distance." There is also a further discussion of desks within the context of office furniture systems in "Life in the Office."

References

"Anthropometric Recommendations for Dimensions of Non-adjustable Office Chairs and Tables," B.S. 3079. London: British Standards Institution, 1959, p. 7.

Applied Ergonomics, "General Framework and Workstation Analysis," 1, no. 1, December, 1969, p. 33.

M. C. Eastman, and E. Kamon, "Posture and Subjective Evaluation at Flat and Slanted Desks," *Human Factors* 18, no. 1, (February 1976), pp. 25-26.

Edward T. Hall, "The Silent Language in Overseas Business," *Harvard Business Review* 38 (1960), pp. 87–96.

Darell Boyd Harmon, "Lighting and Child Development," *Illuminating Engineering* April 1945, pp. 199–233.

Darell Boyd Harmon, "The Co-Ordinated Classroom," Grand Rapids: American Seating Company, 1949.

Jiro Kohara, "The Application of Human Engineering to Design - Chair - Bed - Vehicle Seat," Chicago: Institute of Design, Illinois Institute of Technology, 1965.

K. H. Eberhard Kroemer, and Joan C. Robinette, "Ergonomics in the Design of Office Furniture: A Review of the European Literature," Fairborn: Aerospace Medical Research Laboratories, 1968.

A. C. Mandal, "The Seated Man (Homo Sedens)," Klampenborg: Tarbaek Strandvej 49 2930 Denmark, 1979.

Humphry Osmond, and Robert Sommer, "Architecture for Researchers," *American Behavioral Scientist* 4 (December 1961), pp. 32–34.

Oxford Pendaflex, Garden City, New York, 1971, 1977.

Robert Propst, "The Office — A Facility Based on Change," Elmhurst: The Business Press, 1968.

Wesley E. Woodson, "Human Engineering Guide for Equipment Designers," Berkeley and Los Angeles: University of California Press, 1956, pp. 1–78.

Richard L. Zweigenhaft, "Personal Space in the Faculty Office: Desk Placement and the Student–Faculty Interaction," *Journal of Applied Psychology* 61, no. 4, 1976, pp. 529–532.

7 *Interior Design as Nonverbal Communication*

"The whole of environment, from the moment we name it and think of it as such, is a tissue of symbolic forms: the whole of environment is symbol."

(Rykwert, 1967)

Figure 7.1. Nonverbal communication.

When entering any interior space, its *impact* on the senses becomes instant communication without words. While this impact is principally visual, since the eyes are the prime sources of sensory information, the thermal, auditory, olfactory, and tactile qualities of the surroundings are perceived as well. The impression received may be clear and sharp, or merely a fuzzy, ambiguous impression, or nothing may be noticed at all. However, the fact remains that interior spaces do communicate with those who occupy them or see them, and this communication usually takes place without spoken words.

Determinism

There are those who assert that essentially the design of an interior space and its location not only can communicate with those who enter it, but also can control their behavior. They even go so far as to claim that this is the sole behavioral determinant. The ecological psychology group, led by Roger G. Barker and Paul V. Gump of the Midwest Psychological Field Station at the University of Kansas, is the leader in this belief. Their work, meticulously detailed, consists mainly of "non-intrusive, tender-minded, non-destructive" observations of how subjects use interior and other spaces over long periods of time.

Ecological psychology focuses on objects and the physical, built environment rather than on individual people. Although Barker explicitly mentions individual differences in defining his theories and field limits, "the environment is seen to consist of highly structured improbable arrangements of objects and events which coerce behavior in accordance with their own dynamic patterning."

While the reader of this school's works is treated to tidbits of individual behavior (e.g., Anne Matson, in Barker, 1968) that include names, individual actions, and explicit descriptions, the specific actions of human beings lose their importance as they are homogenized and blended into the personless, bland research results.

Mass of Data

The voluminous mass of data that spews forth from Barker, Wright, and their colleagues is staggering in its sheer effusion of numbers: in a study of 119 children they estimated that "these subjects engaged in more than 36 million behavioral episodes in the course of a year." While it is undeniably useful to know that "three children who were observed for an entire day were found to interact with 571, 671, and 749 different objects" and that "the total number of interactions with these objects was 1882, 2282, and 2490," these numbers and their associated assertions still cannot validate a statement by Barker and Gump that "for example, it is possible to study schools in terms of such variables as the social class of students, the training of teachers, and the extent of curricular offerings; but students do not respond directly to these variables."

This kind of statement attempts to shut out all other theories of how and why the environment can affect the actions of human beings in it or the interactions of human beings with it. More important, it almost completely rejects the notion that human beings themselves may acquire abilities to determine their actions and fate in the environment; it also presupposes singular nonverbal communication from the environment to persons in it, "coercing" behavior with no other instrumental factors.

Thing-Oriented Theories

The extremism of this group's thing-oriented theories can be illustrated by such statements by Barker as: "It is not easy, at first, to leave the person out of the observations of the environment of molar behavior," and "The people who inhabit a class are to a considerable degree interchangeable and replaceable. Pupils come and go; even the teacher may be replaced. But the same entity continues as serenely as an old car with new rings and the right front wheel now carried as a spare." To agree with such statements is to deny any progress or change in the educational process in the future; their implied static, unchangeable condition is not a reality.

Nowhere in the works of Barker and Gump is there any evidence of a direction toward research that would identify possibilities and factors for change or prospects for improving the human condition. Barker and Gump seem cognizant of *technical* innovations (television, teaching machines, and so on), but strangely do not proceed beyond a statistical analysis that leaves the rich field of interpersonal relationships untouched. Even with its limitations, the rather didactic approach of Barker and his group did produce some evidence that might relate to theories concerning how many people can successfully communicate at one time in one place (see Chapter 4, "Communication Distance").

*Greater
Participation in
Small Schools*

In their study of school sizes and the resultant effects on student behavior, Barker and Gump found that the participation of students in activities of all sorts is greater in small schools than in larger ones, in terms of sheer numbers of students per activity, responsible positions filled, satisfactions gained, and productivity. They specifically mention that in small schools students "exhibit . . . easier communication, both through greater clarity and decreased difficulty," and "exhibit greater social interaction among inhabitants generally."

While this evidence might strengthen the view that the lesser numbers of students and the lesser distances in small schools might improve communication, there is also the possibility that students are simply more relaxed in small schools. They may feel more at home and not receive the lost and tense feelings communicated nonverbally to them simply by the presence of the big school as a physical reality.

A Barker disciple, Robert B. Bechtel, has explained some of the theoretical underpinnings of the Barker group by his use of the term "undermanning." As interpreted by Bechtel, "undermanning" is "a theory of human scale." He feels that there are a great many benefits for people who operate in small human organizations. Each person has a chance to engage in a wider variety of functions, is more important, has more responsibilities, and can achieve more self-identity.

Behavior Mapping

The work of Barker and his group is somewhat related to the behavior mapping techniques used by researchers Harold M. Proshansky, William H. Ittleson, and Leanne G. Rivlin. Using a psychiatric ward in a hospital as a behavior setting, these researchers have made mass studies from preset observation points of where patients are and what they are doing over a span of time. Both groups have concentrated on determining what activities are occurring and/or the extent of human participation in them. Barker and his group have further developed the concept of synomorph—that an activity must fit the setting in which it takes place, which may be helpful, and might serve as a basis for future researchers who might attempt to identify individual stimulating or inhibiting elements in the environment.

Cognitive Mapping

A third group, the cognitive mappers, have provided useful information describing how human beings perceive the environment and what elements in it are used as cues (nonverbal) to get from one spot to another. Almost all of this work has been done on the exterior, not interior spaces, but because it focuses on the perception of space and on spacial concepts, it might prove in the future to be a useful research procedure in interior spaces. Lynch; Moore; Appleyard; Stea and Downs; Ladd; Appleyard, Lynch, and Meyer; and Piaget and Inhelder are all examples of this approach.

Stimulated by some of the more distorted maps reported by Ladd, the author developed the hypothesis that our perception of the environment may be affected by the sum total of our education and experiences up to any given moment; that differing backgrounds and educations might result in our being affected differently by environmental cues.

Also, it might be possible that differing perceptions of the interior environment may be due to an entirely different set of factors: nonverbal communication from the environment to the viewer may be an integral part of other processes.

Ethological Considerations

Vital clues may lie in the works of Richard G. Coss concerning the ethological studies of "enemy recognition" and the research of Eckhard H. Hess concerning what ethologists call "imprinting." Coss is both an industrial designer and a student of comparative ethology who has extensively investigated what Tinbergen and Lorenz call "sign-stimuli" or visual "releasers." Primarily, these "releasers" are special key stimuli which elicit reliable and appropriate responses from specific species or groups of animals—usually for survival purposes.

For example, the specific enemies of certain mammals, including man, could include poisonous snakes, spiders, and scorpions, in addition to the larger predators such as the great cats. Coss feels that "the spontaneous fear exhibited by man of snakes, scorpions and other insects with many legs suggests that these avoidance responses represent emotional by-products for survival purposes—residual from an earlier evolutionary period." He also cautions, however, that "some of the studies that will be discussed need further confirmation through additional research. The subject is new and the area awaits much study."

Coss says that "the possibility [is] that man may have unlearned sensitivity to specific visual forms resulting from biological evolution." Specifically he explains further in one example that "through fighting and breeding selection pressures exerted by dominant primate males, the inherent sensitivity to staring eyes could be genetically encoded with the neural biochemical material associated with pattern recognition." This statement is supported by a discussion of experimental evidence of the possible mechanisms involved.

What are the specific studies on which Coss bases his theories?

Eyespots and People

One of the more important works cited concerns peacock butterflies and eyed-hawk moths. For example, both of these species display two discoid patterns (eyespots) on their hindwings; the purpose of these is assumed to be to ward off their normal enemies. The praying mantis (among many other species) also flares up its wings to display discoid eyespots in an effort to keep predators away. In some cases the likenesses are accurate enough to look as if the sun were shining into two real eyes.

Proceeding to evidence from studies on human beings, Coss cites research on infants by Robert L. Fantz that suggests that the form of the human face, especially the eyes, is recognized at an early age. It must be noted that the brains of young infants are immature and that learning is severely restricted. Infants appear to be sensitive to circular forms and will gaze at a caretaker's eyes for many minutes rather than at other equally conspicuous forms, such as the mouth and the edges of the face. Moreover, if the caretaker turns his or her head to a profile view, exposing only one eye to view, the infant quickly loses interest and redirects his gaze elsewhere.

Other researchers have observed the same phenomenon in infants as old as four weeks. As a means of investigating the response to staring eyes in mature adults, Coss presented slides depicting various clusters of concentric circles and measured their pupillary dilation response with a special instrument called a pupillometer. The results of these tests indicated that two concentric circles were the most provocative shape.

In another series of tests Coss presented two circles in vertical, diagonal, and horizontal rows on paper. Only the horizontal pair of circles elicited a significantly higher response, indicating that shapes depicting the perceptual aspects of two staring eyes are indeed more potent stimuli than similar shapes depicting fewer eye-like properties.

Sharp-Pointed Forms

Coss has also investigated the emotional responses triggered by sharp-pointed forms, such as compressed zig-zags, which give the deceptive impression of serrated teeth. Using the pupillometer as an arousal indicator, he found that sharp-serrated patterns evoked a significantly greater response than equally complicated rounded patterns—in both American and European adults he tested. Coss at this point again emphasizes the necessity of much further observation and testing before arriving at conclusions. Coss also discusses other aspects of enemy recognition by both the lower primates and humans, especially in terms of aversions to snakes, scorpions, spiders, and cats, and that there may be a partially unlearned basis for this aversion.

In underscoring the possible importance of discoid, snake-like, teeth-baring, cat-like, and spider-scorpion forms as visual releasers, Coss traces their frequent appearance in art and design forms back through the earliest ages of man to their possible use by man's hominid predecessors. For example, the whole tool-making tradition of man's predecessors three to four million years ago may have started with the inherent understanding that sharp-pointed objects, such as broken bones, large canine teeth from dead carnivores, and fractured pebbles could penetrate flesh, and therefore be useful tools and weapons. The sensitivity to sharp-pointed objects may have mediated the selection of these objects for survival purposes.

Coss's approach is cautious and reasoned; it merely suggests the possibility that some of the elements of interior design may communicate nonverbally by acting as provocative releasers of which we have little definite knowledge.

Imprinting

While Coss is concerned with the possible existence of a partially innate source of pattern recognition useful for designers, Eckhard H. Hess has written one of the clearest accounts of experiments in actively "imprinting" animals.

He first describes Konrad Lorenz's experiment with geese. Lorenz removed half of a clutch of eggs laid by a graylag goose so that they could be hatched in an incubator, and left the other half to be hatched normally. As soon as the goslings hatched by the mother were born, they followed their mother goose around since she was the first living thing they saw.

The incubator-hatched half, however, saw Lorenz first, and had not seen their mother: since he was the first living entity they saw, they went quacking after him as their mother.

After visually designating the members of each gosling group, Lorenz herded both groups under a large box. After he lifted the box, the goslings split into the same two identifiable groups, one going toward Lorenz, the other going toward the real goose mother. Lorenz coined the term "imprinting" to denote this tendency of newborn young to follow the first moving object they see.

Imprinting has been found in other birds, insects, fishes, and some mammals—including sheep, goats, deer, and buffalo, according to Hess, and in his own experiments he and his associates were able to imprint mallard ducklings using a decoy with sound, a silent object, or with sound alone; to illumine the possibilities of imprinting, Hess describes other experiments where geese and ducklings have been imprinted with a football and with a box with an alarm in it. Certainly there is the possibility that early human "imprinting" may occur and that varying early visual experience may affect human beings' responses to visual elements in interior design.

Other Methods
It would not be easy to ascertain the differing responses of individuals to interior design elements. One method which seems to offer promise—deep psychoanalytic hypnosis—would certainly peel away the overlying layers of conscious response, but whether this elaborate, costly procedure would even then be able to identify patterns of human reaction to specific design elements may be questionable; yet, it is certainly possible.

Another method is reported by Clare Cooper. She tells about a group of college teachers assembled for a workshop in Humanistic Education; after ten days of "intensive experiences with all kinds of encounter group techniques (movement, fantasy, non-verbal communication, etc.)" each participant was given the assignment of "drawing in as much detail as possible the house and garden in which they had grown up, and then describing it and its associations to another person."

The result was recollection in detailed form of the milieus of childhoods, and the revealed associations with these backgrounds exposed the interminglings of interiors with fundamental feelings deep within the

Figure 7.2. Trying to be a garden again. (arc photo)

human psyche. If this approach could be pursued on a scale large enough to yield replicable results, we might begin to learn typical human reactions to interior design elements and artifacts.

However, before we proceed to examine some of these design elements and their relationships in terms of their roles in nonverbal communication, it might be pertinent to point out that the predominantly rectangular shape of most interior spaces inhabited by human beings is not necessarily the most appealing shape in a historic, or even a cultural sense.

Nonrectangular Forms

As Amos Rapoport points out, the shape of dwellings and rooms around the world and across cultures, as well as through recorded history, has not been always rectangular.

The half globe of the Eskimo igloo, the Samoan domed dwelling, the Mongol yurt, the Masai onion shape, the bean-shaped Cameroons houses, the Ashanti hut, the Sepik river "sleeping bag," the Marsh Arab meeting hall, and the American Indian tepee are all examples of nonrectangular forms that exist today; the examples through history are legion, according to Rapoport, especially "the Roman Pantheon as the ideal dome of heaven." After all, the planet we live on is round and so is the horizon we look at. One of the first forms perceived by an infant is the mother's dome-shaped breast. Could the current worldwide interest in construction of dome and zome dwellings be a somewhat primordial expression of a preference for predominantly round and certainly non-rectangular shapes?

There are some grounds for believing that this might be true. Clare Cooper points out that some of the origins of dwelling forms certainly are mystical and religious; the use of the dome and other circular shapes persists in our religious structures today.

Fireplace as Altar

Certainly the persistence of the fireplace as an interior element cannot be justified on the grounds of utility alone in the presence of the sophisticated light and temperature control systems available to us. While much has been written about symbolic significance of the fireplace, including the use of it as a focus for gathering a family or group together, the photographic comments of Jurgen Ruesch and Weldon Kees seem very pertinent; they show the fireplace as a form of altar, along with bedroom vanity tables, dining room buffets, and dining room chinas, enhanced into this form by the decorative and arranging habits of the owners. As they emphasize, "objects fulfill a highly *symbolic function* when people use them to announce what they are and what they do." Further, they explain, "the effects that objects achieve in terms of their communicative value are dependent not only upon arrangement but also upon variations of *material, shape and surface*" as well as variations in aroma, taste, and temperature.

Thus objects are likely to affect more of our senses than speech—which only affects principally our ears and secondarily our eyes—and than the printed word that is seen by the eyes. Object language may or may not suggest usage; it may suggest status or prestige. Evidence of disuse may also tell its own story.

Therapy and Environment

They made a suggestion: "Psychiatrists need only to study the material environment with which individuals surround themselves to secure fresh insights into their relationships to objects, people and ideas." Not long ago, Alfred A. Messer, professor of psychiatry at Emory University in Atlanta, began to practice in just this manner. He feels that patients are more comfortable and freer to express their more intimate emotions in their own territory—their homes—so he visits each patient on the patient's own turf, staying for two or three days and intensively scrutinizing not only the patient's material surroundings, but family relationships as well. In his opinion, the analyst's territory is the analyst's office and this fact negatively affects the patient's ability to freely react.

Certainly the possibility exists that close and systematic observation of interiors, their objects and arrangements, in short, of the total interior milieu, will suggest much about the psychological problems of the inhabitants, so that a therapist can gather more of the information needed for treatment in a much shorter time. Designers could also use this method to find out the needs of their clients. In doing so, they might use the concept proposed by Erving Goffman, who has devoted "a sort of handbook detailing one sociological perspective from which social life can be studied, especially the kind of social life that is organized within the confines of a building or plant . . . from . . . the perspective . . . of the theatrical performance" to the description of a theatrical framework into which many of life's activities can be theoretically placed.

Environment as Theater

Goffman's division of interior spaces into "front regions" and "backstage regions" emphasizes our use of interiors as parts of a stage and correlates varieties of human behavior to the parts of the interior where each is performed. Interior design is, of course, a silent partner in the preparation of these areas for their diverse activities.

Parlor as Stage

The persistence of the parlor (no matter what it may be called) in some residences as a formal space in which to receive visitors is perhaps the clearest example of a stage in the home. For example, a family in the South had a small parlor in the home where they formerly lived for twenty years; five years ago, when they built a new house, the parlor was included in the plan, though it had shrunk to a space about nine by twelve feet. Except for the very occasional receiving of visitors who are strangers to the family, the space is almost never used; yet it is very formally and completely furnished.

Bruno Bettelheim tells of the parlor of his childhood in Vienna, a quite formal room, austerely furnished and used only for receiving visitors; he laments the tendency of some American families to use their so-called living rooms for this same purpose, emphasizing that meaningful living in the American family usually takes place in other parts of the typical house.

The parlor as a formal stage or first setting in which to receive visitors persists across cultures and across economic strata. Christopher Alexander and his associates emphasize the importance of the sala—the Peruvian parlor—as the most important first element in the intimacy gradient of the private dwelling. The sala is the public space that is always well maintained and furnished as a matter of family pride, no matter how poor or rich the family may be economically. It is the place where strangers are always received (though they may get no further into the house and both the room and its furnishings carry that nonverbal message). Further, as Alexander and his associates found out, it is absolutely necessary that each private home have a sala as the least intimate place to sit in the Peruvian house, the "front region."

Decor in the Living Room

This theatrical concept also formed one of the bases for a study done by sociologist Edward O. Laumann and social psychologist James S. House, which relates the decor of the living room to socioeconomic status, upward socioeconomic mobility, and a host of other attributes.

Laumann and House view the living room as a "front region" stage and concentrate on it; they say:

The living room is the area where "performances" for guests are most often given, and hence the "setting" of it must be appropriate for the performance. Thus . . . more than any other part of the house, the living room reflects the individuals' conscious and unconscious attempts to express a social identity.

They offer their findings "very tentatively indeed" but they feel that decor is rather strongly related both to a family's status and to its behavior in certain areas of life. Their living room study was a part of the 1966 Detroit Area Study, a project of the University of Michigan at Ann Arbor using a random sample of 1,000 households. The researchers did not determine socioeconomic status or attitudes from the living rooms visited. Rather, the respondents' socioeconomic status was determined by other means and then related to the presence or absence of certain characteristics in their living rooms.

Included as one part of the study, interviewers took a visual inventory of each living room they visited. Laumann and House, in analyzing the results of the inventories, found four styles of decor distinguishable by status and attitude:

1. High-status modern: sleek, functional furniture; abstract paintings and sculpture are typical.

2. High-status traditional: French or early American furniture, a piano, a fireplace, and potted plants are typical.

3. Low-status traditional: Floral-designed carpets, translucent curtains, and religious objects are typical.

4. Low-status modern: A television set and general disorder are typical; however, Laumann and House note that this pattern seems more the result of impoverishment than real stylistic preference.

On the high-low status scale, such objects as Bibles, photographs, knick-knacks, books, wall mirrors, cut flowers, and wood-paneled walls tend to group in the middle.

On the modern-traditional scale, such things as picture windows, encyclopedias, phonographs, knick-knacks, Bibles, and old-fashioned bulky furniture also tend to group in the middle.

They also found that:

1. Those with modern decor tended to be upwardly mobile in terms of father-son occupational mobility. That is, the son tended to have a better job, a higher spot on the socioeconomic status scale than his father.

2. Those with traditional decor demonstrated no such mobility. Sons tended to occupy the same spot on the socioeconomic scale as their fathers.

3. Those with traditional decor tended to be the so-called upper class, the white Anglo-Saxon Protestants not climbing out of their social level or that of their parents; they were, in short, the Establishment.

4. The persons with modern decor also tended to be Catholic and to be descendents of the "New Migration," the southern and eastern European families who came to the United States after 1900.

5. Those with traditional decor tended to be Protestants and members of the "Old Migration," the northern and western European families that settled in the United States before the Civil War.

6. The group with mixed decor was quite mixed in background and mobility, containing Irish and German Catholics and others who do not fit the patterns of those with clearly modern or traditional decor.

Though Laumann and House are careful to emphasize that their findings are neither definitive nor final, their study does indicate the importance of interior design (or the lack of it) in nonverbal communication of certain attributes of the owners.

*The Business
Milieu*

It is also possible to learn much about a business simply from the look of its interior without a word being said or written. One example, a corporation known to the author, insists on nonmatching office furniture, draperies and carpets, as well as a certain number of pieces which are made in its model shop especially to look homemade. This corporation, a research organization, wishes to project an informal image which is also made to seem unplanned and therefore flexible, as befits an organization which changes its activities as its research directions change.

Another example, also a corporation known to the author, was at its beginning solely a research organization, but now progressed to the point where its manufacturing activities far outweigh its research efforts in terms of personnel, capital, and space devoted to each. This client now places great emphasis on the more formal aspects of its interiors, especially those which will be seen by outside visitors. Original art and custom pieces are used to promote the image of solid respectability with progress.

The first corporation has no formal reception area as such; visitors may be able to find a seat in the rather informal research library. The second corporation has a reception area that could seat as many as twenty visitors at one time, but there are only three widely scattered

Figure 7.3.
Combination library, research, and reception area.

easy chairs in the whole space; a definite attempt is made to give the visitor an impression of dignity and deliberation.

Reception Areas as Stages

In a way, these reception areas resemble stage settings (just like living rooms) and there is no more evocative expression of interior design as nonverbal communication than a well-designed stage or movie set; the set is essential for determining the climate of the action and interaction on the stage.

Sometimes the business stage can be set with just a few small props. An example is an insurance agency with a seemingly humdrum, prosaic office. However, to differentiate it from its competitors, the owners have adorned its walls with a collection of antique etchings of fire-fighting scenes and with a collection of fire marks (plaques formerly attached to buildings to indicate which company had insured the building). This choice of wall decor carries the message that this agency is far more deeply interested in insurance than in just selling and servicing policies; it also creates an impression of established character and permanence. Yet, there are specifics which influence this communication process.

The explorations of Ruesch and Kees demonstrate that it is possible within limits to control certain aspects of traffic, communication, inter-

Figure 7.4. No, we don't want you to interact.

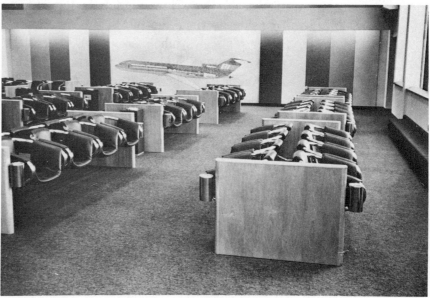

action, and conversation through the arrangement of furniture; one example they both mentioned and photographed was the perennial table between two chairs which sets a formal conversational distance and "tells the guest that no excessive intimacy is expected."

Certainly the total look of an interior space, as it is communicated to a person who enters it, somewhat influences the view of those expected to use it and what they are expected to do in the space. Formal or casual, period or eclectic, "for show" or "meant to be used" are some of the more obvious alternatives.

Here is an extreme example from Ruesch and Kees: "Wallpaper can indicate the activities that are expected to take place in the room, and the one who chooses it can convey to visitors and family members alike instructions that they might be unwilling to accept if set forth in verbal terms."

Significance of Chairs

Single pieces of furniture are sometimes eloquent. Chairs by themselves can be highly expressive. Winick and Holt trace the development of chairs from strictly seats of the mighty, literally seats of power in 1000 B.C., to their "more general use around the 1490's; they became a standard article during the 16th century."

"The use of chairs as symbols of power is well established," continue Winick and Holt. They mention the Pope's use of an ancient oaken chair "considered since the third century to have been St. Peter's" throne. Other seats as symbols are listed, such as the county seat, a seat on a stock exchange; "judges are referred to as the bench on which they sit," and Apollo's prophetess at Delphi sat on a tripod.

Joseph Rykwert also focuses on the symbolic aspects of chairs and sitting as he emphasizes the significance of the fetus in a sitting position in the womb as the first position each of us assumes. One of the illustrations of his article is a picture of a Byzantine mosaic showing God sitting on a throne, and he points out that cathedrals were so named because a particular church "is where the bishop has his seat or cathedra." Thus the phrase "ex cathedra" or from the throne, chair, or seat of power, has been derived.

Chairs are so used today. Office furniture dealers must offer a carefully graded series of "executive" swivel chairs both in terms of comfort and in terms of back height to the typical hierarchically organized clients. The highest back and most comfortable seat belong to the top person who runs the organization; progressively lower backs and less comfort characterize the chairs for the lower echelons of the organization.

When office workers in large offices are members of a union, management must be careful to choose one or two types of chairs that are likely to fit almost anybody and be comfortable for each worker and then stick to those types; the introduction of a new type of chair has become an issue in more than one labor-management bargaining session.

Desks and Space Allocations

Sizes of desks are also used to indicate rank in the business and professional worlds. Except where interior space is exceptionally cramped, the 60-inch-by-30-inch desk seems to be the minimum, and of course this size is dictated by the human factors or ergonomic approach which determines how far a seated person can reach to get work materials without getting up. Most manufacturers' standard desk lines increase in size in 6-inch steps until 42 inches by 84 inches is reached; that seems to be about the limit for standard executive desks (on which a seated executive cannot reach all the work materials). However, some practical executives do buy L- or U-shaped desks which provide much more useful work space than the usual two pedestals with a top.

Of course the sizes and positions of office spaces themselves tell quite a story without words. Edward T. Hall has this to say:

Anyone watching the anxious faces when space allocations are being made prior to an organization's move can't help recognizing the tremendous importance space plays in our lives. Space allocations are inevitably and quite correctly read as a type of communication.

While this discussion barely scratches the surface of interior design as nonverbal communication, it does indicate some of the perceptual and symbolic aspects of the subject. It also delineates some philosophical bases and some possible pathways for future research.

References

Christopher Alexander, Sanford Hirshen, Sara Ishikawa, Christie Coffin, and Schlomo Angel, "Houses Generated by Patterns," Berkeley: Center for Environmental Structure, 1969.

Donald Appleyard, "Styles and Methods of Structuring A City," *Environment and Behavior* 2, no. 1 (June 1970), pp. 100–117.

Donald Appleyard, Kevin Lynch, and J. Meyer, *The View From the Road*, Cambridge: The MIT Press, 1964.

Roger G. Barker, *Ecological Psychology*, Stanford: Stanford University Press, 1968.

Roger G. Barker, and Paul V. Gump, *Big School, Small School*, Stanford: Stanford University Press, 1964.

Robert B. Bechtel, *Enclosing Behavior*, Stroudsburg: Dowden, Hutchinson & Ross, Inc., 1977.

Bruno Bettelheim, "How Interior Environment Affects People," Paper presented at NEO-CON, the Merchandise Mart, Chicago, June 22, 1969.

Clare Cooper, *The House as Symbol of Self*, Berkeley: Institute of Urban and Regional Development, University of California, Working Paper #120, 1971.

Richard G. Coss, *Mood Provoking Visual Stimuli: Their Origins and Applications*, Los Angeles: University of California Press, 1965.

Richard G. Coss, "The Ethological Command in Art," *Leonardo* 1 (1968), pp. 273–287.

Richard G. Coss, "The Perceptual Aspects of Eye-Spot Patterns and Their Relevance to Gaze Behavior," in *Behavioural Studies in Psychiatry*, ed. Hutt, S. J. and Hutt, Corinne, New York: Pergamon Press, 1970.

R. L. Fantz, "Pattern Vision in Newborn Infants," *Science* 140 (April 19, 1963), pp. 296–297.

Erving Goffman, *The Presentation of Self in Everyday Life*, Garden City: Doubleday Anchor Books, Doubleday & Co., Inc., 1959.

Edward T. Hall, preface in "Spatial Behavior of Older People," Leon A. Pastalan and Daniel H. Carson, eds. Ann Arbor: University of Michigan—Wayne State Institute of Gerontology, 1970.

Eckhard H. Hess, "Imprinting in Animals," *Scientific American*, March 1958, pp. 3–7.

Florence C. Ladd, "Black Youths View Their Environment," *Environment and Behavior* 2, no. 1 (June 1970), pp. 74–79.

Florence C. Ladd, "Black Youths View their Environment: Some Views of Housing," *American Institute of Planners Journal*, March 1972, pp. 108–115.

E. O. Laumann, and J. S. House, "Living Room Styles and Social Attributes: The Patterning of Material Artifacts in a Modern Urban Community," *Sociology and Social Research*, no. 54, (1970), pp. 321–342.

Kevin Lynch, *The Image of the City*, Cambridge: The MIT Press, 1960.

Gary T. Moore, "Conceptual Issues in the Study of Environmental Cognition," in "Environmental Design: Research and Practice," ed. William J. Mitchell, (Proceedings EDRA 3/AR 8) 30.1, Los Angeles: School of Architecture and Urban Planning, University of California, 1972.

J. Piaget, and B. Inhelder, *The Child's Conception of Space*, New York: W. W. Norton, 1948.

Harold M. Proshansky, William H. Ittleson, and Leanne G. Rivlin, eds., *Environmental Psychology*, New York: Holt, Rinehart and Winston, 1970.

Amos Rapoport, *House Form and Culture*, Englewood Cliffs, N.J.: Prentice-Hall, Inc., 1969.

Amos Rapoport, "Symbolism and Environmental Design," *Journal of Architectural Education* 27, no. 4 (1974), pp. 58–63.

Jurgen Ruesch and Weldon Kees, *Nonverbal Communication*, Berkeley and Los Angeles: University of California Press, 1956.

Joseph Rykwert, "The Sitting Postion - A Question of Method," *Arena/Interbuild* (Architectural Association Journal), no. 83 (June 1967), pp. 15–21.

Thomas F. Saarinen, *Perception of Environment*, Washington: Association of American Geographers, 1969.

David Stea and Roger M. Downs, "From the Outside In Looking at the Inside Looking Out," *Environment and Behavior* 2, no. 1 (June 1970), pp. 3–12.

"The Shrink Who Came to Dinner," *Human Behavior* 1, no. 2 (March/April 1972), p. 24.

Charles Winick, and Herbert Holt, "Seating Position as Non-verbal Communication in Group Analysis," *Psychiatry* 24, (1961), pp. 171–182.

II *Specific Uses of Facilities*

8 *Spaces for the Elderly*

In the chapter on the handicapped there are a great many design directions that apply to design for the elderly. "Only 20% of older people suffer from *no* chronic illness of limitation on their mobility," according to Lawton.

To help student designers and architects at least partially experience the sensory world of the elderly, Leon A. Pastalan, of the University of Michigan's Institute of Gerontology, has developed an "empathic model." He equips his students with a set of ear plugs to diminish their hearing acuity, a set of special eyeglasses to fog their vision, and a local anaesthetic to dim their other senses. The result is that the students temporarily have the sight, hearing, and sense of touch of a person 80 years old or more.

Greater sensitivity to the needs of the elderly, whether from using Pastalan's "empathic model" or from other methods, should enable us to design a great deal more than just shelter, feeding, recreation, and health care into facilities for the elderly—our objective should be to enrich the quality of life in these places as well as to provide creature comforts. However, to do this, we must identify the user needs of this part of the population—those over 65—and solve the posed design problems in nursing homes, convalescent homes, rest homes, hospitals, or single family homes—wherever they may live. We might even be able to improve present facilities, for instance.

Who Are the Elderly?

Out of a total population over 65 of 16,559,580 in the United States in 1960, 510,000 were in institutions. By 1967 the number of elderly had increased to 18,796,000 and the number in institutions had increased to 780,000. The percentage had risen from slightly less then 3 percent to slightly more than 4 percent of the population. By 1975 more than 10 percent of the United States population was over 65 years old—22.6

million people, according to figures from the Department of Health, Education and Welfare. HEW expects that by the year 2000 there will be a 40-percent increase in this number—to 31 million.

Lawton emphasizes that from 1960 to 1967 the number of patients in state and county mental hospitals decreased more than one third from 520,000 to 340,000. A significant portion of this drop involved elderly patients being taken from these mental hospitals to institutions for the aging, but part of the decrease was also due, no doubt, to better methods of treatment becoming available, including the increasing use of therapeutic drugs. One implication of this group of figures is that the population of our institutions for the elderly may be composed of the least mentally competent portion of our aged population. Another implication could be that the mental hospitals had been the repository for many who were merely indigent, unwanted, or otherwise handicapped while being "old."

Diminished World of the Elderly

Still, the thousands of patients who were taken from mental hospitals and placed in other institutions were not miraculously cured. The newer drugs have helped and many of the patients were no doubt differentially diagnosed, but the fact that this happened pinpoints one condition of the institutionalized elderly: "The elderly person's world diminishes as the result of his deficiencies in sensation, perception and/or mobility," according to Lorraine Hiatt. To these deficiencies must be added forced institutionalization and the social and mobile limitations of institutional constraints.

Those with the most severe perceptual impairments were formerly diagnosed as mentally ill and placed in mental hospitals. Now, many of these same patients have been placed in institutions for the elderly that also receive new patients who formerly would have entered mental hospitals. These new patients are being diagnosed as impaired, rather than as mentally ill.

This fact of sensory, perceptual, and physical impairment must become one of the most important determinants in any design for the institutionalized elderly, and especially for interior design, which affects their environment the most in terms of sensation, perception, and mobility. Lawton refers to this impairment as a "reduction in competence," and associates it with the fact that the elderly who enter institutions are likely to come from the least economically endowed portion of the population; therefore, their "disadvantaged" state becomes a factor that compounds their feelings of incompetence and renders them more susceptible to influences of the environment.

Aging and Mentally Ill Are Not the Same

This sensory and physical impairment and its differential diagnoses are confusing to the designer because useful research on the needs of the institutionalized elderly is just in its beginning stages. Designers' use of the existing literature as a starting point and as a source of direction is complicated by the fact that some researchers and analysts whose work seems most potentially helpful constantly refer to research (done either by themselves or others) on the aging and the mentally ill almost as if these research results might be interchangeable in their usefulness as guidepoints for interior design, as well as other design disciplines.

Perhaps they are interchangeable, to some extent—but as we will see from the very small amount of relevant material available, there are some very striking differences in the microenvironmental needs of the few mentally healthy aged and mentally ill populations which have been conceptualized.

Differing Perceptual and Social Needs

Both types of populations share mobility losses, the aged due to lessened abilities, and the mentally ill due to confinement. Assessments of the perceptual and social needs of the two populations differ markedly, however.

Sommer is very specific about his feelings,

I am willing to accept the fact that most schizophrenic mental patients have a reduced desire for conversation and interaction with others and given the opportunity, most schizophrenics will avoid a meaningful relationship. However, I am not willing to accept this description as applying to the elderly.

He feels that even though some elderly people may be senile, they still want to interact and still want to be emotionally involved with other people. If they withdraw when institutionalized, the institutional atmosphere itself may be the cause of withdrawal, he thinks. Koff points out that privacy and places for the expression of sexuality must be provided in institutions for the elderly.

Lawton wants to change that environment by "humanizing" it; he suggests a more stimulating use of vivid colors and patterns as well as textures on the walls and floors, and that the usual institutional furnishings be supplemented with decorative pictures, plants, and birds in cages.

As we shall see more fully in the next chapter, Kiyo Izumi champions a quite opposite point of view in his suggestions for the interior design of facilities for the mentally ill. He wants to avoid overstimulation of typical mental patients because he feels that they suffer from distortion of perception rather than the deficiencies of perception suffered by the elderly. Overstimulation, he feels, would merely increase these perceptual distortions and confuse mental patients, thus making it much more difficult for them to recover; therefore he wants to keep the interior colors and textures as unambiguous and unobtrusive as possible with the exception of directional devices.

Regarding the need for privacy and personal identity, Lawton and Izumi are essentially saying the same thing about these needs in both populations. Lawton asks for private territory as well as private shelves and drawers for personal items for the elderly; Izumi asks for as much mental patient privacy as possible saying that

Each patient needs a place to retreat to when he feels threatened. This place of his own can serve its function even if it is quite limited in size. . . . Each patient needs encouragement to preserve his own individuality and identity so that he will not be lost in the mass of other patients.

Another important difference between the elderly and the mentally ill becomes evident in approaches to planning interior spaces for social interaction.

Elderly Prefer More Intimacy

Lawton wants to increase opportunities for social contacts by using floor plans that provide varying sizes of social space, and allow for easy communication among them. Sommer wants to plan smaller institutions for the elderly with more single bedrooms and wants the residents to be able to bring with them their own furniture and other possessions. Nahemow wants to enhance "the feeling of ownership" by allowing nursing home residents to decorate their own rooms and by providing bulletin board surfaces; she also advocates that residents be responsible for cleaning their own rooms.

De Long emphasizes that the aging tend to compensate for the loss of people in their lives (family members and friends) by becoming attached to familiar objects; they tend to "substitute objects for people." To most interior designers this bringing of objects from home is anathema, but allowing it seems vital to the health of the elderly; "they seem to interpret giving up cherished items as giving in to death."

Matter of Life and Death

While institutional maintenance personnel are also inconvenienced by these items brought from former homes, the importance of the continued presence of familiar objects is certainly a matter of life and death to some elderly people entering an institution for the first time, according to research by Bourestom and Tars, and Bourestom and Pastalan. Calling the phenomenon "transfer trauma," Archea and Margulis described how the above Michigan research became the basis for a Nursing Home Relocation Program published by the Pennsylvania Department of Public Welfare.

Briefly, Bourestom and Pastalan "had documented increases of up to 100 percent in the mortality rate for elderly persons affected by forced transfers from one . . . setting to another. Furthermore . . . increases in mortality were directly related to the degree of environmental change . . . and to the victim's cognitive and physical decline," according to Archea and Margulis.

Later, a situation developed in Pennsylvania where the enforcement of fire and safety regulations would cause from 2000 to 6000 elderly people to be moved from unsafe nursing homes. Using the Michigan research as a basis for calculation, moving only 2000 people could boost the normally expected death rate of 250 people to 450 people within a year, and only 16 people had died in nursing home fires in Pennsylvania the year before.

Therefore, the Nursing Home Relocation Plan was published based on the Michigan study developed as a result of the research: the elderly to be moved are familiarized with their new environment little by little until they are thoroughly familiar with it before they move. While this procedure does not eliminate the "transfer trauma" problem, it does sharply reduce the number of deaths.

Not only do the elderly prefer familiar surroundings, but De Long says that the elderly in his experience prefer to be closer together in smaller spaces; they want closeness of persons and things that a younger person might find irritating. Because of their sensory impairment, he feels that the elderly prefer much more intimate contact than younger Americans in social relationships, including quite a bit of touching.

Space Allocation and Furniture Arrangement   Sommer, in a study to help an internist friend find out how to promote more social interaction in a ward for elderly at a state hospital, focused on the importance of space allocation and arrangement of furniture in a lounge.

Although a great deal of money had been spent to improve the interior decoration of this lounge (it had been completely renovated with new furniture), "the ladies' mental state was unchanged." Sommer found, after long observation and experimentation, that much of this was due to the arrangements of the furniture, and some of it was due to the type of furniture used.

He discovered that the chairs and sofas were placed in straight rows around the walls, and back to back in the center of the room for the most part, with a few chairs around columns facing away from the columns in all directions.

He found the reasons for these arrangements in the desire of the maintenance people for ease of cleaning, and in the desire of the nurses for ease of observation, as well as the whole staff's institutional desire for order and neatness; also, "highways" for food service and cleaning vehicles are thus formed.

As Sommer points out, once these furniture arrangements are put into effect, they become "sacred" and "the way things belong" in an institution. The patients and nurses are not consulted, and are not expected to object, no matter what the effect of these arrangements may be. He felt that the placing of the furniture had the effect of arranging the patients' lack of social interaction.

Unfortunately, these arrangements were sociofugal, which means that they served to isolate the patients from each other, rather than bringing them together. It was almost impossible for patients sitting in the chairs around the columns to talk to each other, and with the infirmities of hearing losses and lessened muscle movements, it was difficult for the patients sitting side by side in the chairs around the walls or in the center rows to turn the necessary 90 degrees to talk to each other.

To foster a more sociopetal (serving to bring people together, rather than to set them apart from each other) arrangement "to allow people to converse, interacting when they want to," Sommer removed some of the sofas and introduced square tables, thirty inches on a side. Chairs were placed around the tables, rather than in the former rows. Sommer used square tables rather than round ones to give the patients a sense of secure territoriality: "With round tables, a person never knows where his territory ends and another's begins."

He also selected this arrangement in order to break the very large rooms into smaller spaces. (He mentions that the room was made to look larger and more institutional than it really was by the floor tiles which "were all the same pattern and ran the same way.")

After the changes had been in effect for some time and after the patients had been gently given suggestions as to the use of the new arrangement, Sommer was able by observation to record definite increases in interaction among them.

Grouping of Social Spaces

Another method for increasing social interaction is the grouping of social spaces in a central location, consisting of the lobby, community room, office, elevators, and mail room with chairs strategically located to facilitate sitting and watching, often mentioned as one of the prized activities of the elderly. Newman agrees.

Additionally, Byerts and Conway suggest that "elderly people seem to love ceremony; a flexible multi-purpose room, slightly elevated at one end for a stage, should always be provided for programs, awards, ceremonies and plays." Lawton also suggests that the common dining area be placed near a room with comfortable seating which might be the same chairs for sitting and watching; the meal and the times just before and just after it are high points in the social life of any institution.

De Long outlines a more general way to look at the space requirements of the elderly. He feels that they need three "functionally different" types of space in the institutional setting—semi-private spaces for personal behavior, semi-private–semi-public spaces for social behavior, and public spaces for public behavior. He says that "private rooms decrease aggression and increase cooperation; semi-private semi-public spaces increase cooperation, participation and social awareness."

Opposite Views on the Mentally Ill

Opposite to these views encouraging social interaction for the elderly are those of Izumi on the design of institutions for the mentally ill. One of his four prime principles of design is "to create spatial relationships that reduce the frequency and intensity of undesirable confrontations," He explains that:

A mentally ill person should not be faced with an undue number of choices in his daily life, particularly in choosing companions from a large number of strangers. Spaces should be arranged to permit each patient to interact with a small group without being confronted by unfamiliar faces.

Humphry Osmond has put it another way:

Sick people (the mentally ill) whose perception is inconstant can only interact with a very small number of patients . . . if patients try to interact with more than this number they become confused, and will therefore be forced to reduce social interaction to a point where they are more or less isolated.

Therefore, in the Osmond-Izumi sociopetal mental hospital design, a collaborative effort of both men, "corridors have been eliminated" to cut down "the frequency and intensity of undesirable confrontations."

They were also eliminated for other reasons: Mayer Spivack's "Sensory Distortions in Tunnels and Corridors," and "Psychological Implications of Mental Health Center Architecture" describe at length how the harsh, shiny surfaces and interminable lengths of typical institutional corridors combine to produce visual and auditory illusions which can become quite disturbing to a patient in any hospital, though they may be barely irritating to healthy persons. Izumi also mentions these effects.

Importance of the Hallway

Yet for the elderly, Hiatt and Ostrander find that

The hallway is perhaps the most extensively used and multi-functional location in many nursing homes. Hallways not only function as traffic arteries, but also serve as lounges, meeting places, wheelchair storage space, promenades, dining rooms, and staff conferral sites. Most nursing stations are also prominently located along corridors.

One of the most important problems they found in hallways or corridors was the disorientation produced in some patients, resulting from their psychologically confused state and resulting from insufficient color coding, or inadequate signage in others. Hiatt also points out that the normal aging process produces increased sensitivity to glare in the elderly and suggests that glare be sharply reduced in facilities for the elderly, especially in bathrooms, dining rooms, and hallways; she mentions the yellowing phenomenon in slightly different terms from Harmon.

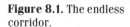

Figure 8.1. The endless corridor.

Following are excerpts from Hiatt and Ostrander's "Research Hypotheses with Implications for Design" in regard to hallways:

1. The length of the corridor may be optically reduced through certain design elements.

    a. Color variation, lighting, and textural variations in floor and wall coverings may reduce the length of the corridor.
    b. Longer corridors are more disorienting (all things being equal) than are shorter corridors.

2. Residents may be able to use hallways as a "promenade" or walkway, especially when the hallway itself is thought of as a room.

3. Hallways are more effective when not used for wheelchair storage.

    a. Alternative arrangements should be made for wheelchair storage to alleviate hallway clutter.
    b. Wheelchairs and walking aids should, however, be accessible to the resident, preferably stored in the bedroom.

4. Many hallways create hazards due to lighting difference.

    a. The change in lighting from lounges and bedrooms to the hallway creates difficulty in light adaptation for aged individuals.
    b. This problem will be particularly in evidence during the daytime and on bright days.

5. A double loaded corridor, separated by a service island, will muffle patient noises and be more satisfactory without the service island, especially if door openings are staggered so that "my door doesn't open exactly opposite yours."

6. Firedoors should be easy to open from either side after they have closed.

   a. Firedoors should not close so fast that a person can get caught in the door.

   b. A staff member should be able to open a firedoor manually once it has snapped shut.

Hiatt also suggests that color contrasts, light against dark, and complementary colors against each other, be used instead of simply a conglomeration of bright colors which tends to confuse the elderly. Increasing the ability to perceive and organize the microenvironment is quite important to maintain levels of mental activity in the elderly, she feels.

Izumi suggests an alternative to color variations as environmental cues; while he proposes it primarily for the blind, it certainly might be considered for the aging:

The more interior the space, it should be smoother, softer, and quieter and as one moves closer to the outside, the materials on the walls and floors become harder and rougher and the corridors or spaces should become larger. Increasing number of light sources and other elements can be clues to help one out from the inner world. The blind are greatly aided by the tactile quality of the floor and, for example, by starting with a very deep pile carpet in the remote interior and next a harder felt type carpet, then to a softer resilient floor such as vinyl, or rubber, then a parquet type floor to terrazzo or tile and finally to a very rough, textured stone floor. Such an arrangement of floor covering can be quite effective in providing the necessary clues to tell them where they have been, where they are and where they are going.

Parenthetically, Izumi (as quoted by Esser) is much concerned with the confusion and disorientation caused by visual ambiguities in the interior environment. While this will be discussed more fully in another chapter, he mentions "plastic table tops that look like wood so that (especially elderly) patients hesitate to use a knife on these tables, or doors with knobs placed in the middle panel so that (especially ambivalent) patients have a hard time deciding which side to open."

Tactile Spaces

Izumi's proposal for tactile coding finds a responsive chord in De Long's statement:

> It is not surprising that the senile are typically confused, disoriented and bumping into walls. Architects and designers are building visual spaces—the elderly need tactile spaces. . . . Whereas architects are building visual, linear spaces based upon the grid, the elderly require tactual, point-integrated spaces based on the use of landmarks.

Signage

However, it should be reiterated at this point that signage is most important in the continued, as well as the initial orientation of the aging. As Hiatt and Ostrander mention, signage must be legible and at the right height so that patients can read it.

> Signs on windows are frequently difficult to read. Name plates may be more useful if placed next to the door on the wall than if on the door. . . .Residents seemed to view their name on their door (or doorway) with great pride.

Hall also feels strongly about signage:

> Signage is still so bad that most people have difficulty getting around in a strange environment. . . .Work with the aged can actually produce principles by which it would be possible to get virtually anybody from one place to another with a minimum of confusion. These principles are sorely needed today.

Certainly one of those principles is the use of large letters, probably white on a black background. (See Chapter 2.)

Therapeutic Corridor

Consonant with the Lawton-De Long-Ostrander-Hiatt view that social interaction should be encouraged, the concept of the "therapeutic corridor," originally developed for use in general hospitals, should certainly be considered for adaptation and use in space planning for institutions for the aging.

While prior examples exist at the Menninger Clinic in Topeka, Kansas, and at Tufts University Medical Center in Worcester, Massachusetts, a more recent corridor designed with the help of Ronald Beckman of Research and Design Institute in Providence, Rhode Island, at the South County Hospital, Wakefield, Rhode Island, should be examined as a possible partial solution to the problem of encouraging social interaction in institutions for the elderly.

The usual eight-foot corridor was broadened to eighteen feet so that it could contain alcoves on both sides which hold the necessary furniture and space for medical consultation, family visits, dining furniture for casual meals, a small library, a game area, and writing space. It also includes a water fountain and low, open telephone booths which can be used even by patients in wheel chairs. Informal in aspect, it provides a place where patients can be with their families and visitors outside the cramped confines of the usual hospital room.

Called the Borda Wing, the South County Hospital's installation was designed for patients who are not bedfast, and who do not need the total care required by patients who cannot get out of bed at all. This is similar to the situation in some institutions for the aging, and by turning the corridor into a sort of "street" with many activities possible in it, Beckman has added a new option for corridor design.

Telephone Booths, Walkers, Chairs, and Wheelchairs

Unfortunately for wheelchair patients, not only are specially designed telephone booths quite rare, but most nursing homes and other institutions for the aging do not provide adequate space and movement paths for wheelchairs, either the standard type, or the geriatric wheelchair. Walkers, of course, are another feature of the institutions for the aging. In an institution studied by Hiatt, 41 percent of the residents were in wheelchairs, and in another study of six nursing homes, Hiatt and Ostrander report that "from fifty to sixty percent of the residents come with their own chair or walker." As they clearly point out, provisions must be made in interior space planning for these prosthetic devices in several ways; also the suggestion has been made that institutional staff might work toward getting clients out of wheelchairs.

Emphasizing that the high proportion of residents using wheelchairs or walkers means that space must be left for them in the television viewing areas, and in front of the window areas in the lounges so that a chair may be wheeled up within seeing distance, they say:

In fact, one of the most functional resident lounges observed would have seemed barren to the average interior designer. . . . [this] was an open space with only four to six pieces of fairly easily movable furniture on a carpeted floor surface.

Incidentally, they suggest the provision of extra, "easily accessible," stackable and/or storable chairs for visitors.

"A second problem results from the differences in chair heights," they continue:

Geriatric wheelchairs literally tower over the coventional living room furniture. Wheelchairs, although somewhat higher than the conventional lounge chair, are still lower than the geriatric wheelchair. The resulting hodgepodge may create a demand for row seating in front of the focal activity or television.

Hiatt and Ostrander list a variety of problems associated with wheel-chair design, and as Hiatt points out, "almost 55 per cent of nursing home residents are in wheelchairs."

1. The sling seat becomes extremely cramping or uncomfortable for many people. Pillows, sponge materials, or blankets are often spread over the seat to provide cushioning.

2. Loose cushioning frequently slides out the rear of the seat.

3. Foot pedals are too high or too low for the patient's leg length.

4. Fabric backing on wheelchair provides less support than geriatric wheel-chair.

5. Braking devices on wheelchairs are hard for people with arthritic hands to manipulate.

6. Brakes on wheelchairs often do not grip sufficiently to give the person a feeling of security.

7. Wheelchair arms are too high for some people to comfortably rest their arms on. Residents often *look* infirm because their arms are raised to an uncomfortably high level.

8. Narrow tubular construction of wheelchair arms is uncomfortable for resting arms.

9. Wheelchair arms do not fit under many tables due to table rims or ledges and arm height of chairs.

10. Protruding metal footrests on wheelchairs often bump into objects or other people.

11. Small wheels on front of wheelchairs catch in rugs and make it difficult for the individual to navigate.

12. Removable arms on wheelchairs (available on some models) would permit person to slide into bed, shower, or other chair.

13. Lack of support of canvas sling under the front of the legs; people put pieces of wood under legs.

14. Leg rests often cut into the mid-calf creating circulatory problems and discomfort.

They also find that geriatric wheelchairs are "almost impossible to be moved by the person occupying them, thus severely reducing that person's mobility." "Reduction in visual access because of chair construction" is another problem.

Nahemow particularly emphasizes that "parking spaces" for wheelchairs should be provided wherever activities may go on; she also feels that making a nursing home barrier-free will have another important benefit. She says that "it is hoped that this easy accessibility will break down some of the barriers which currently exist between the ambulatory and the non-ambulatory. Physical barriers help to create social barriers; a barrier-free environment should serve to encourage easy interaction between people as well as a feeling of competence in dealing with the environment itself."

Tables and Chairs Must Relate

Hiatt and Ostrander comment on chair-table relationship:

1. There will be a greater amount of personalized social interaction during a meal served at tables that have a proper chair-table fit, than those that do not.

2. There will be more negative affect in a misfit situation than a good fit situation.

3. There will be more food eaten where there is a good fit than where there is a misfit situation.

4. There will be more anxiety and/or stress behavior where chair and table do not fit than where there is a good fit.

5. Different amounts of time devoted to eating and to verbal socializing will be found between fit and misfit seating arrangements.

6. The chair-table relationship is particularly important in dining rooms, recreation rooms, and therapy spaces where a table is essential to the performance of the activity.

7. Geriatric wheelchairs would be more satisfactory to mentally capable residents if they could be moved close to the table. In fact Hiatt would like to "throw out all geriatric wheelchairs and use an auto crusher on them."

8. Table width should be coordinated with the length of a geriatric wheelchair. This means that two persons in geriatric wheelchairs may sit across from each other at the table and yet each one will be able to sit close enough to that table to eat or work.

It seems at the minimum, tables around which chairs are to be used by the aging should be adjustable in height.

In relation to social interaction taking place around tables, Hiatt and Ostrander say that "residents congregate around tables of a normal height but could not readily congregate around coffee tables." It is quite difficult for the aging to reach a coffee table from a wheelchair, geriatric wheelchair, or a conventional chair; their movements are limited. One of their comments on chairs in general is important:

The human factor aspects of the aged user of chairs should be studied. If we were to physically describe the occupants in the extended care facility several physical characteristics would be representative of a sizeable proportion of the resident population:

1. Limited arm strength
2. Limited hand or grip strength
3. Short stature (of European aged)
4. Skin easily bruised
5. Heavy or overweight, or
6. Slender build and little padding around the pelvis
7. Limited strength in feet or leg muscles
8. Lower back problems of spine curvature

It Is Not Just 18 Inches

A search of the literature reveals almost no usable human factors hard data on seating for the aged; in fact a myth has grown up that 18 inches is *the* proper height for geriatric seating. Nothing could be further from the truth. The author feels that although total adjustability in geriatric seating would answer many of the problems delineated by Hiatt and Ostrander, the fact remains, however, that the necessary research has just not been performed in this area.

Still designers keep trying. The British journal, *Applied Ergonomics*, reported a chair designed in Denmark, produced in Sweden, with nine posture settings; however, the chair is not adjustable in height, and one photograph of it with an aged model indicates possible heavy pressure on the lower thighs just above the knees due to improper height for the model.

Toilets and Chairs

The designer of this chair, E. C. Hansen, feels that the upholstery should be able to breathe and that it should have a rough surface. This does not solve the recurrent problem pointed out by Hiatt and Ostrander—the fact that incontinent patients use a chair of any type as a commode, and that these accidents are fairly frequent. A rough, woven material such as that recommended by Hansen is not that cleanable. As a part of this problem Hiatt and Ostrander note that only one of the six homes they studied had a lavatory adjacent to the twenty-nine lounges in the six facilities. Implicitly they suggest that more toilet facilities near lounge and activity areas might help with this problem as well as increasing the attractiveness of these areas to the residents.

Toilet facilities in institutions for the elderly leave much to be desired, however. One of the real horror stories of interior design for the aging has been told in "The Bathroom," by Alexander Kira. As he points out, the weight of anatomical evidence is that a squat position is most nearly correct for ease of defecation; yet we persist in the use of high water closets. Unfortunately, the physical act of squatting exercises the same muscles human beings use in the defecation process; lack of this squatting exercise weakens these muscles and contributes to difficulties in defecation.

As Kira emphasizes, these difficulties increase with age and he emphatically recommends the use of lower water closets; the lower the closet, the greater the ease of defecation, *over the whole life span.* Some time after Kira's book was first published in 1967, American Standard, the plumbing manufacturer that partially sponsored Kira's study, exhibited a new line of bathroom fixtures, the design of which was somewhat based on Kira's design criteria. When I asked their spokesman why the lower water closet that Kira strongly recommended had not been designed or introduced, he informed me somewhat testily that the American public was not ready for such a radical change. They had lowered the height of one toilet in their line—one inch, however. A dip of the colors in the right direction, perhaps, but far from the meticulously researched recommendation for which they were paying dearly.

Tubs and Showers Need Attention

Kira emphasizes safety as a prime consideration in the design of tubs and showers, pointing out the necessity of providing "adequate support, seats (and handsprays . . .)." He suggests a height of approximately 18 inches for the seat; it is probable that he selected this height for reasons of stability (as well as safety). Since the use of a shower seat takes place only for short periods of time, this selection should not be considered an extension of the "18-inch myth" for long-term comfort mentioned earlier. The Ministry of Housing and Local Government recommends a maximum height for the tub rim of 15 inches. (See "Designing for All of Us" for further recommendations.)

More Toilets Needed

With regard to the provision of private toilets in nursing homes, Izumi cites a study which showed that "in a nursing home for elderly women, a high rate of incontinence was traced to the lack of private or privacy in toilet facilities."

This is but one example of an insensitivity in planning the interior environment with a definite, undesired effect on the ultimate client, the person who occupies it. Environmental analysis, the reality-oriented, inquiring approach that reaches the needs of the human client (represented by the Ostrander and Hiatt examples, among others) offers real hope for producing the clues that designers should consider.

Design Checkpoints

1. Consider as much portable furniture as possible, especially chairs, so that they can be moved to suit interaction needs.

2. Consider adjustable-height chairs to fit the varying body sizes of the aged.

3. See that any upholstery for seating is resistant to urine and feces; be sure also that it can be washed.

4. Consider making provisions so that the elderly can bring some of their own interior furnishings with them when they transfer to an institution.

5. Consider adjustable-height tables for eating and working so that wheelchairs can be used with them, making sure that the placement of the legs or pedestal will accommodate wheelchairs.

6. Consider the use of color as directional cues, and be sure that lighting is adequate for weakened, aged eyes. Avoid strong yellows or purples.

7. Make sure that signage is quite plain, legible, and well lit.

8. Make sure that telephone booths can be used by people in wheelchairs.

9. Provide for storage for wheelchairs and walkers in all parts of any

facility for the aged; however, they should not be stored in corridors unless special provisions are made for them.

10. Design bathrooms carefully, using all available technology.

11. Make sure that enough toilets are provided in the right locations, considering the ranges of movement of elderly people.

12. Investigate the possible use of the Fokus bathroom system in institutions for the elderly.

References

John Archea and Stephen T. Margulis, "Environmental Research Inputs to Policy and Design Programs: The Case of Preparation for Involuntary Relocation of the Institutionalized Aged," Task Force on Environment and Behavior News Letter, American Psychological Association, #9, May, 1976, pp. 5–9, mimeo.

N. Bourestom and S. Tars, "Alterations in life patterns following nursing home relocation," *The Gerontologist,* no. 14 (1974), pp. 506–509.

N. Bourestom and L. Pastalan, "Forced Relocation: Setting, staff and patient effects," Final Report to the Mental Health Services Development Branch, National Institute of Mental Health, Ann Arbor: Institute of Gerontology, University of Michigan, 1975.

Thomas O. Byerts, *Fact Sheet on the Elderly,* Washington: Gerontology Society, 1975.

Thomas O. Byerts, and Don Conway, eds., "Behavioral Requirements for Housing for the Elderly," Washington: American Institute of Architects and Gerontology Society, 1973. (Publication also sponsored by the Association for the Study of Man-Environment Relations and the National Tenants Organization.)

Alton J. De Long, "The Micro-Spatial Structure of the Older Person," in "Spatial Behavior of Older People," ed. Leon A. Pastalan, and Daniel H. Carson, Ann Arbor: The University of Michigan–Wayne State University Institute of Gerontology, 1970.

Aristide Henri Esser, "Environmental Design Needs Empathy to Combat Pollution," Thiells. Text based on a seminar presentation, "Social Pollution as an Aspect of Environmental Design," November 2, 1970, at the College of Architecture, Virginia Polytechnic Institute and State University. (mimeo)

"Furniture for the Elderly," *Applied Ergonomics* 3, no. 2, (June 1972), pp. 118–119.

Edward T. Hall, preface in "Spatial Behavior of Older People," ed. Leon A. Pastalan, and Daniel H. Carson, 1970.

Lorraine Hiatt, "A Case Study of the Role of the Near Environment in Mediating Social Interaction in the Infirmary of a Geriatric Center," Ithaca: Dept. of Design and Environmental Analysis, Cornell University, 1971. (mimeo)

Lorraine Hiatt, "Environmental Changes for Socialization," *Journal of Nursing Administration,* 1977.

Lorraine Hiatt and Edward R. Ostrander, "Interim Report of Findings-Spatial and Physical Considerations in the Nursing Home Environment," in "Gerontology Project Group: Research in Environmental Analysis and Design for the Aging, Report Number One," ed. Joseph A. Koncelik, Edward R. Ostrander, and Lorraine Hiatt, Ithaca: Dept. of Design and Environmental Analysis, Cornell University, 1972.

Kiyo Izumi, *Psycho-Social Considerations of Environmental Design*, New York; National Society of Interior Designers, 1968.

Kiyo Izumi, "LSD and Architectural Design," in "Psychedelics," ed. Bernard Aaronson and Humphry Osmond, Garden City: Anchor Books, Doubleday, 1970.

Alexander Kira, *The Bathroom: Criteria for Design*, New York: Bantam Books, 1967, and Viking Press, 1976.

Theodore H. Koff, "National Overview of the Elderly Population," *Journal of Architectural Education* 31, no. 1 (September 1977), pp. 5–7 and 16.

M. Powell Lawton, "An Ecological Theory of Aging Applied to Elderly Housing," *Journal of Architectural Education* 31, no. 1 (September 1977), pp. 8–10.

M. Powell Lawton, "Ecology and Aging," in "Spatial Behavior of Older People," ed. Leon Pastalan and Daniel H. Carson, 1970.

M. Powell Lawton, "The Human Being and the Institutional Building," in "Architecture for Human Behavior," ed. Charles Burnette, Philadelphia: Philadelphia Chapter, American Institute of Architects, 1971.

M. Powell Lawton, "The design of life-supportive and life-enriching housing for the elderly," Philadelphia: Philadelphia Geriatric Center, n.d., circa 1971. (mimeo)

M. Powell Lawton, Bernard Liebowitz, and Helen Charon, "Physical Structure and the Behavior of Senile Patients Following Ward Remodeling," Philadelphia: Philadelphia Geriatric Center, n.d., circa 1970. (mimeo)

Lucille Nahemow, "New York State Veterans Home, Oxford, New York, 1 Behavioral & Research Objectives," Albany: Division of Medical Care Services & Evaluation, State of New York Health Department, n. d., circa 1974.

Oscar Newman, "Design Guidelines for Creating Defensible Space," Washington: U.S. Government Printing Office, April 1976. Stock #027-000-00395-8. (National Institute of Law Enforcement and Criminal Justice, Law Enforcement Assistance Administration, U.S. Dept. of Justice) in "Psychiatric Architecture," ed. C. Goshen, Washington, D.C.: American Psychiatric Association. 1959.

Humphry Osmond, "Some Psychiatric Aspects of Design," in "Who Designs America?," Laurence Holland, Garden City: Anchor Books, Doubleday, 1966.

Leon A. Pastalan, "Designing Housing Environments for the Elderly," *Journal of Architectural Education* 31, no. 1 (September 1977), pp. 11–13.

Leon A. Pastalan, "The Empathic Model," *Journal of Architectural Education* 31, no. 1 (September 1977), pp. 14–15.

Jean W. Progner, "The Sociologist and the Designer Can Be Friends," *Design & Environment* 2, no. 1 (Spring 1971), pp. 52–55.

"Some Aspects of Designing for Old People," London: Her Majesty's Stationery Office, 1974. (Ministry of Housing and Local Government)

Robert Sommer, "Small Group Ecology in Institutions for the Elderly," in "Spatial Behavior of Older People," ed. Leon A. Pastalan and Daniel H. Carson, 1970.

Mayer Spivack, "Sensory Distortions in Tunnels and Corridors," *Hospital and Community Psychiatry* January 1967, pp. 24–30.

Mayer Spivack, "Psychological Implications of Mental Health Architecture," *Hospitals* 43, January 1, 1969.

9 *Toward Mental Health*

"The most important aspect of any design consideration that may stem from the understanding of the needs and preferences of the mentally ill is its applicability to any buildings used by and for any human being, ill or otherwise."

Kiyo Izumi (Architect)

"The mentally ill need what we all need—an ordinary world."

Mayer Spivack

Figure 9.1. Entrance at Cleveland State. (arc photo)

Design control for many structures now lies with government agencies, foundation trustees, corporate boards, and business executives, who hire and pay the designers; yet they are not the ultimate users of homes for the elderly, educational institutions, prisons, and mental hospitals.

Although the designers they choose are responsible to them, they are not the persons for whom the designs are conceived, the ultimate user.

For Kiyo Izumi, architect-planner, in 1954, the ultimate user client was the mentally ill human being, and the paying client was the Province of Saskatchewan. Izumi had been asked to prepare architectural studies for the renovation of the existing mental hospital, the Saskatchewan Hospital at Weyburn, and also for the construction of a new hospital.

Building Classes: Sociofugal and Sociopetal

At that time, Humphry Osmond was the superintendent of the Saskatchewan Hospital, and Izumi used Osmond's notes of the functions of a psychiatric ward as a basis for his architectural design for a new hospital. Osmond coined two new words to describe his feelings about certain qualities of buildings. He felt that they could be divided into two general classes: *sociofugal* or *sociopetal*. Sociofugal buildings prevent or discourage the formation of stable relationships among people, while sociopetal buildings foster, encourage, and enforce relationships. In conjunction with Izumi he developed the architectural concept of the hospital as a semicircle with large group space in the center, space for individual retreat at the outer edges, and space for small groups in between. In this way the mentally ill patient was given options to be alone or with a small of large group. This architectural concept has generally been called the Izumi-Osmond hospital concept and quite a few hospitals embodying these "sociopetal" concepts of design have been built in various parts of the world.

Understanding Patients' Perceptions

At this point, however, after the design concept had been formulated, Izumi felt that "many of the significant and more detailed psychiatric considerations and their architectural counterparts still eluded me." A research team was therefore formed, consisting of Humphry Osmond, psychiatrist and psychopharmacologist, Robert Sommer, psychologist, Francis Huxley, social anthropologist, and Izumi, architect. Their mission was "to determine what architectural elements might have psychiatric significance."

The other members of the team fully explained to Izumi their perceptions of their patients' problems in terms of their own specialties. In particular, they told him about the half or more of the chronic beds in typical mental hospitals that are filled by victims of schizophrenia. One

9.2

Figure 9.2. Nothing to do . . . (arc photo)
Figure 9.3. What did they do before television? (arc photo)

9.3

of the differences between schizophrenics and normal persons is the way in which they perceive the world around them; another difference is, of course, their behavior. The perceptual distortions experienced by schizophrenics frequently seem bizarre to normal people. Osmond said "a vivid example is that of a patient who patted a black retriever and saw his arm blackening with the retriever's glossy fur, which had seemingly invaded him up to the elbow." Such perceptual distortions involve all the senses and their often complex interrelationships. Kahan sums it up this way: "The schizophrenic's 'computer system' of receiving and interpreting data from the various parts of his body is out of order, and the messages he receives from his eyes, ear, nose, fingers, therefore are wrong."

Izumi was familiar with these descriptions of perceptual distortions but since he felt that the information was "secondhand," he sought a way to learn more so he could design more effectively for the therapeutic welfare of the ultimate user—the schizophrenic. Therefore, under supervised conditions, Izumi tried to simulate the mental state of schizophrenics through the use of drugs. While doing this, Izumi placed himself in rooms and situations that a typical mental patient might encounter. The impressions he gathered as a result of such experiences were incorporated in a set of design principles.

Izumi's Design Principles

Sommer, of course, was a member of the design team and familiarized Izumi with the then available literature; Izumi then came up with four principles that he felt should be the essence of mental hospital design:

1. Each patient must be able to have privacy when he needs it.
2. There must be no ambiguity in "architectural design and detail." Doors must be made to look like doors; there must be no visual confusion between the two. Ambiguity produces uncertainty in well people, but for mental patients it may produce real problems.
3. The environment must not be intimidating.
4. The environment should be planned so that it does not force the patient into unwanted and frequent confrontations with other patients or staff.

It is noteworthy that Izumi was able to translate these principles into a very usable form as he incorporated them into the Canadian Standards for Mental Health Facilities, 1965. Excerpts from these standards can be found in chapter 1.

9.4

Figure 9.4. Before . . . (arc photo)
Figure 9.5. After. (arc photo)

9.5

The Izumi-Osmond Mental Hospital Design

In contrast to the multiple-occupancy wards and bedrooms of the typical mental hospital, the Izumi-Osmond design provides for single, private bedrooms which are optimally arranged in a circle, with a nursing station in the center; the individual rooms radiate from the center as spokes do in a wheel.

Izumi cites an investigation of the perceptions of mental patients which indicated that their senses relate better to circular interior spaces than they do to rectangular interior spaces; for this reason and because the planet we live on is round as the horizon is round, he felt that the larger spaces in his mental hospital design should be round.

Since the rooms can be seen from the nursing station, support and supervision are instantly visible and available; however, privacy is preserved since no patient can see into another's room, and the individual spaces give each patient the needed "place to retreat."

As the plan evolves toward the center "small group areas" and along with the nursing station at the center, a "large group area" is provided for; corridors are eliminated, and along with the sizing of the group areas, this helps prevent "undesirable confrontations." With the large sizes of the typical mental hospital dormitories and dayrooms, which often hold 100 or more patients in a single interior space, Osmond described the resultant situation:

The psychotic people, all gravely ill, are trapped in a kind of eternal cocktail party . . . the nineteenth century psychiatrists could not show that as groups of people become larger so the complexity of interactions increases enormously—as anyone at a cocktail party soon discovers. It is hardly surprising that at such parties much alcohol, a valuable if erratic social lubricant, is required to cut down our apprehensions. But we now know that while in a group of two people there is only one possible two-person interaction; in a group of four there are six; and in a group of eight, twenty-eight. In other words, in terms of this simplest kind of reaction alone, an eight-person group is twenty-eight times more complex than a two-person group.

With this geometric ratio of increasing, undesirable interactions, it is no wonder that Izumi and Osmond wanted to cut down the number of patients who are forced to interact in the large spaces.

Here are some details of the spaces that are designed to limit the number of undesirable interactions. The plan provides for individual toilets in each bedroom, along with a washbowl if the budget permits. On lower budget projects, Izumi has designed toilet rooms so that each toilet is visually separated from every other for privacy, and as much aural protection as possible is designed for as well. Individual closets and other spaces for personal belongings are planned for in the bedrooms.

Izumi found that noise from another patient room was much more disturbing than noise from other sources. Therefore great care was used in soundproofing the walls between the bedrooms, as well as between the bedrooms and other spaces. Osmond suggests that carpet also be used for this purpose.

The bedrooms are clearly defined, even to the ceilings, so that the patient can feel the room as an entity in itself; even the closets can be perceived as being completely inside each room. This gives a sense of personal possession to each patient; a different colored bedspread also helps a perceptually confused patient know his own room. Each ceiling in each room is designed to look as if it belongs only to that room, rather than looking as if it is part of a plane that goes on and on.

Surfaces throughout the hospital, which would otherwise reflect faces, as well as light bulbs or tubes have been either chosen or treated so that they are nonreflective, since otherwise they would confuse patients with impaired perception. One sheet of glass at a slight angle from the wall line is used for the principal part of each window; bug screens and dividing bars are eliminated as visual distractions. Each window has returns on the sides to show the patient that he is on the inside, but with the large main part of the window, he has an unconfused means of "visual escape."

Visual Illusions

Great care was taken in the design to prevent visual illusions, so that no ambivalence could occur in patients' minds as to what is what. Doors are specified to look like doors, and doorknobs look like doorknobs. Izumi had found clocks and signs with no visible means of support particularly disturbing to patients, therefore "we used no clocks or signs that might appear to be floating, insecure or defying gravity."

With the perpetual disturbances present in the mentally ill, good signage becomes an absolute necessity. The more legible signage is, the better chance it has of penetrating these perceptual disturbances. Hall's admonition in this regard for institutions for the aging could be doubly reinforced for mental institutions.

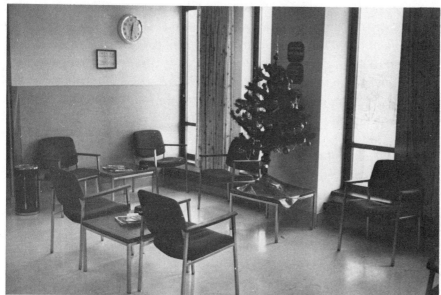

9.6

Figure 9.6. Lounges
with light (but strong)
movable chairs.
Figure 9.7. Very formal,
institutional waiting
area, courtesy of
maintenance.

9.7

Other design elements which might trigger patient illusions, such as patterns in cloth wherever it might be used in the hospital, were eliminated also. Izumi felt that a knotty pine ceiling has no place in a mental hospital; patients might think that the knots are eyes staring at them; even heavily grained wood might form pictures of a terrifying type. According to Izumi, perforated or fissured ceilings are just as disturbing, so the best solution is probably wood.

Other Design Considerations

So that the patients might feel at home wherever they are in the hospital, the same nondisturbing oatmeal colored drapes were used throughout Yorkton as a decorative, unifying device; chests and dressers in the bedrooms and desks and credenzas as well as tables in the offices all have the same white laminate tops and gray drawers.

Beds are placed against the wall to make the patient feel more secure, and the beds are lower than typical hospital beds so that patients can get in and out of them easily, even in the dark.

Single chairs are specified in the day rooms, rather than multiple seating sofas, in order to reduce strain among patients; a patient doesn't have to decide who to sit next to on a sofa, or whether to do so or not. Another strain-reducer was the provision of more single chairs in any given space than the number of patients expected to occupy them. This way, there was always an available chair, which fact reduced the hesitancy of patients to enter a seating area. Otherwise, the frequent phenomenon of "favorite chairs," a typical feature of institutional life, takes over. Patients have their chosen seats, which become their territory, especially in the median portion of the dominance hierarchy; a patient in the lower range of the dominance hierarchy might not be able to sit down at all if there were not more chairs available than there are patients to sit in them.

Hall says "for the institutionalized psychotic, laying claim to a territory is more basic than speech (in some instances). At least it is still manifest in mute patients." He also reports observations of ward dominance hierarchy that are consonant with the findings of Esser, Chamberlain, Chapple, and Kline, and that "space was the 'currency' of one of the large, seldom visited wards in Washington D.C.'s St. Elizabeth's Hospital." Hall also quotes Winick and Holt: "the preference for individual chairs indicated that a human being must experience his own body bor-

Figure 9.8. It looks like a prison, not functionalism. (arc photo)

der as well as a need for a 'life space' in the literal sense. It appeared, however, that the degree of preference for individual space was a function of the degree of neuroses."

Izumi also has strong feelings about furniture arrangement:

People do not arrange themselves in space according to the assumptions of many architects and interior designers. I find that interior decorators in particular make the wrong assumptions on what proper furniture arrangements should be. The furniture is usually arranged at right angles. This has a certain formality, and is done in relationship to the furniture itself rather than to people. In fact, I suspect it is easy to draw with a T-square and triangle.

Sensitivity To Human Needs

Osmond and Izumi share a concern for the well-being of the user-client. As Osmond describes it:

Supposing we found ourselves in a schizophrenic patient's world, what would do us most harm and what would help most? It seems in principle very simple.

Figure 9.9. An outdoor area connected to the indoors helps. (arc photo)

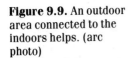

Anything that makes heavy demands upon the patient's impaired perceptual apparatus will harm him. This means not only avoiding ambiguous and muddled design, but also avoiding too much complication, even though it may be aesthetically interesting.

Osmond also explains what he wants:

A true functionalism could develop depending not upon what architects believe human beings should feel about the design of buildings, but upon the perceptions and needs of actual human beings under the many differing conditions of their existence. This social functionalism would not be an arbitrary matter, depending upon the fads and fancies of a particular school of architects, but would derive from the way in which the people who are going to inhabit the particular building perceive the world around them, and the activities they want to undertake in the space the architect is providing for them.

Just as Osmond's desire for a true functionalism applies to all buildings, almost all of the foregoing design criteria for mental hospitals apply to general hospitals as well, since any hospital patient is not in his accustomed interior and shares many of the perceptual and behavioral needs of the mental patient. However, the methodology involved is most important: find the ultimate client-user and design for his or her needs.

Some Organizing Principles

Designers have begun to look at these user needs in terms which make it possible to make use of two basic concepts:

1. The concept of *pattern language* originated by Christopher Alexander and associates:

The essential feature which every pattern has, is that it forms the basis for a shared agreement in a community. Each one is, therefore, a statement of some general planning principle so formulated that its correctness, or incorrectness, can be supported by empirical evidence, discussed in public, and then according to the outcome of these discussions, adopted, or not, by a planning board which speaks for the whole community.

Patterns are open-ended, they can be applied to any design problem, and they can be easily updated. Briefly oversimplified, a pattern consists of defining the need for a space in which to conduct an activity or a series of activities, then describing how the space might be designed, along with the rationale for the design, which consists of reasoning, as well as references to applicable human reactions and behavior patterns as described in the literature.

As an extension of this process, Alexander and his associates have also evolved a method of relating external and internal spaces to each other, using the same general method. An example is a pattern that they developed in 1970 for the entry portion of any residence in an urban area. They suggest basic discontinuities between street/parking place and the door to the residence proper, such as changes in materials, change in levels, and changes in direction within the entry. One specific suggestion is that the floor of the living areas of the resident should be at least one step below the floor just inside the entry.

The general reasoning behind these suggestions is that human beings develop a separate behavior for the street and public areas; psychologically, the discontinuities mark the change in atmosphere from street to home—thus allowing the person who enters the residence to drop his street-oriented tension and guardedness. He then is able to relax and interact with the people in the residence, having had the stimulation of these transitional interior features to help him be ready for it.

2. Abraham H. Maslow proposed a hierarchy of human needs. Archie Kaplan summarized these for designers as:

Level One—these are physiological, for food, clothing and shelter and include freedom of movement to avoid stagnation, meeting anthropometric and biomechanical requirements, and providing comfort in relation to the necessity for alertness.

Level Two—safety, security and territorial needs, which emphasize the necessity for environmental cues to time and space.

Level Three—social needs: for belonging, love and friendship; these involve being able to see other people and activities, being able to express emotions, and being able to express ideas.

Level Four—ego needs: for self-esteem, and for instance, to be able to exert some control over one's immediate environment.

Level Five—the highest need: for self-actualization, to be the person you can be and want to be.

For detailed discussion of the use of patterns and their organization according to Maslow's hierarchy see arc's "Handbook: Changing Places & Settings." Arc has also been the leader in designing mental health facilities with the participation of both staff and patients in the design process.

With the help of arc and others, the author conducted a study to test the theory that the staff and patients view the interior environment in different ways—and therefore to try to find out whether or not both should be consulted in the redesign of an existing mental health facility. This study was done at Chicago-Read Mental Health Center and is fully described in the case study on that hospital.

Design Checkpoints

1. Refer to "Architectural Considerations for Mental Health Facilities," the Canadian Mental Health Facility Standards prepared by Kiyo Izumi, Architect-Planner.

2. Be careful in the treatment of corridors so that they do not seem to be endless or intimidating.

3. In day rooms, recreation areas, and the like, be sure that more chairs are provided than there will be patients to use them.

4. Check both the patients' and the staff's opinions about the existing interior environment, when redesigning a mental health facility.

References

Christopher Alexander, Sara Ishikawa, and Murray Silverstein, "A Pattern Language Which Generates Multi-Service Centers," Berkeley, Calif.: Center for Environmental Structure, 1968.

Christopher Alexander, and Barry Poyner, "The Atoms of Environmental Structure," in "Emerging Methods in Environmental Design and Planning," ed. Gary T. Moore, Cambridge, Mass.: MIT Press, 1970, pp. 308–321.

Christopher Alexander, Murray Silverstein, Schlomo Angel, Sara Ishikawa, and Denny Abrams, *The Oregon Experiment,* New York: Oxford University Press, 1975.

arc (architecture/research/construction) Michael Bakos, Janet Biederman, Richard Bozic, David Chapin, Charles Craig, Kenneth Exposito, Barbara Hartford, Steven Kahn, and Robert Reeves (Walter Kleeman, and Laura Taxel, special consultants), "Handbook: Changing Places & Settings," Cleveland: arc Research Division, Cleveland Development Center, Ohio Department of Mental Health and Mental Retardation, 1975.

Aristide H. Esser, Amparo S. Chamberlain, Eliot D. Chapple, and Nathan S. Kline, "Territoriality of Patients on a Research Ward," in "Recent Advances in Biological Psychiatry," ed. J. Wortis, New York: Plenum Press, 1965.

Edward T. Hall, "Spatial Relations and Man's Physiology and Psychology," paper given at the Conference on Medicine and Anthropology, Arden House, Harriman, New York, November, 1961.

Edward T. Hall, *The Hidden Dimension,* Garden City: Doubleday, 1966.

Mardi J. Horowitz, Donald F. Duff, and Lois O. Stratton, "Personal Space and the Body-Buffer Zone," *Archives of General Psychiatry"* (December 1964), pp. 651–656.

Kiyo Izumi, "LSD and Architectural Design," in "Psychedelics," ed. Bernard Aaronson and Humphry Osmond, Garden City: Anchor Books, Doubleday, 1970.

Coryl LaRue Jones, "Planning, Programming and Design for the Community Mental Health Center," New York: Mental Health Materials Center, 1966.

F. H. Kahan, *Brains and Bricks*, Regina, Canada: White Cross Publications, 1965.

Archie Kaplan, "Maslow Interpreted for the Work Environment," A talk given at NEOCON 8, Chicago, The Merchandise Mart, June 1976.

Abraham Maslow, "A Theory of Human Motivation," *Psychological Review,* 50, 1943, pp. 370–396.

Humphry Osmond, "Design Must Meet Patients' Human Needs," *Modern Hospital,* March 1966.

Humphry Osmond, "Some Psychiatric Aspects of Design," in "Who Designs America?" ed. Laurence B. Holland, Garden City: Doubleday, Anchor Books, 1970.

Robert Sommer, *Personal Space: The Behavioral Basis of Design,* Englewood Cliffs, N.J.: Prentice-Hall, 1969.

Robert Sommer, *Design Awareness,* San Francisco: Rinehart Press, 1972.

Mayer Spivack, "Healing Surroundings," *Human Behavior* 6, no. 3 (March 1977), p. 34.

C. Winick, and H. Holt, "Seating Position as Non-Verbal Communication in Group Analysis," *Psychiatry* 24, (1961), pp. 171–182.

John Zeisel, "Fundamental Values in Planning with the Non-Paying Client," in "Architecture for Human Behavior," ed. Charles Burnette, Philadelphia: Philadelphia Chapter, American Institute of Architects, 1971.

10 *Residences: Some Observations*

For the majority of Americans, participation in the design of the places where they live just does not happen, especially for apartments, mobile homes, and tract homes that make up the majority of places where we live. These kinds of homes are not designed by the users, though the mechanism of the marketplace does influence their design to some extent; builders do build what they think will sell.

Design for a residence should begin with a floor plan to determine sizes of spaces, necessary adjacencies, and number of rooms; how critical this process can be is detailed below.

Implications of Floor Plans

Brent Brolin and John Zeisel, architect and sociologist, respectively, broke new ground with their observational study and resultant proposed architectural designs for inhabitants of the North End of Boston. Using as a base the previous research by Herbert Gans on the West End, which was similar to the North End physically, ethnically, and demographically, Brolin and Zeisel found evidence that the floor plans of dwelling places could interfere with the living patterns of those who live there.

Among the working class families of Italian origin they studied, it was customary for men and women to gather without intermixing for social occasions; unless separate groups could gather, the typical lifestyle could not be preserved. They also found that the cooking area had to be large enough to accommodate women visitors, and that areas for adolescent girls must be within sight of the boys' areas.

Zeisel reports the floor planning needs of working class families of Puerto Rican origin in New York; one of the findings is that the living room is a place of reverence; therefore it must be separate from the kitchen. The entrance must be near the kitchen so that the woman of the house can see who comes and goes as she spends most of her day in the kitchen; this works well, since an entrance directly into the living room would not be appropriate in these families' eyes.

He also describes the attitudes of moderate income southern blacks in South Carolina in terms of housing floor plans. This group needs a separate dining room; it cannot be a part of either living room or kitchen. This need is explained in terms of a historical desire, that has become a social need, to get away from cooking odors.

Other ethnic groups need the same kind of analysis, as can be seen from diverse vernacular floor plans around the world reported by Amos Rapoport. These reports have a message for designers; floor plans must reflect the behavioral patterns and desires of those who live on them, and unless the techniques of participatory design are used, this will not happen.

Use of Scale Models

Several experimenters have used variations of a simple, low-technology technique to involve users in participatory design—the changeable scale model of a proposed environment.

Leo Zrudlo used a scale model kit at the scale of one-half inch to one foot to help Inuit Eskimos to plan housing in the Arctic; the effort was successful, and as a result of participatory design, a house was developed using the "principle of creating a trap for the cold air in winter at a lower level in the house where the heating system would be installed, and placing the living areas on the upper levels where the heat would rise by natural convection." This concept also resulted in less total volume and less exterior wall area, thus reducing construction costs.

A similar technique was used by Sam A. Sloan in helping thirty-five families of the Spokane Indian tribe to design their own homes. Sloan provided each family with a changeable model house at a one-inch-to-one foot scale, and each family was successful in designing its own home.

Models for Mental Hospital Design

Another version has been used successfully by arc for patient and staff participation in the design of interior spaces at Cleveland State Hospital. A model of the space to be redesigned was constructed from ordinary cardboard to a scale where one-quarter inch equals one foot. The scale model seemed to be quite comprehensible to both patients and staff and proved to be quite useful for mental hospital design where staff and patients participated in the design. Changes were made with a knife or scissors—easily.

**De Long's
Revolutionary
Research**

However, the most advanced and revolutionary research in the use of scale model environments is that of Alton J. De Long. De Long, associate professor of architecture at the University of Tennessee–Knoxville, has been working with model environments for several years to try to unlock the secrets of how to design spaces appropriate for their intended human use. Frustrated by the inordinately large amounts of time and money necessary to perform experiments utilizing traditional methods of analyzing microenvironmental use, he long ago turned to scale models as a possible method of performing environmental analyses useful to designers at much smaller costs in time and money and it looks as if he is right.

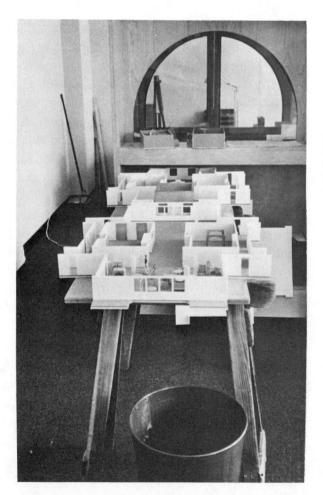

Figure 10.1. Arc model for the use of patients, staff, and designers in planning changes for mental institutions.

De Long says:

Instead of slowing down and attenuating behavior in environments (as traditional methods would dictate), we have been compressing the behavior into shorter time intervals through the use of "compressed" environments.

By reducing the scale of the environment, we are attempting to reduce and compress the execution rates of the behavior so that proportionately more behavior can be elicited in a given time frame.

The use of scale models changes a person's perception and sense of time; it currently appears that *the perceived time-frame is equivalent to the spatial scale.* We can therefore say that *time passes faster in scale environments.*

Finding that informants working in his scale environments (his subjects were untutored in the design process) became tired after working more than one hour in them, De Long sensed that his subjects were compressing their thinking and working in the same ratio as the scale: in *one* hour they were going through *twelve* hours of experience and work, it seemed.

So, De Long began to try to find out what was actually happening. He initially figured that his subjects' experiential time-frame would be 1/12 of real-time in a 1/12 scale environment; however, the first results he got from careful observations and interviews did not come out that way.

The first results showed that subjects were only experiencing 1/5.2 real-time instead of 1/12. However, in this initial observation, the subjects were "reporting the time-intervals experienced in scale to an investigator timing them—so they were also simultaneously operating in a full-size spatial scale, or real-time (the investigator)."

For the next set of observations, De Long removed the investigator and had the subjects start and stop a timing device themselves; this procedure resulted in an "average experiential time-frame over all intervals experienced, large and small, of 1/8.5". However, this set of observations also brought up the fact that as the time intervals got larger, the perceived time-frame approached 1/12—from 5 to 10 minutes, the perceived time-frame was 1/7.7; for 15 to 20 minutes, it was 1/9.1; and for more than 30 minutes, it was 1/11.1. This last result is, of course, close to the 1/12 ratio. And, what has happened in his observations of untutored subjects bears this out.

He reports that whole dwellings can be designed by unsophisticated subjects in periods from 4½ to 9 hours, using one-inch-to-one-foot scale models.

Right now in his laboratory at the University of Tennessee is a one-inch-to-one-foot scale model of the planned new Art and Architecture building for the University of Tennessee, one-third of it, that is. The model is thirteen feet wide, eighteen feet long, and over four and one-half feet high; it includes model furniture and model human figures, and took 4,000 student man-hours to build. The building is planned to cost more than nine million dollars and De Long feels that in this way, people can experience the space before it is built. I can agree with that, because I found that you can lie down in the courtyard of the model and get a good idea (I felt) of how the space would be when it is built and used.

However, I do not feel you could do this if the scale were any less than one-inch-to-one-foot, and using this same scale, De Long has performed some other experiments that indicate a substantial future saving of time and money for those of us who are interested in finding out how users perceive and perform in the microenvironment.

De Long agrees with Edward T. Hall, the noted anthropologist, that the average person deals with space every day and is "fluent in the language of space." So, he decided to try to replicate Hall's observations of "proxemic zones" in both full-size and in scale-model environments. He succeeded, finding that the accuracy of his subjects' perception only varies "at an almost constant 6 to 7½" between full-scale and scale-model environments. He has also replicated some of Robert Sommer's experiments with the "distance for comfortable conversation" with remarkably similar results.

De Long says that "the fact that essentially the same behavioral data can be elicited in a 1/12 scale model implies that behavioral relationships are independent of spatial scale. In other terms, there is no reason why a person cannot accumulate a valid baseline of experience through exposure to a scale environment." He feels that a 1/12 scale is "ideal" for getting behavioral information because it is large enough for a subject to imagine being in it and large enough so that a subject can accurately assess and report how he would feel and react in it.

He also believes that the importance of scale environments in the socialization process for human beings may be greater than we have previously realized. He points to the earlier social maturity of girls than boys in our culture, and wonders whether or not it might be due to girls' tendency to play more with dolls and doll houses, which are after all forms of scale-model environments.

Further, De Long sees the possibility that the use of scale-models to speed the perception of time and quicken the solution of design problems may have significance far beyond his present use of the procedures. He points to the work of John B. Calhoun, the ethologist, who has related significant advances in human intellectual capacities to increases in the human population. "With every doubling of human population a conceptual revolution emerges which completely alters the perspective people utilize as well as their means of coping with the world," De Long says, pointing out the significance of Calhoun's vision. De Long feels that as the world becomes more crowded and less space is available for each of us, some of the effects of reduced-scale environments will be felt; some of the resultant problems might then be solved much faster with the use of scale-model environments to anticipate problems that will occur as our human population increases.

The use of scale-model environments to try to solve our design problems faster and better is certainly a key objective for DeLong, but he feels that he may be on the track of finding better ways to solve other kinds of problems faster for human beings—so he continues to experiment and to try to refine the processes he has discovered.

Although at the present state of his work he regards the 1/12 scale as the most productive one for behavioral results, he is now experimenting with other scales, notably 1/8 inch to 1 foot, 1/96 scale ratio, and his preliminary results indicate that time seems to pass more quickly in the 1/96 scale model environment.

Incidentally, he will shortly publish electro-encephalagraph (EEG) measurements of his subjects confirming higher rates of brain activity while they are working with models.

De Long is continuing to refine his methods and to test other aspects and uses of the scale-model environment; this observer finds his experiments the most exciting work going on in the environmental design field today.

Arguments for Participatory Design

There are powerful arguments for the necessity of participatory design. Habraken says, "We must, I think, refuse to see the housing process as anything other than a story of human bondage. It sounds a trifle too easy when one uses the words 'freedom,' 'creativity,' and 'beauty.' I much prefer expressions like 'possibility to act,' 'involvement and identification,' and 'integrity and honesty.' "

Another meaning of participatory design is the possibility of changing what you design to suit changes in the lives of those who live in a residence. Coryl LaRue Jones has this to say in regard to "Design as a Change Process": "The architectural and planning professions now realize that it is necessary to design for change rather than permanency. The fixed edifice is a very costly error, even in residential construction. . . . The Japanese proverb states it well: When the house is finished, it is time to die." Amos Rapoport agrees, "It would seem that the introduction of system building offers an opportunity of providing loose fit and changeability and to reconsider the matter of open-endedness and personalization."

Yet, generally, we do not take advantage of the systems we have. It is rare that we see a residence that uses an industrial building system; however, Baraban describes a house using one and using demountable interior partitions to boot. It was designed by Marc Harrison of the Rhode Island School of Design and uses lead sheet in the interior partitions and some of the ceilings to deaden sound as well as drop seals on the doors for the same purpose.

From *The Architects' Journal* we learn that there is experimentation in England with the "PSSHAK (system) in which the main structure of the building (support structure) is separated from the internal fittings of the dwellings (assembly kit) allowing each tenant to fix his plan before the prefabricated kit is fitted into the flexible structure."

In the present situation in the United States, most people buy or rent what is already built and designed not for individuals but for large classes of people. What would happen in the housing marketplace if some of housing were flexible and changeable as well?

The Bedroom

For some of the parameters of bedroom design we turn to a study done for the United States Department of Housing and Urban Development by the Environmental Design Department of the University of Wisconsin under the direction of Byron Bloomfield. This report emphasizes that there must be enough space in the bedroom to start with—for easy movement around the sleeping unit and so that getting out of bed doesn't result in bumps and falls; the arrangement of the bed and other furniture must be done so that this is possible. The study also states that the bedroom should not

be visually or physically so small that surfaces (seem to) approach a person to the point of building up body tension. The ultimate goal of the sleeping area is to provide a restful place that allows the human mechanism to relax. . . . Surfaces which define the basic sleeping area should generate a restful psychological and physiological feeling . . . wall surfaces should not have coarse textures and visually strong design patterns which stimulate the nervous system of the human body.

The report also recommends that the colors used should stay within general contrast limits of 3:1, and certainly should go no higher than 7:1.

The use of pure color should generally be avoided in the bedroom area because the human mechanism tends to build up an avoidance toward a surface which communicates too rapidly.

Also:

High contrasts would create an unrestful feeling while . . . relaxing . . . within the bedroom area.

While these general recommendations are well founded in the literature and available data, further it is the author's feeling that individual requirements in the bedroom should take advantage of excellent equipment on the market available to provide a changing visual and auditory setting in the bedroom. With the film and projection devices now obtainable, it is possible to provide rather inexpensively any color or scene on bedroom walls, and then to change it instantly, if you wish, but always under the control of the human beings who occupy the bedroom; the relatively new techniques of holography should also soon be available for residential use. The same is true of the auditory milieu; with multi-channel high fidelity audio equipment it is now possible to bring any sound you wish to any room using records or tape.

Both the auditory and visual environment can now be changed almost at will to fit the desires and needs of the human beings who use a particular bedroom—but only if the bedroom is first protected from the unwanted intrusions of noise and light from the outside.

Intimate Contacts and the Bedroom

In "The City as a Mechanism for Sustaining Human Contact," Christopher Alexander makes a convincing argument for the necessity of *intimate contacts* between human beings as vital factors in their mental well-being. He stresses the fact that more and more of us live in cities and while we have increasing numbers of contacts with others in cities, the quality and intimacy of these contacts is lessened as the number of them increases. Yet the minimum need for human intimate contacts remains and increases as the number of casual contacts increases.

However, in all of this one matter has been largely neglected: the *place* where it happens. Certainly any deep, intimate contact between human beings must occur in a place where there is complete privacy—and privacy is *the* necessity for the barriers-down relationship between two human beings (or more) that constitutes intimate contact.

When this kind of contact occurs in an interior space (and it occurs there more frequently than in exterior space), "we lead an indoor social life," according to Erving Goffman—the chances are greater that it will take place in the bedroom than anywhere else in the dwelling, especially where there are more than two people living together there.

While many other activities take place in bedrooms, certainly it is the preferred site for love, sex, companionship, and private conversation in an intimate relationship between two people; the walls of the bedroom are a prime factor in making privacy possible here by separating the occupants from the exterior and the rest of the interior.

Robert Maxwell has done one of several studies of the relationship of walls to human behavior; he relates the relative impenetrability of walls to codes of premarital sex behavior in a cross-cultural comparison involving ninety-three societies around the world. His range of penetrability goes from open walls through grass, leaves, and hides to stone, brick, and concrete. Briefly, he found that as the impenetrability of walls increases, the number of restrictions on premarital sex activity increases and that as walls are more penetrable and open, the number of restrictions decreases. He also relates his data to temperature means and extremes, suggesting that the need for thermal comfort may be a salient factor in determining what kind of walls a society may build. We live in a society that uses the more impenetrable types of walls, suggesting both our need for thermal comfort and the development of mores that require this type of physical barrier for the development of intimate contacts and relationships.

As far as the bedroom is concerned, however, the wall must be so constructed that it provides two principal types of privacy in order that intimate contacts between human beings may occur there. The first is visual privacy, which is the lesser problem of the two. You cannot see through most walls and doors, and it is a rather simple task to make sure that the window coverings are composed of materials that will not allow someone outside the window to see what is going on inside. Of course, for some individuals who are extremely light sensitive, draperies or blinds that completely block light coming from outside are required.

The second kind of privacy, acoustical, is a bit harder to come by, but the competent interior designer must be able to provide the degree of acoustical privacy that is necessary. Sometimes the problem starts with the inner composition of the walls themselves; they are just too thin and we have draped entire walls to correct this problem. Erving Goffman tells of British researchers interviewing residents of public housing projects to find that the walls were occasionally so thin that whole conversations could be heard and understood by neighbors; these invasions of privacy produced greatly inhibited behavior. Parsons also points out that it is just as important that sounds inside the bedroom do not reach the outside as to protect the bedroom from intrusive sound. Thin and/or poorly insulated walls do not make good spaces for facilitating intimate contacts and you cannot assume that a wall is sound deadening enough until you experience the acoustic atmosphere next to it.

Underlining the importance of privacy in the bedroom Montgomery recounts McQueen's response of homeowners to the question: "Which of the following, if any, detract from a harmonious sexual life?" Answers included: "Lack of ½ bath adjoining master bedroom—33.6%; children's bedroom too near parents—22.7%; lack of soundproofing—24.5%; lack of privacy for family members—14.5%."

Unfortunately, interior designers often cannot affect the construction of walls, but they can provide some of the acoustical and visual protection necessary for that most precious process—intimate human contact.

Reducing Noise

The effects of carpet as a noise-reducing agent are well known. Certain types of carpet laid over certain types of underlays on the floor can lessen ambient noise by as much as 70 percent averaged over the audible sound frequencies and therefore are rated as having a noise reduction coefficient (NRC) of 0.70, after being rated on the basis of standard tests under laboratory conditions; carpet and pad also reduce impact and vibration noise as well. Carpet on the walls will lessen the sound pressure level even further. The NRC varies with the type of carpet.

So important has this characteristic become that most carpet mills have their carpets tested and give the noise reduction coefficient as part of the specifications for various types. The accepted test is ASTM C-423-66.

The type of underlay also is a determining factor in the amount of noise reduction achieved. Although most carpet noise reduction coefficients are determined using 40-ounce all-hair underlay as the standard material, certain carpet manufacturers have tested their carpets using other materials that can double the noise reduction coefficient in certain situations. Of course, laying carpet without any underlay at all can lessen the amount of noise reduction by almost half.

Draperies can also be quite efficient in reducing noise levels. Robert Marshall credits certain types of draperies hung against walls with a noise reduction coefficient of 0.55; this is based primarily on the sound absorption qualities of the drapes.

PPG Industries has developed a system for rating the sound absorption, heat insulation, and brightness control of draperies. They point out that:

Because of the "fullness" created by pleating, draperies have a greater surface area in contact with the air. Therefore, they stay cooler than blinds or shades and do not *reradiate* as much energy to people near the windows. Light-colored fabrics stay cooler than dark-colored fabrics because they reflect, rather than absorb, much of the solar energy reaching them. . . . All fabrics have a beneficial effect in reducing noise, but the most effective are those which are very tightly woven and relatively heavy in weight.

Draperies and carpet are not the only interior furnishings that help reduce noise levels—planning and close attention to interior finishing details are also important factors. Materials used in doors, the way doors close, wall coverings, and what is inside the wall (insulation is not that expensive), the design of air conditioning systems, windows, and their closures (double panes help)—all can be very important to the control of noise. In the home, selection of household appliances for their aural qualities can help, especially garbage disposal units, dishwashers, blenders, washers, and driers. Insulation of the walls that separate these from other rooms must be selected properly.

The Bathroom

Another device that can be selected for its quietness is the toilet—though it usually is not. This brings us to another key area that is not known for its contribution to health and safety—the bathroom.

Alexander Kira was the principal investigator in a five-year study of the bathroom sponsored by the Cornell University Agricultural Experiment Station and by the American Radiator and Standard Sanitary Corporation's Plumbing and Heating Division. This study is the most nearly complete and penetrating one that has been done on any interior area and is a model for what should be done for other areas. It approaches the problems of America's "unmentionable room" from historical, cultural, anthropological, psychological, and ergonomic points of view.

Kira felt that the typical American bathroom was being built "more for the convenience of plumbers than people," and further that "social and psychological taboos" surround even the mention of the bathroom and its uses and "seem almost to have built up into a culture-wide embarrassment . . . the simple and inevitable body functions have come to be regarded as unspeakable and vulgar." For instance, he describes the bidet as "an innocent washing fixture" that is designed for simple cleanliness "but through misunderstanding and misinformation it has become a sex symbol." Kira thinks that might be acceptable if we cleaned ourselves thoroughly between the legs in some other fashion, but he says, "The blunt fact is we do not."

Kira is quite concerned about the safety hazards of the bathroom, especially in the cleansing process; he mentions that we have to stand on slippery surfaces, sometimes clean with our eyes shut and meanwhile we have to reach all parts of our bodies with soap and water.

Kira's specific criticisms of existing bathroom fixtures include:

1. The lavatory or basin is too small and little changed from the Victorian era.

2. The bathtub is unsafe and uncomfortable.

3. The shower is cramped and unsafe.
4. The toilet is the "most ill-suited fixture ever designed."

He also felt that little thought has been given to improved storage, ventilation, lighting, heating, and especially sound-proofing.

Some of the design changes for the bathtub and shower suggested by the study to answer these and other criticisms are:

1. Contouring the bathtub for built-in lumbar support.
2. Maximum rim space for sitting when bathing children or cleaning out the tub.
3. The narrowest possible rim span at the center of the tub for ease in grasping when getting in or out.
4. A permanent slip resistant bottom as a safety feature.
5. A tri-wall surround made from fiberglass reinforced plastic to eliminate grout and help the cleaning process with rounded corners.
6. Two fixed shower heads—one at shoulder height so that you don't have to get your hair wet if you don't want to, and one high enough to cleanse a tall person from head to toe. A concealed flexible hand spray to reach body recesses easily is also suggested.
7. Self-draining storage space, plus multilevel soap dishes.
8. A fold-down utility tray plus a fold-down seat.
9. Recessed built-in lights at the top.
10. An automatic whirlpool with variable heat, volume, direction, and air content for both pleasurable and therapeutic use.
11. A beveled edge on the tub to use as a head rest.
12. A controlled splashless arc of water was suggested for the lavatory, and lower height as well as a completely redesigned seat are recommended for the toilet.

Many other recommendations are made for these fixtures as well as for all facets of the bathroom.

In the course of the study, Kira and his team measured people carefully in relation to all of the activities usually performed in the American bathroom; they took photographs of the use of present equipment; as they progressed they developed experimental, improved models, and photographed people using these. The study was based on the premise that:

equipment should be adapted to people and to the physical actions involved in the performance of activities. . . . The criteria for design, therefore, include the heights, reaches, breadths, ranges of movement and other characteristics of the people who will be using the equipment.

As an example of new light on old problems, Kira's search of the literature, as well as the study's emphasis on measuring human performance in the bathroom, produces a new answer to the problem of counter heights comfortable for the standing worker, whether the worker is an assembler in a manufacturing plant or a cook in a kitchen. In connection with his work on "How high should the basin be?" Kira ran three separate tests that confirmed earlier ergonomic studies (notably Ellis) that had shown that, assuming a reasonably relaxed standing posture, the best work height for the hands is one to three inches below the elbow.

The Kitchen

These findings clearly call for adjustable height counters, in kitchens and manufacturing plants, as well as wherever work is performed while standing—yet the seemingly rigid, frozen, unchangeable counter height in American kitchens is 36 inches, as well as in many other places. Still, any height on either side of the narrow range of one to three inches below the level of the elbow is uncomfortable, and, assuming long periods of work at a counter of the wrong height, unhealthy as well, especially in view of Harmon's findings of specific health defects related to lack of height adjustability of desks and seating for school children. My friend who is four feet eleven inches tall solved this problem by seeing to it that her new house had a kitchen counter 29 inches high, which is a comfortable height for her, but that option is not open for most people.

We need kitchen work surfaces that are adjustable in height. This goes against Grandjean who recommends a uniform height of a little over 35 inches for sink, stove, and other kitchen work surfaces for standing tasks. However, even he cites basic work by Bratton, as shown in Steidl and Bratton, that shows a range of preferred work surface heights of from 30 inches to 37 inches in the form of averages related to elbow heights. If this data could be translated into individual preferences, the range of preferred heights might be greater. On the measured elbow heights of 500 homemakers in New York in 1938, preferred heights might range as much as 10 or 12 inches. In Ward and Kirk we find that this range could be between 30.34 and 39.33 inches for variety of standing work performed by British subjects in the kitchen. Grandjean also quotes a study by Bloch and Muller presumably done with German subjects that showed a range of preferred ironing heights (also derived from averages) of more than 9 inches.

Hoag and Van Dyke propose adjustable height kitchen work surfaces and show drawings of how they might be made; they propose a 30-inch to 39-inch range, but say that it might be necessary to have a 30-inch to 42-inch range. They say that "the shortest subjects in particular noted that fatigue was greater while working at the standard counter (36 inches high). The reason for the fatigue was obvious; the shorter woman was required to mix . . . with her elbow well away from her torso. In two cases, the upper arm was nearly parallel to the floor."

Another argument for adjustable height work surfaces and shelves in the kitchen is that as we grow older our body dimensions change: we shrink in bodily size, as Grandjean points out. We *need* kitchen work surfaces that are adjustable in height.

References

Christopher Alexander, "The City as a Mechanism for Sustaining Human Contact," Berkeley, Calif.: Center for Environmental Structure, 1966.

arc (architecture/research/construction) Michael Bakos, Janet Biederman, David Chapin, Richard Bozic, Charles Craig, Kenneth Exposito, Barbara Hartford, Steven Kahn, and Robert Reeves, (Walter Kleeman, and Laura Taxel, special consultants), "Handbook/ Changing Places & Settings," Cleveland: arc Research Division, Cleveland Developmental Center, Ohio Department of Mental Health and Mental Retardation, 1975.

Architects' Journal 23 (February 1977), p. 334.

Regina Baraban, "A House for our Times:," *The Designer*, Three/77, 20, no. 242 (March 1977), pp. 28–30.

W. Bloch, and H. P. Muller, "Untersuchungen über die arbeitstechnisch richtige Höhe von Bügeltischen," *Industr. Organisation* 23, pp. 208–210.

Byron C. Bloomfield, "Performance Requirements, Reston Low Income Housing Demonstration," Madison: Environmental Design Dept., University of Wisconsin, 1967. (mimeo)

Esther Crew Bratton, "Working Position and Fatigue in Household Economics and Management," Ithaca: New York State College of Home Economics, Cornell University, 1959.

Brent C. Brolin, and John Zeisel, "Social Research and Design: Applications to Mass Housing," in "Emerging Methods in Environmental Design and Planning," ed. Gary T. Moore, Cambridge, Mass.: MIT Press, 1970. Also published in slightly different form as "Mass Housing: Social Research and Design," *Architectural Forum*, July-August 1968, pp. 66–71.

Alton J. De Long, "Coding the Environment," in "Psyche and Design," ed. Wolfgang F. E. Preiser, Champaign: University of Illinois at Urbana–Champaign, Department of Architecture, 1976 and Orangeburg: The Association for the Study of Man-Environment Relations, 1976.

Alton J. De Long, "Architectural Research & Design: The Art & Architecture Building Project," *Free Flow* 1, no. 2 (November 1976) pp. 1–10.

Alton J. De Long, "Time, Space and Geometry: Design Problems in the Promotion of Man," *Portfolio* 1 (Spring 1977), pp. 25–30.

Alton J. De Long, "Proxemic Zones and Context: An Empirical Analysis," in "New Directions in Environmental Design and Research," ed. Walter E. Rogers and William H. Ittelson, Washington, D.C.: Environmental Design Research Association, 1978, pp. 348–364.

Douglas S. Ellis, "Speed of Manipulative Performance as a Function of Work-Surface Height," *Journal of Applied Psychology* 35, 1951, pp. 289–296.

Herbert Gans, *The Urban Villagers,* New York: Free Press, 1962.

Erving Goffman, *The Presentation of Self in Everyday Life,* Garden City: Anchor Books, Doubleday & Co., Inc., 1959.

Etienne Grandjean, *Ergonomics of the Home,* New York: John Wiley & Sons, 1973.

Etienne Grandjean, "Ergonomic Aspects of Aging and the Built Environment," in "Proceedings—6th Congress of the International Ergonomics Association," Santa Monica: Human Factors Society, 1976, pp. 145–148.

N. J. Habraken, "Supports Responsibilities and Possibilities," *Architectural Association Quarterly* 1, no. 1, 1968/69.

Darell Boyd Harmon, *The Co-Ordinated Classroom,* Grand Rapids: American Seating Company, 1949.

Laverne L. Hoag and Robert H. Van Dyke, "A Human Factors Evaluation of the American Kitchen," Santa Monica: Proceedings of the Human Factors Society Meeting, 1975, pp. 120–123.

Coryl LaRue Jones, "Planning Process *vs.* Personal Process," Paper presented at the workshop, "A Process for Designing Mental Health Facilities," at the Environmental Design Research Association Conference (EDRA 8) Urbana, Illinois, April 19, 1977.

Alexander Kira, "The Bathroom: Criteria for Design," New York: Bantam Books, 1967 and Viking Press, 1976.

Robert Marshall, "Carpet as an Acoustical Material," *Canadian Interiors* 7, no. 1 (January 1970), pp. 36–39.

Robert Maxwell, "Onstage and Offstage Sex: Exploring an Hypothesis," *Cornell Journal of Social Relations* 1, no. 2 (1967), pp. 75–84.

Phil K. McQueen, "Relationships Among Selected Housing, Marital and Familial Characteristics," Unpublished dissertation. Tallahassee, Florida: Florida State University, 1964.

James E. Montgomery, "Impact of Housing Patterns on Marital Interaction," in "Human Needs in Housing: An Ecological Approach," ed. Karen Natrass, and Bonnie Maas Morrison, Washington: University Press of America, 1976, pp. 82–90.

Henry McIlvaine Parsons, "The Bedroom," *Human Factors* 14, no. 5 (October 1972), pp. 421–450. The bibliography attached is excellent.

"PPG Industries Feneshield Fabrics," Pittsburgh, Penn., 1976.

Amos Rapoport, "The personal element in housing:an argument for open-ended design," Royal Institute of British Architects, *RIBA Journal,* July 1968, pp. 300–307.

Amos Rapoport, "House Form and Culture," Englewood Cliffs, N.J.: Prentice-Hall, 1969.

Rose E. Steidl, and Esther Crew Bratton, "Work in the Home," New York: John Wiley & Sons, 1968.

Joan S. Ward, and N. S. Kirk, "The Relation Between Some Anthropometric Dimensions and Preferred Working Surface Heights in the Kitchen," *Ergonomics* 13, no. 6 (1970), pp. 783–797.

John Zeisel, "Fundamental Values in Planning With the Non-Paying Client," in "Architecture for Human Behavior," ed. Charles Burnette, Philadelphia: Philadelphia Chapter, American Institute of Architects, 1971, pp. 23–30.

Leo Zrudlo, "Planning with the Inuit - Participatory Design in the High Arctic," *Journal of Architectural Education* 29, no. 3 (February 1976), pp. 11–12.

11 *Interior Ergonomics in Outer Space*

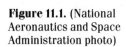

Figure 11.1. (National Aeronautics and Space Administration photo)

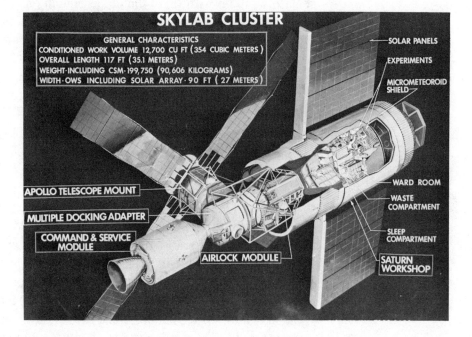

Skylab is history and its interior design and space planning problems turned out to be quite similar to those faced by interior space planners everywhere, except for those posed by the Zero-G completely closed system.

Would you believe that one of the needs foreseen for future spacecraft design is more windows? According to C.C. Johnson, chief of the Spacecraft Design Division of the National Aeronautics & Space Administration, the 18-inch-diameter window in the Skylab wardroom permitted the greatest use of "those great human sensors . . . a pair of eyes." The two earth viewing ports in the Multiple Docking Adaptor were also well used.

Would you believe that the sound level was a problem, as it is even in most well-designed offices? Charles (Pete) Conrad, Jr., the first Skylab mission commander, at one early point complained that the crew was shouting so much that they became temporarily hoarse. He also reported that the sound-pressure level in the workshop aboard the orbiting Skylab at one point was 64 dBA, while the wardroom and bedroom at the same time registered about 55 dBA. These rather high levels might have had something to do with the difficulty in communicating. Since 55 dBA is near the upper limit usually set for desirable background office noise, that level would seem to be a little high for a bedroom area. The Russians have concluded from their own spacecraft studies that 40 dBA should be the upper limit for any part of a manned spacecraft.

We read in the newspapers about the temperature problems encountered by Skylab when one of its heat shields was torn away during the launch process. Most interior designers have had to cope with temperature problems here on earth, where it is quite a bit simpler to deal with them than it is in the hostile environment of outer space. However, the low humidity level in Skylab made it possible to work in relatively high temperatures in the initial period, when the workshop was beginning to cool down after the new heat shield had been installed.

Zero-G did not seem to be an insurmountable problem, according to Conrad. Published pictures of the astronauts aboard Skylab show, among other things, a medical examination under way while the examiner is sitting in a "normal" position (as far as the picture is concerned), while his fellow crew member being examined is "upside down" in relation to the examiner. In leisure moments, the astronauts were able to float freely inside Skylab, without apparent strain or discomfort, and were able to relax in whatever spot they found themselves after bouncing off the walls, ceiling, or floor. Any position seemed natural to them in the weightless environment of Skylab. This demonstrated ability to move freely in all directions probably will result in the elimination of most flooring from the cockpit area of the Space Shuttle, leaving large holes to permit freer movement, according to C. C. Johnson.

Normal Day-Night
Cycles Disrupted

This weightless, Zero-G environment was also cut off from the normal day-night cycles of earth life, because the first Skylab mission was launched four hours earlier than was originally planned and because

Figure 11.2. Astronaut Owen K. Garriott, science pilot of the Skylab 3 mission, is stationed at the Apollo Telescope Mount console in the Multiple Docking Adapter. (NASA photo)

there were initial periods of very intense activity that resulted in work periods as long as eighteen hours at one stretch. Gradually, the astronauts' normal work-sleep cycles were disrupted. As a result, toward the end of the flight it was necessary to gradually adjust their work-sleep cycles to approximate normal earth cycles, so that they would be rested and at their physical fitness peaks for the exacting maneuvers necessary for successful reentry and splashdown.

Weightlessness produced another problem: items handled by the crew would not always stay in their normal position and would float around the cabin. The filter screen on the spacecraft's air exhaust system not only sucked these items into one place, where they could be recaptured, but also took care of loose screws, washers, rivets, and bolts left over from the space vehicle manufacturing process.

To ease the problem of floating stray items, there probably will be more "flat, smooth and continuous surfaces in the Space Shuttle to eliminate corners and crevices, where things can get caught and then become hard to retrieve," according to C.C. Johnson. This somewhat conflicts with the demonstrated usefulness of astronauts' wedge-fitted shoes, which were sized to slip into the triangular shaped floor grid to form a necessary restraint system for some activities.

Weightlessness, however, turned out to have another real advantage. The crew members were able to easily move items that had a "mass equal to their own." Also according to Johnson, this has implications for Space Shuttle design, making it possible to, perhaps, simplify some of the equipment planned for that project.

One would expect grid flooring in this Skylab spacecraft, because it started out as an S-4B third stage from a Saturn Five launcher: two aluminum grid floors formed the base for the laboratory and crew quarters in the 10,000 cubic feet liquid hydrogen tank, while the rest of the volume in the liquid oxygen tank next to it was used as a waste container. Its original use as fuel tanks dictated its size and configuration, making it much larger (117 feet long) than the 40-foot long, 12-foot diameter (4,100 cubic feet) mock-up that McDonnell-Douglas had used for some of the early mission simulation studies. This size gave the three-man crew volume far in excess of the 150- to 700-cubic-foot minimums recommended by earlier studies (depending on the duration of the flight) to prevent various difficulties resulting from confinement in smaller spaces. In fact, according to Cooper the Skylab workshop alone was "33 times as large" as the Apollo crew compartment and 100 times as large as the Gemini crew compartment.

No Claustrophobia in Space

In fact, Skylab's 12,763 total-cubic-foot volume was so spacious for the three-man crew that Conrad ventured that this spaciousness might have been partially responsible for the lack of sensation of motion sickness during the flight.

No claustrophobia was reported by the first Skylab crew either, and the large amounts of volume available may have been responsible. At least a cramped feeling has been reported in Russian space studies and claustrophobia has been mentioned prominently as a possible hazard to manned space flight in the several feasibility studies sponsored by NASA over the past several years.

Habitability

These were deep and penetrating studies that probed the possibilities thoroughly and focused on the concept of spacecraft "habitability," de-

Figure 11.3. This overhead view shows the layout of the crew quarters of the Orbital Workshop, the largest component of Skylab. The large section at the top is the general control and working area. At the right is the wardroom where crewmen prepared and ate food and spent leisure time. At lower center is the Waste Management Compartment or "space bathroom." At the left is the Sleep Compartment. (NASA photo)

fined as "how fit an environment is to live in," or "the perception of the quality of life in an environment."

How is habitability to be evaluated? Psychometric and sociometric measurements are to be made using the entire spectrum of measuring tests available to the behavioral sciences, including biofeedback methods, which are predicted by some space scientists to be the most useful future tool in evaluating the habitability of the space environment. In fact, one of the early studies stated implicitly such an objective when it suggested finding out "how an environment is supportive to an individual's needs for behavior in areas of duty, leisure, sleep, as well as body function." In a later paper Wortz and Nowlis state flatly, "We can measure habitability."

Although the pressure of work was arranged for Skylab (flight duties as well as scientific tasks) so that both the variety and quantity of things to be done would not leave time for boredom, ennui is expected to be a problem for long flights to our solar system's planets and beyond in the future. For those missions, space scientists want to make sure to provide "perceptual and behavioral richness" in the space environment. They specify some of the necessary factors as negative space, positive form, personal territory, personal space, mobility, and trafficability, as well as visual, tactile, auditory, and olfactory elements that are changeable. The importance of this richness is underscored by Wortz and Nowlis. This perceptual richness must be present, but integrated, in order to prevent disorientation in Zero-G. One way to help with this process is to ensure that the individual crew member can change the visual and physical elements of interior space in the craft, especially in the personal compartments.

Inflatable Walls Will Help

Inflatable, reversible, and movable walls, with different colors and textures on each side and lighting that can change in color (while altering the patterns on the walls and ceilings by means of varying filters), are among the ideas being considered for future spacecraft. Also suggested are interchangeable wall hangings and panels, not only interchangeable within a compartment but also from compartment to compartment.

While white is recommended as a basic color for the interiors of spacecraft (because it acts as a psychological space expander and makes an excellent background for the interplay of color and pattern changes), dichromatic paint is also prescribed, because it provides apparent color changes as the physical viewing point of the observer changes. However, the floor should be darker in color and coarser in texture than the ceiling and walls; this is based on normal earthbound, good ergonomic practice. Removable pigments are suggested to be given to individual crew members so that they can decorate the walls and ceiling with their own temporary graffitti and works of art on long flights to the stars.

Future spacecraft designers are urged to investigate two recent discoveries, ferroelectric ceramics, which change color when an electric current is passed through them (they can be made in thin chips), and liquid crystals. All liquid crystals change color with changes in temperature, and some of them also change color when placed in an electrical field.

A double door system for the personal compartment is a possibility with a translucent outer door to let in some light from the general lighting system and an opaque door to shut out light for sleeping. This dual door system is also important in privacy and acoustical control.

In the general interior space planning of a spacecraft or station for occupancy of twelve or more men, Edward T. Hall's concepts of proxemics and the prevention of crowding are emphasized as design parameters. The prevention of territorial acts in the outer space environment is likewise pinpointed as a design objective, with the suggestion that acceptable and functional demarcations of individual territory be used in such a way that individual territorial needs are met. Hall's further assertion that "touch and visual spatial experiences are so integrated that the two cannot be separated" is given as one reason for making sure that textures are varied throughout future spacecraft.

People-Initiated Changes

In many of these suggestions for changing light, colors, textures, and form, provision is made for the individual to initiate the changes. Some space analysts believe that it is impossible at this point to predict the tastes of a future crew of any particular space station or spacecraft, and they do not want "to create an environment that is totally alien to the tastes of the crew." They also feel that getting the crew's participation in the space planning of the spacecraft interiors will get them ego-involved and set the stage for positive feelings on their parts about the craft. These analysts also believe that giving the individual crew member control of light, color, texture, and pattern, as well as to a certain extent the arrangement of a personal compartment, will perform an important function in satisfying needs for personal expression, as well as needs for territory.

Moreover, in terms of the need for privacy, it is important that the space traveler be able to control this inner space in the sense that it must be used for a variety of activities, in addition to sleep, on a long flight: looking at and listening to a projected individual audio-visual console, grooming, dressing, reading, solitary games, games with others, voluntary isolation, and other person-to-person social interactions.

Wortz and Nowlis' study of the U.S. Navy's Tektite II program emphasized not only the importance of having private bunk areas, but also "that crew members did not disturb each other when they were in the privacy of their own bunk areas."

Circadian Light Cycles

While much attention is given to the individual control of interior space, including lighting control, Righter et al recommend that for long flights, the general interior lighting in spacecraft should be "varied on a daily schedule to promote the maintenance of normal circadian (24-hour biological) cycles." In other words, the traveler in space will still operate biologically on the 24-hour Earth day cycle, and to prevent biological disorientation, this cycle will have to be preserved in the lighting. Control of circadian cycles on the relatively short Skylab flight was accomplished by commands from Mission Control. In the near future "the [Spacelab] crew will work a 16 hour day and all sleep at the same time. Work on the second simulation with split work/sleep schedules was too disruptive."

Audio-Visual Console

A proposed individual audio-visual console with keyboard is also suggested as a personal connection to Earth. While it would still be used for mission-related communications, maintenance, and emergency alarm instructions, off-duty uses could be for study, recreation, and private communication with family and friends on Earth. Data from the Tektite II program also support this proposal as a method of increasing the positive habitability of the space station or spacecraft.

Interior Space Use

Dual use of interior spaces would seem to be indicated. But with the exception of the multiple uses suggested for the individual crew compartments and the further exception of the wardroom, which can be used for exercising, meals, and assemblies as well as for leisure social activities, the uses of interior spaces for more than one purpose is discouraged by some space scientific authorities. One example given in support of this view is space for medical care, which, some feel, should not be used for any other purpose. In contrast, others give detailed sets of compatibility data for determining which different uses can be made of the space, depending on the need, the mission, and the size of the crew.

Corner Interactions

Spacecraft interior planners want to avoid any excess volume for long flights and want to make the most efficient use of volume while maximizing the feeling of spaciousness as perceived by the crew. One fully documented example of this is the methods used and the decision made about the size and shape of future dining tables, while providing for adequate aisle space.

First they studied the literature, emphasizing work by Sommer and Osmond on social interaction at tables. They found the well-known result that conversations are more likely to occur across the corners of rectangular and square tables than anywhere else at tables of those shapes. They also found, of course, that square or rectangular tables occupy more interior space per person accommodated than do round tables.

Round Tables in Space

So, as a compromise, this major study recommends round tables, 48 inches in diameter, to make the most efficient use of volume, while providing adequate opportunities for conversation and social interaction. Warning is given that the tables should have the capability to change in shape in the event that "extreme cultural differences exist within the crew," evidently referring to Hall's work in delineating the different distances at which human beings socially interact, depending on cultural background.

This study also emphasizes that the results of experimentation in the area of social interaction around tables are not conclusive or necessarily "universally applicable." It points out that "what is desirable is flexibility and congruence between design and function, so that there can be a variety of shapes, and crewmen can be involved or not as the occasion and mood demand."

Since this particular study as well as others done for NASA continually refer to "missions" and use typical U.S. Air Force wording and formats, there is a certain military flavor in this material, and almost all the men who have gone into space have been members of the armed forces. It is hard not to wonder if, had they read the chapter on Communication Distance, their choice of table shapes would have been the same.

Women Crew Members

Space scientists have accepted the possibility that there may be female members of future spacecraft crews. Righter also pointed out that only a few additional features would be necessary in future spacecraft for women that were not already planned for the male astronauts, simply, additional volume for storage and disposal of feminine hygiene supplies plus a separate female urination system which is being designed into the

Space Shuttle. Disposal of feminine hygiene supplies would have to be in a separate receptacle, to keep the planned waste disposal system from becoming too complicated.

This study also mentioned the fact that this additional volume might be compensated for by the probability that space women might require less volume themselves, since they are typically five inches shorter and weigh thirty-five pounds less than men when they are 30 to 34 years old, which is also the age of the typical astronaut candidate.

Thus, we could expect that space women, being smaller, would require less food and oxygen, which could make a significant difference in the number of scientific experiments which could be carried aboard instead of food, oxygen, and typically heavier men.

Other reports have been cited that women are more resistant to radiation (always a hazard in space travel), less likely to have heart attacks, and not as likely to be adversely affected by noise levels, extremes of heat or cold, loneliness, or pain.

The fact that space women might require less volume in future craft in another way was borne out by studies performed during the Navy's Tektite II project, where it was found that women used the quite confined sleeping area for other leisure activities as well, while the male members of the Tektite II crew found their identically sized sleeping areas much too confining for any other activities, making it necessary to plan more volume in future spacecraft where there will be only male crew members.

An investigation on the effect of menstruation on women's reactions was also cited. There seems to be little to worry about here in terms of the future space women, since no deleterious effect was found on work performance, endurance, or fatigue. One instance was cited about a woman who set a world track record when she was in the midst of her menstrual period. It was pointed out, however, that altitude or pressure changes may produce a slight change or delay in the menstrual cycle, and that this may occur in Zero-G, but that it would produce no bad effects.

While the United States has not sent any women into space, the Russians, of course, did send up a woman cosmonaut in 1963, Valentina Tereshkova. However, somebody at NASA must believe that women should be astronauts because during the period between 1959 and 1961,

NASA tested twenty-five female space candidates and passed thirteen of them as fit persons to travel into the environment of outer space. Very little has been heard about this program since until recently. On April 14, 1977 ten women, 35 to 45 years of age, were to enter NASA's Ames Research Center Human Research facility for tests to determine NASA's future "medical baselines for non-pilot men and women who will make up the bulk of research personnel carried on the shuttle." It is also worth noting that of the 4,625 applications NASA had received up to June 30, 1977 for the Space Shuttle program, "about 925 of the applicants are women."

The atmosphere of the American space program is changing, and it is probably only a matter of time until the first American woman goes into

Figure 11.4. Skylab 4 crewmen William Pogue (above) and Gerald Carr place trash into the airlock of the Orbital Workshop. Carr is holding two other trash bags while a third is floating free in the zero-gravity of space. (NASA photo)

outer space. After all, the first multinational crew was a reality on the Apollo-Soyuz Project.

Parallels to Cities   As the diversity of space crews increases, we cannot help but be reminded that the whole world is fascinated by outer space and its problems. These problems are ergonomic, and because the environment of spacecraft and space stations resembles those of the world's crowded cities—the limits on the amount of physical room available, the limits on the amounts of fuels available, the dangers of human self-pollution, the physical risks, the likelihood of crowding phenomena, territorial constraints, and absolute dependence on mechanical systems for life support—the solutions of these problems can be useful research reports for the future of our life on Earth.

References

Aviation Week and Space Technology, April 9, 1973, p. 52 ff.; June 4, 1973, pp. 30–33; June 11, 1973, pp. 49–51; June 18, 1973, pp. 14–15; July 9, 1973, p. 18; July 16, 1973, pp. 68–69.

Aviation Week and Space Technology, April 11, 1977, p. 22; May 9, 1977, pp. 43–44; July 4, 1977, p. 20.

John R. Baratono, Arthur A. Rosener, Bill F. Fowler, Edward W. Karnes, and Melvin L. Stephenson, "Architectural/Environmental Handbook for Extraterrestrial Design," Springfield: National Technical Information Service, 1970. Accession Number N71-17560.

Henry S. F. Cooper, Jr., "Life in a Space Station-I," *The New Yorker,* August 30, 1976, pp. 34–66.

"Habitability Data Handbook, Volume 2, Architecture and Environment," Houston: National Aeronautics and Space Administration, Manned Spacecraft Center, Habitability Technology Section, Spacecraft Design Division, 1971. MSC-03909.

"Human Factors in Long-Duration Space Flight," Washington: National Academy of Sciences, 1972.

Joan McCullough, "The 13 Who Were Left Behind," *MS,* August 1973, p. 41, ff.

C.E. Righter, D.P. Nowlis, V.B. Dunn, N.J. Belton, and E.C. Wortz, "Habititability Guidelines and Criteria," Springfield: National Technical Information Service, 1971. Accession Number N71-17769. The importance of this study is underlined by the fact that it is the only one mentioned in "Marshall Space Flight Center Design Standard 512A - Man/System Requirements for Weightless Environments" Paragraph 3.2 Architecture/Volume. MSFC-STD-512A was released and published December 1, 1976. It should also be noted that E.C. Wortz and D.P. Nowlis, who are cited separately, were among the authors of the 1971 study.

Russell Schweickart, talking to Peter Warshall, "There Ain't No Graceful Way," *The Co-Evolution Quarterly,* Issue no. 14, June 21, 1977, pp. 44–47.

E.C. Wortz, and D.P. Nowlis, "The Design of Habitable Environments," *Man-Environment Systems* 5, no 5 (September 1975), pp. 280–288.

12 *Life in the Office*

How can the interior designer affect the quality of life in an office? The answers are myriad and important because there are going to be more and more office workers in more and more offices, especially in the twenty-four largest metropolitan areas that account for 65 percent of all the office jobs in the whole United States, even though these twenty-four areas have only 34 percent of the total population of the United States in them. For the United States as a whole, the number of office jobs is more than that for any other form of employment in 1980, 44.8 million white collar workers as opposed to 29.5 million blue collar workers. Using 1965 as a base figure, the number of office jobs will be two and one-half times what it was in 1965 by the year 2000.

The wages that will be paid to this increased number of office workers will count for 92 percent of the total costs of office operation, with rent or depreciation accounting for 2 percent, and maintenance accounting for 6 percent, based on thirty-year depreciation schedules. Therefore, increasing the productivity of the labor that accounts for so much of the total cost becomes a prime objective of any efficient management.

Planning and design of the space where these workers will spend about half their waking hours can be done in such a way that they are happy with it; this is one way that the interior designer can affect the quality of life in an office in a meaningful manner and increase productivity. Another way to ensure the economic success of an office is by designing it so that it functions efficiently, and the interior designer must be able to do this, too.

Office Landscape

To identify some of the ways in which these objectives can be met, let's take a look at the development of a recent major office design advance: *office landscape*. Office landscape started in Germany about twenty years ago from the concepts of Eberhard and Wolfgang Schnelle of the Quickborner Team, a firm of management consultants from the town of Quickborn in Germany. In German the word is "Burolandschaft," and in Swedish, "Kontorlandskap." Office landscape was *not* started by an interior designer or an architect—it was started by management consultants, and the original objective was efficiency in the use of personnel and space.

From a design point of view, a very simple definition of office landscape would be: an office without full-height partitions that is laid out in a communications-oriented fashion (not necessarily at right angles) to maximize use of space and ease of contact among those workers who need to be near each other in order to work effectively.

The soubriquet '"open plan," sometimes used incorrectly to describe landscaped or semilandscaped offices, is not accurate because open-plan offices, sometimes known as bull pens, have existed for about 100 years. In these older offices, you will find the rigid geometric patterns of serried row after row of desks, lined up like soldiers on parade, perpetuating the hierarchy of straight lines and right angles, which also represents the traditional hierarchy of management.

As a matter of fact, the Quickborner Team is dissatisfied with the translation of "Burolandschaft" to "office landscape" in English because they feel that this overemphasizes the plants and trees, which are a highly visible feature of it, but are not absolutely essential. What is absolutely essential is the communications survey that precedes the planning of every successful office landscape, and a second survey that determines the space, equipment, and degree of privacy required for every person who works within the landscape. These two surveys are the heart of the present theory and effectiveness of office landscape.

1. *Communications Survey*—This survey, usually lasting two weeks, asks everyone in the groups who will be in the landscape to identify each telephone conversation by source and/or destination and length. All visits, visitors, and written communications are similarly noted. The purpose is, of course, to determine who needs to be how close to whom.

The density of communications between any two people is given a weighted number. Groups are also weighted and rated. Computers are frequently used in this phase to find out the weight and strength of the needed connections between persons and groups, so that physical closeness can reflect the needs for communication closeness.

2. *Second Survey*—This survey determines the equipment and space required for each worker in the landscape; this space consists not only

of the space needed for individual workers and their equipment, but also the space they need to get to and from their work position.

If these two surveys are properly performed, the needed information is available about the real process and flow of work in that office. You discover from the surveys what really goes on, not just what you think goes on. This analysis of process is the heart of office landscape, and the design of the space cannot properly proceed until this needed information is ready for use.

To put the planning for an office landscape in motion, Robert Propst advocates modeling and pregaming, in addition to the two surveys. Propst's employer, Herman Miller, Inc., sells a modeling kit based on the office furniture it makes, as many other office furniture manufacturers do. But Propst carries this a good bit further by describing a method whereby the proposed landscape can be modeled, then photographed or sketched so that it can be programmed into a computer and simulated three-dimensionally. With light pen capability to change, add, delete, or rotate the display, it offers a very attractive tool in planning office landscape.

Why No Partitions?

The simple fact is that most partitions, even though they may be the movable kind, are seldom moved. Partitions in general are erected in one position and stay that way; they become fixed features of the office space. They not only box in people, but they box in thinking, too. However, probably most important, they actually hinder communication between the people who are behind the separate partitions.

The function of office landscape is to facilitate communication and to facilitate change as well as expansion. The seemingly random pattern of many landscapes is due to the fact that groups of people who must communicate with one another are grouped together and groups who need to communicate with other groups are put close to these other groups. A certain percentage of the space is left open and becomes a safety valve for growth as the size and importance of various groups changes.

When these changes occur, they can be implemented, usually by an in-house staff overnight, at costs that are quite low in relation to changes that involve moving partitions or walls. Canadian National reported that work places (offices) can be relocated at a cost of 12 to 15 cents per square foot, compared to $3 per square foot for conventional private offices. Eastman-Kodak in Rochester reported that office landscape re-location costs are 10 percent of conventional moving costs, showing a 95 percent saving, 34½ cents per square foot for landscape changes against $7.50 per square foot for conventional changes. Eastman should know—they had 11 major rearrangements in a six-year period. While these cost figures have escalated since, it is probable that the ratios have remained relatively constant at about $1 per square foot for landscape changes against $20 per square foot for conventional changes. Cost savings of 10 to 25 percent have been reported for initial installations (no partitions needed) and more efficient use of space has produced further savings from 10 to 60 percent. Also, and more recently, John Pile reported results from an unpublished General Services Administration study which show that landscape office planning reduced space needed per work station from 150 square feet to 135 square feet, reduced initial occupancy installation expense from $4.18 per square foot to $3.47 per square foot, annual maintenance costs from 89 cents per square foot to 46 cents per square foot, and replacement costs from 15 2/10 cents per square foot to 12 7/10 cents per square foot. These figures are for government installations, of course.

User Satisfaction

The previously mentioned, Canadian National (CN) and Eastman in the same study both indicated a high degree of user satisfaction. CN reported 92.5 percent of its users expressed complete support or support with qualifications, while Eastman showed even higher satisfaction percentages over a three-year period.

Eastman has one of the more successful landscapes in the United States, and so did du Pont in Wilmington; both of these are research- and growth-oriented organizations. It probably was not accidental that they both turned to office landscape, because office landscape is best suited to that kind of organization.

Fixed rows of desks and fixed partitions are symbolic of fixed ideas; by itself, getting rid of them will not automatically get rid of fixed modes of thinking. What really happens is that businesses wanting to be efficient and grow get interested in office landscape as a tool to reflect their organizational aims.

They realize that landscape is not based on the typical vertical chain of organizational command; it is based on who actually contacts whom and why, on actual linear communication. For landscape to accomplish its purpose, the business that uses it must be flexible enough in its concepts to let its office processes reflect the actual communication needs rather than reflect the quasi-fiction of an organization chart. However, a high level of technical expertise is required for office planning and design, especially in certain areas.

The Building

First, the building into which the landscape is to be placed should be considered. If the building is a new one to be built, it can, of course, be designed specifically for the requirements of office landscape. If, however, it is to be placed in an existing building, the success of the plan may depend on how well the available space fits the use.

Large blocks of about 10,000 to 20,000 square feet with no barriers in them except for columns are best. The central service cores found in some office buildings are a definite hindrance, since there should be a minimum of about 65 clear feet between the boundaries of the space to be used in any direction; long narrow spaces are not suitable. One American authority indicates an undivided space at least 60 feet by 60 feet as a minimum, and 80 to 100 employees as a minimum for a successful landscaped office. The most detailed and useful analyses of space, size, and shape suitability for the various kinds of office use can be found in *Planning Office Space* by Duffy, Cave, and Worthington.

One dividend resulting from the use of this type of open space is the ease of heating, air conditioning, and ventilating it; with the major wall barriers nonexistent, both planning and installation are simplified. This kind of "interior design was also found to be an effective energy conservation technique. Large open spaces—without high partitions—make it possible to dissipate the heat gained due to lighting and people evenly throughout the interior of the building. Furthermore, such a design enables more effective use of conditioned air through the simple transfer of air from one area to another before it is reconditioned," according to the General Services Administration.

Early in the planning, acoustical factors must be thoroughly considered, and most of the landscapes designed so far have benefited greatly from the advice of acoustical consultants, all of whom insist on acoustical ceilings. Some consultants insist that there be no large sound reflective surfaces. For instance, though almost all installations have carpeted floors, acoustical requirements have dictated the placing of carpet on walls as well as draperies on walls and windows in some installations, depending on the sound characteristics of the equipment to be used. This does not refer solely to the number of office machines and the sound level of their operation; in the early designs desk side panels and the outer shells of filing cabinets proved to be quite reverberative, which kept the sound level too high. The designers were more management consultants than anything else, so they seized on this finding to require that desks have no filing drawers (they are more like work tables in this configuration) and that the materials filed for everyday use be put in moveable open frame carts. The filing material itself then absorbs sound, and in a mild way functions as a set of visual triggers for action, since the file folders are no longer hidden from view. At the same time to reduce clutter, these early designers banished any material not referenced at least once a month from these portable files, since storage was provided elsewhere for less active material. Screens used for visual separation and also used as bases to hang work station equipment on are now acoustically rated for their ability to attentuate sound. Several factors intervene here to determine the acoustic characteristics of the landscape, before the construction and therefore the effectiveness of the screen itself is considered.

Acoustical Requirements

Acoustical requirements in offices consist of:

1. Privacy of speech at both low and normal voice levels
2. The ability to perform normal office work with no distraction from the normal sound of another worker's voice

In achieving these requirements, a major factor is the distance between workers in the landscape, or how crowded it is, since the effect of sound lessens as the distance from the originator to the listener increases. This distance varies with the amount of square feet provided for each worker and in typical landscapes it will be in the following ranges:

Square feet provided per worker	Least distance between workers
110 sq. ft.	8 ft.
120 sq. ft.	10 ft.
130 sq. ft.	12 ft.
140 sq. ft.	14 ft.

In these ranges, which are those usually found due to the expenses of acquiring and maintaining the space, an acoustically absorbent barrier is necessary to meet the acoustic requirements.

Another factor is the orientation of a speaker to those who can hear him. It would be ideal if all office landscape workers faced away from each other in opposite directions, but that is not feasible in view of the typical space constraints above. Therefore, the most effective attainable

Table 12-1. Recommended Noise Criteria for Offices and Workspaces

NC (or NCA) Curve	Communication Environment
Offices	
NC–20 to NC–30	Very quiet office; suitable for large conferences. Telephone use satisfactory.
NC–30 to NC–35	"Quiet" office; satisfactory for conferences at a 15 ft. table; normal voice, 10 to 30 ft. Telephone use satisfactory.
NC–35 to NC–40	Satisfactory for conferences at a 6 to 8 ft. table; normal voice, 6 to 12 ft. Telephone use satisfactory.
NC–40 to NC–50	Satisfactory for conferences at a 4 to 5 ft. table; normal voice, 3 to 6 ft; raised voice 6 to 12 ft. Telephone use occasionally slightly difficult.
NC–50 to NC–55	Unsatisfactory for conferences of more than two or three people; normal voice, 1 to 2 ft; raised voice 3 to 6 ft. Telephone use slightly difficult.
Above NC–55	"Very noisy." Office environment unsatisfactory. Telephone use difficult.
Workspaces, Shop Areas, Etc.	
NC–60 to NC–70	Person-to-person communication with raised voice satisfactory, 1 to 2 ft; slightly difficult, 3 to 6 ft. Telephone use difficult.
NC–70 to NC–80	Person-to-person communication slightly difficult with raised voice, 1 to 2 ft; slightly difficult with shouting, 3 to 6 ft. Telephone use very difficult.
Above NC–80	Person-to-person communication extremely difficult. Telephone use unsatisfactory.

Note: Noise measurements made for the purpose of comparing the noise in an office with these criteria should be performed with the office in normal operation, but with no one talking at the particular desk or conference table where speech communication is desired, i.e., where the measurement is being made. Background noise with the office unoccupied should be lower, say by 5 to 10 dB.

NASA. *Habitability Data Handbook*, MSC-03909, p. 3–44.

goal is usually set at 90 degree orientation of workers to each other in the closest proximity, that is in the normal approximately rectangular divisions of the space.

Best results are achieved by acoustically efficient screens about 82 inches high and with no more than a ¾ inch open air space between the bottom of the screen and the floor. The most economical configuration of the screens themselves is in a Y shape which produces an even more effective orientation of 120 degrees. One reason for this is that it takes a minimum of 10 to 12 feet of screens to acoustically separate two workers on either side of the screens, but in the Y shape, 14 feet of screens can effectively serve three workers.

All of this assumes a typical background noise level of 45 to 50 decibels, although some designers recommend a level as high as 55 decibels. If this level is too low, it can be raised by the addition of "white noise" (unintelligible sound across the principal audible frequencies) produced electronically.

Federal Acoustic Requirements

The prime importance of the acoustic environment in open offices is underlined by a General Services Administration, Public Buildings Service (PBS) Guide Specification, #PBS T 4–13500, for an Integrated Ceiling and Background (ICB) System. This guide specification recognizes that the acoustic atmosphere of any office is a product of several interrelated elements in it: the ceiling with its lighting (light fixtures can reflect and reverberate sound) and air handling components, the screens, the furniture, any office machinery to be used, and the floor. Proposed density of people and equipment is also a factor. According to Corlin and Falluchi, "an increasing number and variety of sound shielding and attenuating enclosures are appearing on the market to fit individual pieces of office machinery; these are being used in many kinds of offices."

Because the interrelationships among all the elements of the acoustic atmosphere are quite complicated, and because absolute quantitative measurements do not exist for evaluating the diverse qualities of the resulting environment (including the acoustics), PBS relies on a human jury to evaluate contractor proposals under this Guide Specification, and has fostered the concept of a Speech Privacy Potential, which can be evaluated in a numerical way as a prime part of it.

Screens with or without Components

While screens with acoustically absorbent surfaces and without attached furniture components are effective as visual and sound barriers when used with separate desks, files, and cabinets, the component systems that are attached to sound absorbing screens have definite advantages in the better utilization of space and the height adjustability of the components. This adjustability allows for the differences in the physical dimensions of the office workers, although attaching components somewhat reduces the sound attenuating efficiency of the screens.

Well-designed component systems attached to screens have another most important advantage over the use of conventional furniture: they can be easily moved and changed to fit different functions as the organization and requirements within it progress and change. This is consonant with the essence of the office landscape concept, which thrives on flexibility for change.

However, even well-designed component systems to be hung on screens have a real disadvantage to the purchaser; manufacturers typically make sure that screens *and* components will only fit each other *if* they are made by the same producer. So the purchaser then becomes tied to one source for screens and components.

It is also the author's belief that screen-hung components are cramping, both physically and psychologically, but it cannot be denied that the use of screens with components reduces the amount of floor space needed by 20 to 30 percent and permits 16 percent greater occupancy without crowding, according to Ruff.

Task Lighting and Energy Conservation

One of the components appearing on screens and every other kind of work station is a lamp or light source attached to the work station and controllable at the work station. The general high levels of lighting formerly specified are giving way to light sources concentrated on the task—to save energy. Jeff Miller of Hunter/Miller + Associates says:

Task lighting cuts energy use in the office by more than 30 per cent. For each square foot of office space, the old guidelines typically assign: 5 watts for lighting, 5 watts for air conditioning, and 2 watts for other services. Task lighting cuts the lighting load in half—to 2.5 watts per square foot. Since 50 per cent of the air conditioning is needed to offset heat from lamps, a 50 per cent drop in the lighting load cuts the air conditioning load by 25 per cent. This yields another saving of 1.25 watts per square foot. The total saving comes to 3.75 watts—or better than 30 per cent.

Figure 12.1. Task lighting with some indirect lighting as well. (Steelcase photo)

Another energy-saving design element was stressed by the General Services Administration: "Light colored floors, walls, and ceilings were found to lend themselves more readily to energy conservation by providing greater interreflectance between interior surfaces, which contributes measurably to more effective lumens per watt of artificial illumination on the task." Reflectance percentages for most paints and laminates are readily available from manufacturers so that designers can keep interior reflectances high to save energy.

Power and Communication

To keep the office landscape truly flexible, especially in view of the energy shortage, power and communications sources must be easily movable. Propst and others recommend that these be located in the ceiling, transmitted to each worker's position through easily portable pipes or poles which are now commercially available. Since almost all office landscapes are carpeted over concrete floors, locating these sources in the floor was not a truly flexible arrangement, even with loose-laid carpet tiles, until the advent of flat cables for both electric and telephone service. It now looks as if flat cable and carpet tiles will prevail.

Two relatively unsolved difficulties with office landscape designs are:

1. Some activities that go on in every office demand more privacy than a landscape system can provide, such as hiring, firing, and the discussion of very confidential financial or planning matters. The only solution to

date has been to provide some spaces with ceiling-to-floor partitions and resultant greater privacy. Also, some organizations are simply not suited to landscape.

2. With a landscape, the status of a private office is gone, and the temptation to the designer is to specify larger or more expensive furniture to identify status; if the designer succumbs to this, the flexibility and interchangeability of the system is compromised. One idea might be to indicate organization levels by finish or species of wood; at least this solution would offer some visual variety after the organization has shifted around several times.

Management Philosophy

Probably office landscape reflects the management philosophy of those who commission it. Because management theory and philosophy are in a constant state of flux, and because further changes in thinking and implementation can be expected, landscape naturally becomes attractive to those decision-makers whose thinking is also flexible and attuned to the changes in requirements that are always appearing in the world of the office.

Who Is for Office Landscape?

However, office landscape is not for everyone; it is not suitable or desirable for every office. How does the designer determine what type of office will satisfy the needs of each client?

Francis Duffy

Francis Duffy and his associates, Colin Cave and John Worthington, have developed a set of theories that can help and they have put them into successful practice. They have come up with a very useful basic concept for office buildings and their contents. These architects separate the "shell," the building itself which cannot easily be changed, from the "scenery" which can and should be changed to suit changing uses by one tenant and/or changing tenants with changing uses of space.

It should be emphasized here that these authors treat office planning and design as a continuing dynamic process; therefore the concepts of shell and scenery are essential for their view of that process. They say that there are "cycles of changing use in an office building"; that "the building shell is useful for, say 40 years with a refit at 25 years"; that "the office 'scenery' is replaced at shorter intervals"; that "changing 'scenery' can keep an office building useful throughout its life"; that elements of scenery are considered on a five- to seven-year-use basis; and finally that changes and adjustments of scenery made by the users "create the 'sets' for the office scene." This last especially has a theatrical ring to it. The scenery consists, of course, of the movable, changeable elements of interior design, the furniture, the partitions, the plants, the screens. Scenery also assumes great tax importance; it can be depreciated much faster than the shell and its attached walls. They also bring forth the important point that the more exactly building shells are planned for an organization's needs at any given time, the more difficult it will be to adapt them for future changes when the organization's needs grow or diminish. They also caution that when shell and scenery are considered together as a design problem, the chances are that future changes will be made more difficult.

Duffy, in another study, also cites the traditional Japanese house "in which only the interconnecting spaces are positive and in which, by removing the 'scenery,' spaces are indeed reversible." However, from the concepts of shell and scenery and of office design and planning as a continuing, dynamic process, Duffy proceeds to a concept that is quite relevant to the designer's problem of satisfying client needs.

Duffy feels that "deep down, the proponents of office landscaping assumed that all organisations were the same and that consequently office landscaping was equally appropriate in all circumstances. This cannot be so." Duffy goes on to point out the different types of office organizations and the variegated types of shells and scenery that can be designed and used to fit each type of organization. In another article, he said further that "office landscaping appeared to offer unlimited freedom but in fact created a whole series of problems in planning and in defining spaces for groups of office workers within endless office floors." Because "most working groups in offices are small and autonomous," they really do not want or have to have the improved communication and they do not like the downgrading of privacy that results from office landscaping.

Duffy suggests adequate analysis of organizations before beginning office planning and design, in terms of the "fundamental user problem of expressing the significance of the individual and the small group while still preserving the integrity of the organisation as a whole." He posits that organizations can be analyzed in terms of their degree of *subdivision*—or in other words, how many partitions are there and what group sizes do they enclose? This will probably be related to the amount of *interaction* that occurs among the staff. He cites a design organization as being low in subdivision and high in interaction—groups of people work closely together.

Duffy also suggests that organizations be analyzed in terms of their degree of *bureaucracy*. Bureaucracy in this sense means strict division of tasks, a definite hierarchy of supervisors, explicit rules for every matter, a sharp separation of administration and ownership and advancement based on technical competence. Therefore, the design organization is likely to be low on bureaucracy and low on differentiation (which is an expression of bureaucracy and is related to the degree of it).

Duffy also mentions that a very largely clerical organization, such as the bookkeeping department of a bank, will probably be high on bureaucracy and differentiation, but low on subdivision, while high on interaction. A corporate headquarters would likely be high on bureaucracy and differentiation; there would be definite separations between the officers, so that the corporate headquarters would be high in subdivision and low in interaction. On the other hand a research organization composed of highly specialized professionals would possibly be high in subdivision and low in interaction to give people a chance to work on their own without disturbance; the research organization would also be low in bureaucracy and would have low differentiation.

Oversimplified, Duffy's purpose in these analyses is to plan and design for each organization individually; he feels very strongly that "scenery should reflect organisational form."

Herman Hertzberger

Duffy has also analyzed the "brilliant initiative" of the Dutch architect, Herman Hertzberger, in his planning and design of an office building for Centraal Beheer Insurance Co-operative Society in Apeldoorn, Holland. The authoritative *Architects' Journal* has called Centraal Beheer "revolutionary."

Hertzberger's "*thesis* is that the individual user is all-important . . . . He accepts the user as a co-designer." For example, in Centraal Beheer, Hertzberger deliberately left parts of the building unfinished to stimulate the users to participate in and complete the decoration by hiding the rough finishes with their own personal touches. That is exactly what has happened; the special ledges that Hertzberger de-

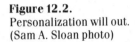

Figure 12.2.
Personalization will out.
(Sam A. Sloan photo)

signed are used for a wide variety of plants. He grouped the ventilation outlets in twos which also become a basis for employee decoration. There are "home-made screens of floor to ceiling ropes," birdcages, dolls, and sprightly posters in great profusion on the rough, unfinished concrete block walls; there are many other personal wall hangings as well.

Hertzberger believes in using very strong form in his "musical architecture," however. He says, "I try to make a building as an instrument so that people can get good music out of it . . . with a bad violin even the greatest violinist cannot get out more than the instrument allows." So, for Hertzberger's thesis to work, the building must be strong and well-designed.

Sam A. Sloan   Another user-oriented architect is Sam A. Sloan. Sloan is an architect from Spokane, Washington who closed his practice to take a Fulbright in Australia and earn his Master of Science in Man-Environment Relations at the University of Sydney. He presented a technique at the Environmental Design Research Association conference in Los Angeles in 1972 that seems quite attractive and meaningful in human terms. As his thesis, he conceived and executed a study in the offices of the Australian Mutual Provident Insurance Society that broke new ground not only in terms of office landscaping, but also in general terms of worker satisfaction everywhere.

His very effective study and its implementation are based on the theories and investigations of Edward T. Hall and of Robert Sommer. In 1963, Hall devised a "system for notation of proxemic behavior." Proxemics as defined by Hall "consists of the interrelated observations and theories of man's use of space as a specialized elaboration of culture." Sloan used this notation system to study the proxemic behavior of the workers in the insurance offices. He also used a test which Sommer had devised to rate personal agression requirements and limits of territoriality.

With these tests Sloan was able to rate each employee as to his personal characteristics and his related environmental requirements. The resulting scale looks like this; (A stands for administrator, C stands for clerk):

Personal Characteristics	Environmental Requirements
A1—unsociable, territorial	passive desk, secluded entry, defined limits
A2—sociable, territorial	active desk, controlled entry, defined limits
C1—sociable, agressive, territorial	active desk, controlled entry, defined limits
C3—sociable, unagressive, non-territorial	active desk, secluded entry, undefined limits
C4—sociable, agressive, non-territorial	active desk, open entry, undefined limits
C5—unsociable, agressive, territorial	passive desk, controlled entry, defined limits
C6—unsociable, unagressive, territorial	passive desk, secluded entry, defined limits
C7—unsociable, unagressive, non-territorial	passive desk, secluded entry, undefined limits
C8—unsociable, aggressive, non-territorial	passive desk, controlled entry, undefined limits

While all these requirements cannot be satisfied in every landscape, still Sloan did "develop a categorization system based upon the entire range of personal characteristics." Reflecting the representation of each category, he designed "an office environment offering the flexibility necessary to repeatedly satisfy varying types of people; each requiring individually designed environmental conditions."

In accomplishing this, Sloan used a device for visual and acoustic separation somewhat different from the typical office landscape. He used hanging cloth panels instead of the acoustic screens usually employed for this purpose. Since these are much less expensive than the screens it would be interesting to test them for their comparative effect on the acoustics of the office landscape.

Sloan did make important tests of his work, however. In his first interviews of the office workers, he found that 61 percent of them wanted a change in their office environment. After Sloan had made his observations and after the insurance society had remodeled the space of the basis of his findings, only 24 percent wanted to change desks. After a year in the remodeled space, dissatisfaction was still down to slightly over half its first incidence, 31 percent. But, a year and a half later, when the company returned the layout to its configuration it had had when Sloan's studies started, the dissatisfaction level rose to 50 percent. Therefore, it is clear that no "Hawthorne Effect" was operating in this situation.

Sloan's study, when added to the communications and equipment surveys described above, was quite productive in terms of employee satisfaction, and might be considered as an additional requirement.

The Future of the Office

We have skittishly skirted the issue of whether or not good office design promotes more productivity; in fact, at this point nobody knows for sure. There is much, largely anecdotal, evidence that it does, but it will take massive and carefully designed studies to pin down the facts. Several studies are underway and it is hoped that the answers will come in a form that designers can use.

Meanwhile, I must ask: "Is the office as we know it obsolete?" The chances are that it is. Why? One reason concerns technical change. Consider the computer. It demands a special interior design climate, literally and figuratively. To house a computer, you need special ventilation and temperature controls, lots of wires and cables with a raised floor to house them, nonconductive flooring, fire prevention and control, and lots of security. You also need a special way of lighting areas containing computers. The CRT (cathode ray tube) terminals cannot be seen properly unless they are free from glare (veiling reflectances). So you have to be very careful how you light any space that has terminals in it. Even the distance from the terminal to the eye must be correct so that people can read what is on the tube. But that is not all.

A presentation at a NATO Symposium on Anthropometrics and Bio-mechanics by Etienne Grandjean, M.D., concentrated on the problems now being encountered with the increasing use of CRTs (cathode ray terminals). Grandjean's study delineates several problems involving operator discomfort while using these increasingly pervasive devices. Because similar devices not using the familiar TV-type tubes are being experimented with extensively, Europeans are increasingly calling them VDTs (visual display terminals) or VDUs (visual display units).

His findings indicate that several adjustments must be available so that the VDT workplace does not cause pain and discomfort for the seated operator. The keyboard surface must be adjustable in height and the keyboard should be independently moveable from the VDT itself; most American VDTs include a permanently attached keyboard that is not moveable unless the whole unit is moved. This moveable keyboard as well as the VDT itself should be on a surface that is not only adjustable in height, but also adjustable in terms of its distance from the operator. This is necessary so that the viewing angle and distance can be changed. It must also swivel so that two can use it, and tilt so that the vertical angle can be adjusted.

Dr. Grandjean also recommends the use of forearm rests for keyboard users and high backrests on chairs, as well as a very flexible, moveable document-viewing platform. It goes without saying that the chair used for this purpose must be fully adjustable.

Dr. Grandjean's recommendations are amplified in a book just published in England, *The VDT Manual.* (See references under A. Cakir, et al.) The business of interior design for the use of VDTs requires great care on the part of the designer.

Computers are getting smaller as the miracles of the semiconductor microchip put more functions in a space about one-third the size of your thumbnail. Add the microprocessor and you get a computer that is housed inside what looks like a very well-designed single pedestal desk of quite normal size. This is available right now.

So, now that it has been miniaturized, the computer can be anywhere because one computer can talk to another. I recently saw a small (less than $1,000) computer in a friend's home that can talk to almost any other computer; all it takes is to dial a regular telephone number. More than forty of this particular model have been sold (mostly for home use) in this town of 37,000 people. Twenty years ago, just one of these desktop computers would have filled a typical bedroom with its tubes, which were superseded by transistors, which were superseded by chips and microprocessors.

The real significance of computers, chips, and microprocessors comes from the fact that "what once were separate devices . . . typewriter, telephone, filing, copier and computer . . . have now become linked . . . not only linked but completely inseparable," as Duffy and Pye have put it. A computer keyboard can connect you to the world. You can be anywhere and do your job. You do not have to be in an office with other people, and the need for having large offices is lessening as communication devices constantly improve. So, the research department no longer needs to be located next to the advertising department—it can be hundreds or even thousands of miles away. Marketing department next to the production control department? Not necessarily. Not now. Why bother with the traditional office building in the future, then?

One central fact is that the increasing concentration of offices in buildings and office buildings in cities is increasing the inconvenience of getting to and from the office, as well as increasing the difficulty of living near the office. These problems do not make the lives of those who work in offices happy ones, and they make the problems of recruiting people for office jobs quite difficult.

To attract workers, offices may have to get out of the crowded, unattractive cities. That is the first step. The next step could be home and office combinations for many jobs for which the requisite communications equipment is available now. Think of some of the activities that are now carried on in homes (even though most homes are not equipped to handle them): filling out of various tax forms, preparing family budgets—these two are at least a bit more complicated than some of the tasks that are performed in offices. Consequently, offices may soon be in or close to the home.

Offices may be in some other places, too. There are other factors in operation in addition to the communications revolution. Further on, you will read about the design of new offices for the Federal Aviation Administration in Seattle, Washington, an example of industrial democracy, where the office workers had options and choices in selecting their furniture. This is far from a trend at the moment, but Duffy and Pye see it as the wave of the future, calling Centraal Beheer the turning point in Europe. They see it as a change in "social management style," with the forces of the open plan being "overtaken by industrial democracy."

They also suggest that we "may be moving from an *employment* economy, in which most of us sell our time in blocks of eight hours, five days a week, to a *contractual* economy in which services rather than hours are sold." They point to the increasing specialization of skills in our increasingly specialized world; many of us may become consultants, form our own organizations, take control of our own lives, and escape the regimentation of working as cogs in large organizations. We may have offices in homes, but we may also use all kinds of existing small buildings. Now we can be anywhere.

Design
Checkpoints

1. Review checkpoints for chairs and desks as well as communication distance. Check the chapters on the handicapped and nonverbal communication.

2. Before laying out an office, carefully check communications patterns.

3. Also check equipment and space needed for it for each work station.

4. Plan for evaluation of both corporate and user satisfaction after the office is put into operation.

5. Relate the office you plan to management philosophy; make sure you fit the environment to its needs.

6. The shape and size of the floor space available for an office may determine how the office can be designed.

7. Plan for meeting the social needs of the users.

8. Treat the design of the acoustic environment as an interrelationship of many components of office design.

9. Make sure power and communication sources are flexible and moveable.

References

The Architects' Journal 7 (April 1976), pp. 677–678.

A. Cakir, D.J. Hart, and T.F.M. Stewart, *Visual Display Terminals—A Manual Covering Ergonomics, Workplace Design, Task Organization, Health, and Safety,* Chicester and New York: John Wiley & Sons, 1980.

Len Corlin and Anne Falluchi, "The Open Plan—Love It Or Adjust!—Users Evaluate Their Experiences," *Contract* 18, no. 7, (July 1976), pp. 51–53.

Herbert W. Dean, "Open Space Planning," Chapter 2 in "Handbook of Modern Office Management & Administrative Services," ed. Carl Heyal, New York: McGraw-Hill, 1972.

Francis Duffy, "AJ Handbook Technical Study Interior 1 Scenery and Change, Office Building," *The Architects' Journal* 26 (September 1973), p. 757.

Francis Duffy, "AJ Handbook, Technical Study, Office Buildings, Conclusions, Section 11," *The Architects' Journal* 30 (April 1975), p. 939.

Francis Duffy, "Building Illustrated, Centraal Beheer offices, Apeldoorn, Holland, Appraisal," *The Architects' Journal* 29 (October 1975), p. 903.

Francis Duffy, Colin Cave, and John Worthington, eds., "Planning Office Space," New York: Nichols Publishing, 1976. (First published in book form in Great Britain. London: The Architectural Press, Ltd., 1976.)

Frank Duffy and Roger Pye, "Offices, the Future Landscape: Paper Factory or Room With a View," *The Architects' Journal* 170, no. 39 (Sept. 26, 1979), pp. 669–675.

Federal Design Matters, Issue no. 5, October 1975. Washington, D.C.: National Endowment for the Arts.

Federal Design Matters, Issue no. 9, February 1977 reported that "acoustical drapery for $1.36 per square foot . . . compared to $2.09 per square foot for (wall) tile provided three times the noise attenuation."

Gordon Forrest, "The Office—Environmental Planning," Ottawa: Office of Design, Department of Trade, Industry and Commerce, Report for the National Design Council, December 1970.

General Services Administration, Public Buildings Service Guide Specification PBS T-4 13500 for an Integrated Ceiling and Background System. (ICB) Washington, D.C.: GSA, 1973.

General Services Administration, Public Buildings Service, "Designing an Energy-Efficient Building," Washington, D.C.: GSA, 1976. Publication#GSA DC 76-3360.

Jack Gordon, "CN User Report: Landscape Office," *Canadian Interiors* 9, no. 3 (March 1972), pp. 24–30.

Dennis E. Green, Unpublished manuscript, 1973.

Roger J. Guilfoyle, "The Chip Invades the Home," *Industrial Design Magazine* 27, no. 1 (January/February 1980), pp. 21–25.

Habitability Data Handbook, Vol. 2, Architecture and Environment, Houston: Habitability Technology Section, Spacecraft Design Division, Manned Spacecraft Center, National Aeronautics and Space Administration, 1971, MSC-03909.

Edward T. Hall, "A System for the Notation of Proxemic Behavior," *American Anthropologist* 65 (1963), pp. 1003–1026.

Michael J. Kodaras, "Laboratory Test and Calculation Procedure for InterRoyal Integrated Office System," New York: InterRoyal Corp., 1972.

Henry Lefer, "The overhead that works for you," *Progressive Architecture*, March 1977, pp. 76–83. An excellent review of ceiling systems and the implications of combining heating, air conditioning, power, and telephone sources plus acoustic modifications in them.

Elton Mayo, "The Human Problems of an Industrial Civilization," New York: Viking Press, 1966.

David Morton, "Anti-gravitational Mass," *Progressive Architecture*, July 1976, pp. 66–69. A description of the building that houses the Los Angeles Southwest Regional Offices of the Federal Aviation Administration.

John Pile, "The open office: does it work?" *Progressive Architecture*, June 1977, pp. 68–81.

Olov Ostberg, "Visual Displays in the Office," *Environmental Design* (Human Factors Society) 10, no. 1 (March 1979), pp. 1–2.

Robert L. Propst, "The Office—A Facility Based on Change," Elmhurst: The Business Press, 1968.

Carl Ruff, "Productivity & the Total Office Environment," *Fortune*, May 21, 1979, p. 21 ff. (advertising supplement paid for by the Business and Institutional Furniture Manufacturer's Association).

Sam A. Sloan, "Translating Psycho-Social Criteria Into Design Determinants," in Proceedings of the Environmental Design Research Association, ed. William J. Mitchell, EDRA 3/AR 8, 14.5. Los Angeles: School of Architecture and Urban Planning, University of California, 1972.

"The Steelcase National Study of Office Environments: Do They Work?" conducted by Louis Harris & Associates, Inc. Grand Rapids: Steelcase, Inc., 1978.

Timothy H. Walker, "From Carpets and Colors to Computers and CRT's," *The Designer* 21, no. 256 (May 1978), p. 24.

Bernard Weissbourd, "Satellite Communities—Proposal for a New Housing Program," Santa Barbara: Center for the Study of Democratic Institutions, booklet reprinted from the Center Magazine, 1972.

13 *University Living and Learning Spaces*

The revolution in communications has made the world a global village—never before has it been possible for so many people to know what's going on halfway around the world in seconds; never before has the world had the means of communicating completely. The most aware part of our global population—the under-21 students—is the group most sensitive to the increased amount and to the improving quality of communication. What has this to do with interior design? Plenty, especially if we take a look at the causes of student unrest and riots in the sixties.

Interior Design as a Force for Unrest

The Cox Commission on the Crisis at Columbia singled out interior design (or the lack of it) as first on their list of forces of unrest and as a negative factor in the quality of student life. The report specifically mentioned the extreme smallness of the double rooms, worn out, nondescript furniture, bad corridor lighting, the lack of any social facilities on the bedroom floors, and the lack of planning for student interaction in the dormitories in general; these negative factors were pointed out as increasing loneliness, isolation, and social awkwardness among the students at Columbia.

There, as at many other colleges and universities, students inhabited interiors that, with almost no exception, were designed for the young population that existed before the start of this century. These interiors were not designed for the knowledgeable, aware students of today.

Nowhere was this more apparent than in the colleges and universities. It was here that the bulk of the unrest surfaced, because this is where the largest concentrations of under-21 youths are. The interiors did not meet their human needs and the students knew it. A lot of this happened because we did not realize the difference between the historical concept of the teenager and the actuality of the teenager who exists today.

Puberty Comes Earlier Now

For one thing, the age of puberty happens earlier—some scientists estimate that puberty comes three years earlier than it did a century and a half ago—and many of our laws are based on age-connected privileges and responsibilities, that is, the ages of puberty 150 years ago.

A world-renowned research psychiatrist, Humphry Osmond, feels that the "psycho-bio-social" needs of young males, particularly, are poorly served by many of today's environments: He feels that young males are interested in and have stronger drives toward the acquisition of territory and status than even toward sex and food. This is heightened because puberty happens earlier. He goes so far as to suggest that unless we better allow for this drive in our architecture, interior design, and city planning, we can expect to continue to experience discontent, disorientation, disturbance, and revolt among the young males in our society.

Automobile as Model

The young male is thus frustrated by the built environment of today. So, what is the easiest way for him to quickly acquire territory, status, independence, and a sense of importance? The answer is, of course, get control of an automobile. Teenage preoccupation with automobiles is now so well known that behavioral scientists are beginning to wonder why and to try to find out.

In some ways at least, the automobile is the prototype of the interior environment that the adolescent wants: the driver can control certain features of the environment, such as who or how many are in the car; the heat and to a certain extent, the lighting; and the ventilation. But perhaps most important, the driver can control the "where"—the car will go most places anyone wants it to. By controlling where the car is and who is in it, the teenager can satisfy one of the most important drives of that age group, the need for privacy.

Importance of the Telephone

This need for privacy is expressed in another obvious way by use of the telephone. By calling one or more of his peers, the adolescent can have instant privacy of social contact and conversation without leaving home or wherever else he may be. Through heavy use of the telephone, the adolescent expresses the need for privacy of contact and conversation certainly, but also sometimes expresses a dissatisfaction with his present environment. The telephone can be an instant method of getting away.

I remember having the only private phone in a dormitory room on the University of North Carolina campus. It was merely an extension of the only pay-phone in the three-dorm group I lived in, but I had sold the administration on the idea of my having a phone because of a campus post I held that year. They felt then that one phone line for 150 students was enough. Today the situation is much changed for the better, but adequate telephone service for student needs should remain on the checklist of the interior designer.

Of course the use of the telephone is not the real problem; it is just a symptom. The real problem and the real obstacle to the acquisition of independence has been legal. Under-21 youths in some states cannot own property, and they cannot buy alcohol, although this situation is changing swiftly. When you think of this mix in the light of earlier puberty, the situation has been explosive, especially where the best-informed youngsters congregate in the universities, colleges, and high schools. The interior design in these places just did not meet their needs at all.

Privacy and Territorial Control
Their urges for privacy and territorial control have much more behind them than just the desire to be alone with someone of the opposite sex. Sim van der Ryn and Murray Silverstein in their book, *The Dorms at Berkeley* (which by the way is still probably the best study available on student dormitory needs), point out that perhaps as many as 85 percent of college students want to study alone most of the time. In fact, many students cannot concentrate unless they have privacy as well as control of heat, light, and ventilation, just as they have control of them in a car.

They all cannot study in double rooms, either. The literature is full of references to the expressed desire of American college students for rooms of their own, "somewhere I can close the door all the way shut and be alone." This really gets nettling where built-in furniture is fixed, cannot be moved, and students in a double room try to study, even silently, in each other's line of sight.

Even the United States Army has recognized this need for privacy by changing its plans for future barracks; they contain clusters of one-to-three person rooms grouped around small living rooms. The army did this to make military life more attractive as it shifted to an all-volunteer force.

Students Do Not Need "loco parentis"

Another factor in this changing situation has been the attitude of today's more intellectually mature student toward educational institutions. He particularly resents the idea that the college administration should control who is in his room or when, and feels that he is also learned enough to decide what he should drink or smoke. He does not want the dean of students to fill the role of his father or mother.

Sometimes he feels that he knows more than his parents do and sometimes he is right. The almost terrifying speed of change and the almost stupefying pace of technology has created a situation where, as Margaret Mead has pointed out, parents can and must learn from their children. After all, today's students are born into a quite different world from their parents; when their parents were born there was no atom bomb, no television, no satellites, and no space exploration.

Human Scale

Another problem plaguing university facilities has been a fundamentally weak understanding of what an interior designer calls *human scale*. This is the usually neglected part of the design process; the neglect is especially evident in the design of facilities for college students, who are certainly one of the most aware portions of our population and who therefore feel the neglect keenly.

Human scale is a catchall term, but basically it means that the interior spaces as well as the furnishings that go into them must be chosen and sized so that human beings who use the spaces and the furnishings feel that the total design is suited to the use. Sommer, van der Ryn, and others point out that students sometimes choose the older buildings on campus or in the town because basically they feel that the larger rooms, thicker walls, and freedom from college authority are more in tune with their sense of human scale.

Human scale has other meanings in the student world, though. We as interior designers were called late in the game to try to improve a bad situation. A college with a student body composed of almost all former slum dwellers was faced with widespread and deep negative reactions to a new dormitory; among other things the students were threatening to riot. As part of the administration's attempts to quiet the situation they asked us what could be done about complaints about the interior itself.

To begin with, the dormitory and its interior had been designed by a firm of architects in absentia—geographically, aesthetically, and sociologically. Evidently no effort had been made to identify culturally the needs of the students who would occupy it. The outer appearance of the building resembles a fort or a hydroelectric dam to the educated eye—it has essentially a strong, permanent look, with much use of exposed concrete, but the writer is sure that the slum dweller's eye looks on it and hears a silent shout: JAIL.

Inside, the architects used the device of leaving the board marks on the surface of the concrete walls of the stairwells; this is of course textural interest for the educated eye, but it means instant association with damp basements to the former slum inhabitant. The architects' choice of furnishings in this dormitory were slim-lined and simple, cleanly designed architectural modern. Here again the faculty view was that this was aesthetically good; the slum dwellers' view was one of alienation; the interior furnishings were too far from their frame of reference and they felt that the furniture was too "spindly" to last very long.

The grayness of the outside and inside concrete (accentuated by a remote, treeless site), the grey blue of the interior exposed concrete (unpainted) block (basement association here also), the typical dropped segmented white ceiling, and the bareness of the recently cleared site

Figure 13.1. Drab classroom ready for crowding.

were relieved only by a vibrant red carpet that only served to point up the surrounding drabness.

We were able to introduce well-designed but much more massive tables and seating in warm colors and patterns; highly figured and colored draperies plus more suitable carpet were installed. While we do not credit the interior design changes with the total reduction of student unrest at this school, we do know from talks with the students that our work helped, and we feel that humanely oriented interior design is one of the important dimensions of "human scale."

Some Classrooms Are Too Large

Perhaps the whole structure of today's university, from the site plans to the interiors, is not in "human scale" as the students see it. Certainly the interiors of most classrooms leave much to be desired for the learning process. Perhaps the majority of learning spaces are wrong for the task, since most of them are much too large for any real degree of intimacy or involvement in the learning process.

If you talk to teachers at any level, you will hear their constant gripes about the size of their classes, except from those who have the exceptional good fortune to have small seminars. It is ridiculous to think of real classroom involvement in the very large lecture halls that some of our universities feature. Of course, the real reason for the objectionably large size of classes is the shortage of teachers, good ones, that is, and the lack of the will to get the money into our educational systems to train and hire more.

However, there may be some hope. Some educators feel that students can be taught successfully in large numbers using television and other visual techniques, assuming that as part of their education, students additionally get the kind of small group discussion and teaching that they need to keep them really absorbed in a subject. If this method is valid, then the teachers we need may be at hand with a slightly different utilization of them needed; however, interior teaching spaces must be designed to allow for use of such a dual system.

However, if students are taught simply in large classes as they are in some institutions, without smaller discussion and seminar groups, this is the faceless kind of education in which neither the student nor the teacher gets really involved, and neither understands the other.

There is evidence that universities and colleges are beginning to listen to student feedback and to plan living spaces for students according to their actual needs. Some of them have too many empty dormitories not to listen.

Ewing H. Miller   In 1967, Ewing H. Miller, an architect who retains a behavioral consultant on his staff to get feedback from students, "found that the lounge in the first of two dormitories he designed resulted in conflict between students who study and students who entertain friends." Instead of the one huge lounge on the main floor he substituted two smaller lounges on different floors in the second dormitory.

He has also designed a series of student residences for Indiana State University that allow for varying student needs and maturing student lifestyles. These are three- and four-story walk-up buildings (a far cry from the high-rise monoliths that put students in filing cabinets and become monuments that the trustees can point to) with three single rooms and one double room arranged around a lounge to form apartments. The rooms contain no built-in furniture except the closet, thus allowing the students freedom of furniture arrangement. Preiser's findings at Virginia Polytechnic Institute (VPI) point to this type of design, also.

What Miller did not say, presumably because the *AIA Journal* probably considers itself a family-type publication, is that his design also provides students with facilities where they can live with whom they please. Another factor in the previously mentioned preference of students for rooms and apartments in older buildings off campus is the plain fact that today's students do not feel that their sexual and cohabiting activities should be supervised by the college or university that they attend. Miller's design recognizes a fact of student life today and offers them a choice that is not available in some schools, though many schools do approach the problem with coed dorms, now widespread.

What Do Students Want?   Educational Facilities Laboratories asked the question: What do students want? Among the answers: "The chance to choose from a variety of living options: coeducational dorms, apartments, suites, special interest dorms, dorms with snack bars instead of dining rooms . . . private telephones, kitchenettes . . . the right to paint rooms and hallways." Many students also want single rooms; Morton described a dormitory at Harvard that continues that university's long-standing policy of single rooms with no more than four students sharing a living room. However, this dormitory, Canaday Hall, is coeducational with men and women on alternate floors. Other universities have responded to student needs in various ways.

Worcester State College in Massachusetts has built Chandler Village that consists of 26 separate low-rise houses. A wide variety of accommodations is provided within these houses: 50 private rooms with shared baths, 25 four-person units with one double and two single bedrooms, 25 eight-person apartments with single, double, and four-person bedrooms, 8 eleven- and fourteen-person communal collectives, four apartments shared by eight students and one faculty member who has a separate, private room, and 24 two-person apartments for married couples or two students. Incidentally, there are six building types in Chandler Village and living rooms, kitchens, and dining areas are provided with all apartments except the private rooms. The only unsuccessful units have been the collectives.

Rochdale Village at the University of California, Berkeley, consists of single bedrooms, 264 of them, plus 97 one-, two-, three-, and four-bedroom apartments; the project has been very successful with a waiting list during the academic year and 80 percent occupancy in the summer.

In one of the few student housing projects built from an industrialized system, Brockport campus, State University of New York, has built 250 low-rise one-, two-, and three-bedroom apartments for students in 27 buildings.

Sonoma State College, Bowie (Maryland) State College, the University of California at Santa Cruz, Stanford University, the University of Illinois at Carbondale, and Southwest Minnesota State College in Marshall have set up temporary or permanent student housing in mobile homes.

More Flexibility

The key word here is more flexibility. The typical involved student is growing and changing and does not wish to be held down by a limited choice of living accommodations. The concept of double rooms is probably wrong for many students, both for the reasons given and for at least one other: the differing lifestyles and increasing desire for individual pursuits among students make a good case for single dormitory rooms. Some dormitories are being built this way, but the most important thing is to give the student a choice of several different kinds of housing.

Some of the universities that have built successful student housing, notably Harvard with Canaday Hall, the Brockport campus of SUNY apartments and SUNY's College at Plattsburgh in a student union building, have built in further flexibility in their structures—demountable partitions—so that as needs continue to change, the structures will be able to change, too. Romaldo Gourgiola said concerning his firm's SUNY—Plattsburgh student union building, "We no longer have definable programs where you do one thing; buildings must be capable of many possibilities; an architect shouldn't freeze the functions."

Vodges in a comparison between two dormitories, one at Harvard and one at Radcliffe, emphasized the importance of room flexibility in the success of one over the other, an important factor being that it was much easier to rearrange furniture in the irregularly shaped rooms of Currier dormitory at Radcliffe than it was in the rectangular rooms of Mather at Harvard. She said, "Flexibility is . . . particularly important . . . to allow for today's rapid social changes. The building should be able to adapt to these changing trends."

Vodges also pointed up the importance of good sound insulation in providing flexibility of space use: "Because many of the common spaces open onto one another, activity in one space often precludes activity in another." Noisy pinball machines in the grill bothered people at concerts and movies in the dining hall and also people looking at television in the living room; therefore, they had to be taken out.

Flexible Interior Arrangements

Students, like other people, want to control the arrangement of their interior furnishings and frequently there is much method in their wishing to do so. Some institutions prohibit the hanging of prints, pictures, rugs, or whatever on the grounds that the walls will be damaged. Good interior design would provide tack boards and picture moldings, as well as interior finishes that are hard to damage and are repaintable.

A possible connection between students' freedom to decorate their dormitory rooms and college dropout rates is conceivable from Hansen and Altman's finding that "those who eventually dropped out of school—two quarters after the last observations were made—reliably decorated *less* than those who stayed in school. . . . Thus decorating may be a long term predictor of dropout rates." They also have the opinion that "territorial behavior and . . . marking and personalizing, may well contribute to viable group functioning."

Anything that prevents students from expressing themselves in a legitimate way is, of course, a bar to their control of territory and their acquisition of status, and essentially this is the frustration they feel when furniture is built-in and they cannot put anything personal on the walls— they feel that the university is confusing a dormitory with a hotel.

The freedom to rearrange the furniture and hang pictures is even more important to women students; in their minds they want to make the appearance of their rooms as individually different as they do their own clothing. This was borne out by High and Sundstrom who reported that "females were more concerned with the arrangement of their settings, and were especially affected by the nonflexible rooms." They also found that high flexibility was related to more frequent room use and "reports of more interpersonal recreation" (as against nonflexible rooms).

High and Sundstrom also point out an economic advantage of high flexibility in student rooms; if the students are limited as to the activities that they can carry on in their rooms, the educational institution may have to provide other spaces for those activities such as take place in "lounges, game rooms, group study rooms, and the like," thus increasing the cost of student housing facilities. For example, built-in furniture, because it is so inflexible, may raise building costs much more than it saves over movable furniture, because additional spaces may have to be built for activities that cannot be carried on in student rooms made inflexible by built-in furniture.

Desk Design

Let's take a look at a typical student desk. I have the naive idea that a desk should be designed for the specific work to be done at it; this simply is not true in any college I know about. To study and write papers, a college student has to have room to write—with a pen or a typewriter (which most students use)—in addition to the books and other materials he or she uses when writing a paper.

Yet, not so long ago we furnished more than one hundred desks to a college for a new dormitory. The tops were only 40 inches by eighteen inches, and these desks had only one pedestal. They gave the student just fifteen inches of filing space and the other two little drawers were much too small for anything but pencils, pens, and paper. This particular dormitory was designed by one of America's most renowned architects, the college is one of America's most educationally advanced, the dorm was financed by United States government funds, but the rooms were just too darned small for a desk any larger than 40 inches by 18 inches.

Actually college work demands a standard stenographic-sized desk— a 60-inch-by-30-inch main top with a 40-inch-by-18-inch return to hold the typewriter. If a college expects the student to produce work efficiently and comfortably, this is what is necessary. A desk of this sort is also needed with enough pedestals with enough drawers to store writing materials, papers, publications, and other materials that the student must have.

Chair Design

Of course, this brings us to the typical straight-backed chair that is very uncomfortably provided to go with the typical undersized desk. This seems to be some sort of torture mechanism left over from America's Puritan heritage. Though the straight chair is much cheaper than a typical office or secretarial adjustable swivel chair, the difference in price is not worth the punishment the student takes.

Actually, the office type of chair is the best solution now readily and relatively inexpensively available, though I do not know of a single institution of higher learning that has been willing to pay the difference to use them in student living quarters. Incidentally, these chairs have adjustable, movable backs for necessary position changes to prevent fatigue and they have rollers so that the student could move from main desk top to typewriter top and back again, if a main top as well as a typewriter top were provided.

However, students do not always study at their desks. Sommer and Gifford found that about half the students they and their associates surveyed (hundreds in several dormitories on eight campuses) study on their beds rather than elsewhere, and the desk shared honors with easy chairs (where they are provided) and the floor in accounting for the other places where students study in their rooms. Incidentally, there was no correlation between grades and where students study, in spite of repeated assertions by college administrators (and regulations in some schools) that students study at their desks and nowhere else.

Redesign the Bed

This points to another necessity suggested by van der Ryn and Silverstein: redesign the bed so that it can be used for studying as students obviously want to use it. An adjustable headrest, lighting attached to the bed, and perhaps even a movable writing surface could be added to the student bed without much additional cost.

Bard College and the University of Massachusetts at Amherst have experimented with "kits" of furniture that can be varied to meet individual student needs. As a part of the same program, the University of Massachusetts has also tried easily movable sound-absorbent screens instead of demountable partitions as a device to increase the flexibility of interior dormitory semipublic spaces.

Acoustic Privacy

This brings us to a major student objection to the living quality of a typical dormitory room—the noise level. Many factors are involved in determining the noise level in an interior. Probably the chief factor in acoustic privacy for the student is the way walls and floors are constructed, although details such as the way windows and doors close are very important. Carpet can reduce the noise level as much as 70 percent and although many dormitory rooms are now carpeted, close attention is not always paid to the noise reduction factor in choosing it. Drapes and wall coverings carefully chosen and installed can in themselves reduce the noise level as much as 55 percent; this factor is often ignored in dormitory planning (see the discussion of bedrooms in the chapter on residences).

The "Showroom" Lounge

If the noise level is too high for studying or the student gets tired of looking at his roommate, the student may decide to try to study in the dormitory lounge (which is usually planned not for student wants and needs, but to impress visiting parents). Here he finds what some students call the "furniture showroom" look or the "hospital waiting room look," which does not go well with the typical size of the student group that wants to use the lounge. This typical size is one student or two students—very rarely more than that. The spaces in the lounges just are not planned for this and the furniture is usually arranged in geometric patterns for mythical student groups of many more than one or two. Or, it is arranged so that it is easy for maintenance people to clean around it; it

13.2

Figure 13.2. Modern, drab, and bleak.
Figure 13.3. The hospital waiting room look.

13.3

is not arranged for a student who wants to study or have a date there. Many of these are still big barren rooms not scaled for intimacy or for the privacy necessary for studying.

He might try to study in the cafeteria but the chances are that it will not be much better. Student eating spaces are usually badly lit for study, more barren than the lounges, and the noise level is much too high. Even the student who goes to the library may not find the desired type of study space. It depends on what type of atmosphere he is looking for.

Libraries

If the student is looking for a place to study where he can eat or smoke, he probably will not find it in most libraries, though actually there is no valid reason why such space could not be made available in most college libraries.

Surveys of college students who go to the library to study show that some of them prefer the carrels, isolated and quiet, while others must have the stimulation of the presence of other people in a quiet atmosphere or even with a definite noise level as a background for studying. Students have different wants and needs, but obviously library planning in colleges seldom allows for the variety of spaces needed.

Make no mistake about it, college libraries *are* used primarily as study halls. Surveys at the University of Michigan and elsewhere indicate that more than 90 percent of the students who use college libraries do not use library materials for study; they use materials they bring with them into the library.

Another study space is the classroom when classes are not in session; however, the space utilization here is low, since no more than about 5 percent of the number of students who could come to classes in session will use an otherwise empty classroom; it is usually one or two or a very small group.

Almost all investigators of the college scene point out the increasing amount of group study and discussion among students, but almost no college consciously plans interior spaces for it.

Despite these other spaces where studying takes place, students actually study more in their rooms than anywhere else, and there is one more aspect of the room itself that contributes to the atmosphere for studying. There must be adequate storage space and it must be organized properly.

Storage Space

The University Residential Building System, a total system of building and furnishing developed by the University of California and Educational Facilities Laboratories, Inc. (of the Ford Foundation), contains within it the most thoroughly researched standards for storage space currently available.

In addition to developing modular shelves and cabinets which can be wall-hung or free-standing, they produced a space-saving way of organizing them. They have also come to the realization that male students require about half as much storage space as female students do. Their typical plans allow about 120 cubic feet of shelves and closed space for women, and about 60 feet for men; this is in addition to desk space, of course. Their prescience was reinforced by a finding that "male and female residents may have different space requirements" from a study of "Room Flexibility and Space Use in a Dormitory" by High and Sundstrom. Parenthetically, the wall-hung desk they use seems much too small, but it is adjustable in height where it is hung, and they do suggest an adjustable-height, swiveling, tilting desk chair.

In fact, the URBS system as planned takes a great step forward in trying to make it possible for the student to have some choice of interior arrangement, since all the furniture is planned to be demountable, free-standing, or wall-hung. They have even planned a bed with a level surface for sleeping that can be sloped for sitting. Unfortunately, URBS has not received widespread use.

Student Participation in Design

What all this indicates is probably much more fundamental than just the specific design of specific interiors for specific purposes. As Robert Sommer has pointed out, more studies have probably been made concerning the residential preferences of college students than on any similar subject, but until the past few years, not many colleges read them or acted on their findings. Now the situation has changed, for many institutions and students are participating in the design of the buildings they use on campuses.

URBS was an early example of the kind of specifications which can be developed by student participation in the design of their living, learning, and social spaces. Among the projects mentioned earlier, student participation in the design process was important in Chandler Village at Worcester (Mass.) State College, Rochdale Village at the University of

California–Berkeley, the apartments on the Brockport campus of SUNY, and Currier House at Radcliffe. Suzanne Stephens asserts that "with regard to new construction, universities and college administrators have begun enlisting students' participation in the programming and planning of their housing. One compelling reason that this is happening is economic, of course. Empty halls meant empty coffers—at least so far as the long-term self-liquidating loans for new construction were concerned."

Another facet of this economic reason is the attitude of the U.S. Department of Housing and Urban Development; a circular sent to all regional offices in 1971 said, "HUD will not approve straight dormitory-style projects unless the long-term prospects for student occupancy are good. . . . Many students, especially upper division and graduate students, no longer want to live in the traditional dormitories. Apartment and suite-style projects, both on and off campus are becoming more and more popular. Apartment-style projects offer better security to lenders because of better student acceptance and the flexibility for assignment as either student housing or family housing."

A Final Straw in the Wind

Less important, but still a straw in the wind, is the changing attitude of a church supported and sponsored college toward furniture for students' use. They came to us to help furnish ten lounges in their women's dormitories. These lounges are for the use of women only—since this college has not yet set up co-ed dormitories.

The order was formally placed through the usual purchasing agent but it did not come about as the result of the usual purchasing process. Before we received the order, we were visited by a committee of students and student advisors who very carefully went through our entire acre of display, and then made their decisions. The decisions were made basically by the students themselves who will be using the lounges; the faculty-student advisors seemed to be just along for the ride.

What did they choose? Just two basic items: tables and pillows. The pillows are two feet square and seven inches thick, covered in a random selection of upholstery roll ends to keep the cost down and provide visual variety. The tables are plastic, molded in one piece, strong enough for a 200-pounder to stand on; the students selected them in four strong clear colors: yellow, bitter green, black, and white.

The students picked this combination so that they can lie on the pillows, prop themselves up to read, and use the tables for reading stands. They must like what they picked out because that was one year, and the next year we furnished eight more lounges with the same pillows and tables, with the added attraction of a few bean bag chairs covered in a heavy duty fabric backed vinyl in similar strong colors. It was a far cry from the "furniture showroom" lounge.

Design Checkpoints

1. Consider various methods of giving students control over their immediate environment: especially movable furniture, tackboards, picture moldings, repaintable surfaces.

2. Check to see that telephone service is adequate, both in quantity and in placement.

3. Consider including single rooms in the basic design.

4. Check to see that desks are adequate in size for typical student use.

5. Think about specifying typical stenographer chairs, one per student.

6. Consider redesigning beds for multiple uses.

Figure 13.4. The furniture showroom look.

7. Check all specifications in terms of acoustic privacy: carpet, draperies, window closures, door closures, wall insulation.

8. See that furniture for lounge areas meets student needs.

9. Provide a variety of spaces in libraries to meet student needs.

10. See that storage needs are met.

11. Consider movable, comfortable seating and desks for classroom spaces.

12. Consult students and former students about all aspects of the design.

References

Associated Press, story in the Springfield, Ohio *Sun*, June 8, 1972, p. 26.

Andrew Baum and Stuart Valins, "Architecture and Social Behavior: Psychological Studies of Social Density," Hillsdale, N.J.: Lawrence Erlbaum Associates, 1977. Also bears the imprint of the Halsted Press Division, John Wiley & Sons, New York.

"Crisis at Columbia—The Cox Commission Report," New York: Vintage Books, Random House, 1968.

Educational Facilities Laboratories, Inc., *Student Housing*, New York, 1972.

Theodore Goldberg, "The Automobile: A Social Institution for Adolescents," *Environment and Behavior* 1, no. 2 (December 1969) pp. 157–185.

William B. Hansen, and Irwin Altman, "Decorating Personal Places—A Descriptive Analysis," *Environment and Behavior* 8, no. 4 (December 1976), pp. 491–504.

Thomas High and Eric Sundstrom, "Room Flexibility and Space Use in a Dormitory," *Environment and Behavior* 9, no. 1 (March 1977), pp. 81–90.

Marshall McLuhan and Quentin Fiore, *War and Peace in the Global Village*, New York: Bantam Books, 1968.

Margaret Mead, "Youth Revolt: Future Is Now," *Saturday Review* 113, (January 10, 1970), pp. 23–25.

Ewing H. Miller, "The Student Quarters That Teamwork Created," *American Institute of Architects Journal* 57, no. 2 (February 1972), pp. 25–26.

David Morton, "Student's Village," *Progressive Architecture* 56, no. 8, (August 1975), pp. 37–41.

Humphry Osmond, "Man's Environmental Needs," *Building Research* 2, no. 4 (July-August 1965), pp. 6–8.

Wolfgang F. E. Preiser, "Behavioral Design Criteria in Student Housing at VPI," Blacksburg: Virginia Polytechnic Institute and State University, 1969. (mimeo)

Sharon Lee Ryder, "Pieceable Kingdom," *Progressive Architecture* 56, no. 8 (August 1975), pp. 56–59.

Robert Sommer, "The Ecology of Privacy," *Library Quarterly* 36 (1966) pp. 234–238.

Robert Sommer, "Personal Space—The Behavioral Basis of Design," Englewood Cliffs, N.J.: Prentice-Hall, 1969.

Robert Sommer, and Robert Gifford, "The Desk or the Bed," *Personnel and Guidance Journal,* 1968, pp. 876–878.

Suzanne Stephens, "Beds of Academe," *Progressive Architecture* 56, no. 8, August, 1975, pp. 35–36.

Suzanne Stephens, "Rust City," *Progressive Architecture* 56, no. 8 (August, 1975), pp. 42–47.

Walter Sullivan, "Boys and Girls Are Now Maturing Earlier," *New York Times*, January 24, 1971, pp. 1, 36.

"University Residential Building System—Phase II Report," Berkeley: Office of the President, University of California, September 1968.

Sim van der Ryn, and Murray Silverstein, "The Dorms at Berkeley," Berkeley: Center for Planning and Development Research, 1968 and New York: Educational Facilities Laboratories, Inc., 1968.

Elizabeth M. Vodges, "A Social/Physical Comparison of Two Dormitory Complexes at Harvard/Radcliffe: Mather and Currier Houses," in "Environment and Behavior, Proceedings Northeastern Undergraduate Conference, April 20, 1974," ed. Jay W. Vogt, Amherst: Institute for Man and Environment, 1974.

Lawrence Wheeler, and Ewing H. Miller, "Behavioral Research for Architectural Planning and Design," Terre Haute, Indiana: Archonics Corp., 1967.

Sally Woodbridge, "The Wheels of Sonoma Grove," *Progressive Architecture* 56, no. 8, (August 1975), pp. 28–29.

Sally Woodbridge, "Berkeley Bravado," *Progressive Architecture* 56, no. 8 (August 1975), pp. 48–51.

John Zeisel, *Sociology and Architectural Design*, New York: Russell Sage Foundation, 1975.

III *Case Studies*

Case Study 1 *The Designer Was Fired*

Background

We will call the client the National Association for Social Equilibration (NASE), and all the rest of the names in this case study have been changed also to protect the innocent, the guilty, and the nasty.

My hiring took place over a protracted length of time. My name was first suggested to do the space planning and interior design for NASE by a member who had known me for years and who was quite familiar with my work in user-oriented office design. After a lengthy interview and a period of months of soul searching by the Executive Committee of NASE, I was hired.

NASE was to move into newly built space in Metropolis, a large American city; a firm of architects (who were members of NASE) had already been hired, and the gross amount of the space, as well as its shape and size, had already been determined before my arrival on the scene.

Although information was really hard to come by, it soon became apparent that the architects had unilaterally decided that there was going to be office landscape, and no buts about it. In fact, they had gone so far as to throw a few very sound-absorbent screens into an area inhabited by twelve people. That was their idea of office landscape: you just put screens in instead of partitions and that takes care of that.

Of course, it did not take care of anything, except to ruin (in the acoustic sense) a space that had formerly been quite useful. This particular space was where a dozen people were negotiating social change over their telephones during most of the day, and there were few office machines around. There was some background noise before the installation of the screens, but afterwards, the screens absorbed what little sound there had been. When I got there, it was so quiet that every person in this space could hear everybody else's telephone conversations. This was certainly not good for cajoling, arguing, social-change agents; yet this was the architects' example that was supposed to make NASE receptive to the inevitable coming of office landscape.

The more I talked to people, the more objections I heard about this particular space and the more resistance there was to office landscape or any other kind of open planning, because a good portion of NASE was composed of social-change agents of different kinds who were also negotiating social change over the telephones, in letters, and in interviews and conferences.

It might be important here to tell you that NASE is an organization composed mostly of volunteers, some of whom are paid in varying amounts and some of whom are not paid at all; a few very specially qualified people are hired for particular purposes and are paid the going compensation for their specialties.

Correspondence

With this background information, perhaps the best way to show what happened would be to give you excerpts from letters sent to NASE (no written replies were received).

Letter 1

Dear Mike,

Enclosed are the very tentative group assignments for floors 4 and 5. These are based on the actual use of space as reported to me, plus information gleaned from the other lists I have.

Several comments:

1. Reception/switchboard might be placed on the first floor.

2. The computer department might be placed in the basement, although a possible location for it on the fifth floor has been indicated; walls for it can be easily and inexpensively built for it there; their Flexowriters especially must have walls to separate them from the other departments, and I've had plenty of experience with Flexowriters and their decibels.

3. The arrangements indicated on the enclosed diagrams satisfy the adjacency requirements indicated by the questionnaires; however, I received only 99 questionnaires and, of course, not all of them were completely filled out. Therefore, some of the samples from individual departments were quite small.

4. I'm sure there will be changes and since some of the department

names differ according to which of your lists I consult, there may be mistakes on that score, but at least this gives us a starting point for discussion; we can talk about this on my next visit.

With kindest personal regards,

Sincerely,

Walt Kleeman

Letter 2

Dear Mike,

Attached is a crude tracing of the general outline of the building in blue with the dotted line in red showing a new wall that suddenly appeared on the plan copies that each department head had been given for the meetings I attended this past Wednesday; I noted this on the plan copies for the fourth floor and had not been previously informed about it.

Obviously, I can't produce department placement plan 1 until I know about this new wall, whether or not it's on the fourth floor or fifth, on one or on neither. It would definitely affect my placement of each group. Please let me know about this as soon as you can.

If this new wall is a reality, it doesn't improve the prospects for the success of open planning, since it reduces the flexibility of the spaces, and reduces one dimension below the 65-foot minimum which is thought to be the smallest space dimension you should have for open office planning. It seems to me that 45 feet might work, but with this new development quite a bit more aisle space will be necessary, which will decrease the amount of space available for work stations.

With kindest personal regards,

Sincerely,

Walt Kleeman

Letter 3

Dear Mike,

Attached is my report of the relevant raw material gleaned from the two days of meetings with the various departments. These are not my recommendations, just a report to you of what I heard.

Since it was reported to me that the architects had not discussed the special needs of the printshop with the people there, it might be a good thing to find out whether the special needs of Files and the Computer Department have been discussed with the architects.

I do not have a copy of the specifications used for the bidding of the building; I would very much appreciate getting one, along with an up-to-date set of prints. I can do much better work if I get these.

If fluorescent lighting is being used, I strongly recommend the consideration of lamping with wide-spectrum tubes (brochure attached) for the health of the people who will occupy the building. I will be glad to discuss the reasons for this when I see you.

On balance, I find a considerable amount of resistance to open planning from a highly individualistic, volunteer oriented organization. Much of this resistance is concentrated in the key people in the organization, but some of it also arises from the natural separatism of departments working together very well with each other within the branches. You will find this indicated in the attached report by the reiteration of privacy needs.

Some of the resistance arises from the architects' unsuccessful experiment in one of the office spaces; have any steps been taken to correct this situation, as I suggested earlier? Since I feel that open planning is quite desirable for the continuing flexibility of NASE, a correction of this problem might change the overall sentiment, though the present sentiment seems to run deep.

I'll look forward to hearing from you after you've had a chance to study the enclosed.

With kindest regards,

Sincerely,

Walt Kleeman

Report of the Meetings—NASE

National Affairs

This division feels that it is the most static in NASE, and feels that it is cramped now. Since its field staff come in and out, an extra space is needed for them, expressed as a need for a multi-use room about 8' x 12' where three people can work and eight to twelve people can get together to confer. This could also serve as quiet space for writing. They also feel a more than normal need for storage space for books, periodicals, and correspondence. The suggestion was also made that eating spaces in the complex be divided into smoking and non-smoking areas; elevators should be designated as non-smoking areas.

Treasurer's Office

Private space is needed for one person who now has it; the five people in one room at present say they work well in this common area and that partitions among them would hinder communication; however, they very definitely want their department separated from others by full, ceiling-height partitions. They have one noisy machine, a check endorser, which does not operate all the time.

Computer Department

This division has temperature and humidity control needs which are unlike any other division *except* Duplicating, which perhaps indicates the location of these two divisions together, possibly in the basement. Noisy machines are also a problem; although the automatic typewriters are slated for removal, they will still have a printer or printers, a burster, and they will receive the typers from Finance (the Telex is considered a printer).

They do have security problems, which further argues for separating this department from the others by walls and location. However, it should be remembered that the Computer Department functions may change and expand, especially if NASE purchases its own computer; this again indicates the basement location where unassigned space exists that could be readily converted to the temperature, humidity, and security requirements.

Programming should be done in isolated spaces, which should be provided.

Although the computer terminal can be separated from the printer, the printer should be placed with the burster.

Office of the Executive Vice-President

The preferred location is between Public Relations and the fund raisers (Finance). However, a separate conference area is needed—for fifteen to twenty persons—which could be used by other divisions—if it is scheduled properly. The actual OEVP could be of a size for the seating of four to five persons in addition to the Executive Vice-President, perhaps with an accordion door separating the OEVP itself from the conference area.

It is very important that the secretary to the OEVP be concentrated with the secretary to the Fiscal Director and with other nearby secretaries so that these two phones are always covered.*

Consumer Information

The final layout and space requirements for this group will have to be done subject to information that I do not yet have. At this time it seems certain that they do need a room for press conferences and film and/or slide showings which could be the same room; the use of the planned auditorium on the first floor for this purpose should be considered. Where their exhibits should be placed seems dependent on the purpose of each exhibit, and might not use office space.

The use of the conference/film showing room for the construction of large exhibits does not seem feasible to me; since the Audio/Visual part of Consumer Information is asking for soundproof and otherwise separate space, including quite a bit of workshop space, this is another operation that might be more feasible in the basement. This should be checked.

Certainly the Files portion of Consumer Information, with its need for 2,500 square feet and need for security and humidity control should be in the basement. Tables for cataloging documents and working space for researchers were mentioned as other needs.

After you read this letter, I would like to discuss this further for final layout, since they are requesting more bookshelves, files, tables for collating press releases, and mostly walls to the ceiling.

*Indicates special attention is needed to these items now.

Governmental Services	Typically, they have three people in from the outside, appointees for orientation or debriefing, and sometimes as many as five; therefore they expressed the idea that they might share the same type of space asked for by National Affairs, and that the common space for this purpose be made a little larger.

GS has a high need for aural privacy for several reasons: the number of phone calls, the fact they have to have a noisy Telex (they claim 95 percent of the Telex use in this division, and that at least 60 percent of NASE telegrams come from GS), and the necessity for privacy in debriefing.

Their present storage facilities are inadequate; they asked for windows that open, space for maps and pin-ups, common bookshelves, smoking privacy, and individual HVAC controls. They also raised the question of whether the planned bathrooms are adequate or not. The A group has a meeting several times per day and needs a bit more space, which might be taken care of by enlarging one office area.

Accounting Department	This department and the treasurer want floor-to-ceiling partitions and hallways separating the department from other divisions, though they like the open communication among themselves in their present quarters. They need more room, and stressed the need for good lighting and a good acoustical environment.

Program	This department needs an office to comfortably seat 4 visitors, needs to be reasonably accessible to OEVP, and needs use of perhaps the same 15 to 20 person meeting room needed by OEVP.

Personnel Department	Although they do not need access to Central Files, they do have 2500 personnel files that should be locked; since these are now in shelf files, they asked for a room around them that can be locked.

They want a discreet entrance, one that people would not have to walk through other office areas to get to them. Then they need their own reception area with space for four people to sit and containing a literature display; an extra work station for short term staff to type at; their own duplicating equipment; more supply space; more bookshelves, perhaps a small library; a place for coats, boots, umbrellas that would not be in a public area; a multi-drawered cabinet for forms; lockers; two private interview areas; a refrigerator; a cabinet for medicines (both to be secure).

They suggest that the Infirmary Area for rest and dressing be located on the first floor, but that there be First Aid stations on each floor; the state and federal laws on this and what must be in the Lounges should be checked.*

Finance

The need for absolute audio/visual privacy for confidential talks, especially those involving deferred giving, was stressed; a room for two would be sufficient for this particular purpose. However, they also want a kitchenette and dining room. They want partitions, perhaps sliding ones. They are willing to house their automatic typewriters with the Computer Department which will alleviate their noise problem.

Files

Again, some sort of a room was asked for, for security; and they asked for a central location.

Tables are needed in two areas to work on; storage space for deactivated files is also needed (the basement again?), as are a window and a sorting counter work station.

Although Mary Jones completed a questionnaire (she showed me a Xeroxed copy briefly), it was not among the ones I have received. Are there a batch of questionnaires somewhere that I do not have?*

Consumer Education

This department needs to be near the Audio/Visual part of Public Relations and they need to be near the printshop. When I told them that it was slated for the basement, they asked to be near a stairway and also suggested that a pneumatic tube might be desirable between them and the printshop.

Because of the odd times that they are accustomed to working—they want their own literature storage and mailing room—they want to control the entire process and want to keep both separate for them.

They want kitchen facilities and want to be separated from others by a wall.

*Indicates special attention is needed to these items now.

Business Management

This department needs telephone privacy, two visitors' chairs, separate space for Joe Green (125 sq. ft.) and for his secretarial assistant (125 sq. ft.); strongly prefers rooms rather than open space (see memo attached). Needs to be near Governmental Services and Program.

Community Relations

Need more storage space, a common work space for mailing, adding machines; more adequate conference space; at least two work stations for temporary staff; their own small reception area. Since they are stable in size and function, they stressed their general privacy requirements and prefer offices, not open space.

Fiscal Director

Needs to be near Accounting and Treasurer, Business Management, Computer Department, OEVP. Needs a minimum 12′ x 11′ space for himself; needs a minimum 12′ x 11′ for Jane Miller; his spaces must be private. Needs new files and a table as a minimum.

Duplicating

In two weeks a report of a Printing Study will be available, which may indicate a change in the size of press, and which may also indicate a 50 percent increase in the size of the paper stock. This should be checked.*

Also indicated a need for a storage room for paper (10,000 lbs.) which needs to be well ventilated, as well as temperature and humidity controlled. Needs a floor drain for their camera plate system, as well as hot and cold running water. Needs a wide double swinging door and room for a 48 inch aisle through the whole area (for passage of paper skids).

Oscar Dean says that these needs have not been discussed with the architects; they must be.*

Conclusion

Dear Mike,

Thank you very much for the check received this week; it has been a pleasure to get to know you, and naturally I am unhappy that your group has decided to terminate my consultant services to NASE. I decided to wait a few days before writing this letter so that I could try to sort out the kind of information that might be useful to your group in the future.

*Indicates special attention is needed to these items now.

First, I question whether or not your group should employ another space planner. One reason I say this is that I received less than half the information I asked for on the questionnaires. You show 199 people on the table of organization I finally obtained on my most recent trip to Metropolis; I only received 103 questionnaires, and after deducting the parts that were not completed on those I received, the equivalent of 94 completed questionnaires was what I ended up with.

Another reason is just a feeling that I have—that I was not getting feedback from your group. I asked specific questions in my letters and reports—no written answers came back; although sometimes I got partial answers on the phone.

I blame myself for lack of detailed information furnished on plan #1; I should not have let myself be pushed into doing it before I had the detailed information I might have obtained in the interviews; this plan being done even violated the sequence outlined in the memo which was attached to the interview forms when they were given to the staff.

A third reason is that I feel very deeply that the staffs of the various organizations are not really oriented to the processes necessary for successful space planning—this attitude extends to the top of the pyramid where the highest percentage of incomplete questionnaire forms occurred.

Further, I feel that open planning is not suitable for the NASE for reasons I made clear in an earlier report. With kindest personal regards,

Sincerely,

Walt Kleeman

Footnote

The big mistake in all of this was to let myself be pushed into proceeding out of logical sequence and without sufficient information. However, the information given does not mention another issue that I believe was crucial: *Assumed violations of personal privacy.*

Naturally, I was curious about the people who did not fill out and return questionnaires—after all, almost half of the members of this employee group did not return anything, and quite a few questionnaires were returned that did not have much information on them. From scuttlebut picked up, what may have happened was that about one-third of the total number of employees refused to fill out questionnaires on the grounds that the questions asked were invasions of their personal privacy.

There is no easy and final solution to this issue. In practice, the only solution that has really worked for me (other than for NASE), is to remove the names from the completed questionnaires as soon as they are returned and substitute code numbers. This must be agreed on at the start of the process; then any information management receives cannot definitely be tied to a particular person.

In NASE, a volunteer organization working for social change, this procedure did not work; honestly, I do not know what would have. Whatever happened, open planning did not work either; two years afterward a visit to the site revealed profuse amounts of permanent, floor-to-ceiling partitions on all floors.

Case Study 2 *The Doctors' Waiting Room*

Design Problem

Redesign a waiting room and reception area in an aged, converted residence for a team of two eye surgeons, an ear, nose, and throat specialist, and six technicians who test eyes, ears, noses, and throats as well as make and fit glasses and contact lenses.

Design Constraints

1. Limited space: the waiting and reception area as it existed before the redesign seated twenty-three people on sofas and chairs; tables held magazines and newspapers.

2. The actual amount of space to be used for these purposes was quite limited because the physicians did not want to alter the structure of the house and the reception space is surrounded by load-bearing walls. They did not want to move to larger quarters, either.

3. At the moment of redesign, the space was sometimes so crowded that patients were sitting on the floor and on an adjacent flight of stairs. Traffic lanes had to be preserved. Basically there were two entrances to the eye surgeons' suite, one of which also functioned as the entrance to the ear, nose, and throat physician's office and treatment rooms. There was, of course, one entrance from the outside which also served as the exit.

4. Questioning of the clients after observation of the reception area in use revealed that a significant proportion of the patients for the eye doctors are middle-aged and beyond, due to the large number of cataract cases they examine and treat.

5. A limited budget, the commonest design constraint of all.

Design Solution

The need for more seating capacity was quite urgent so we:

1. Got rid of the tables; put up wall magazine racks. No ash receptacles or ash trays were needed—all three physicians agreed long ago to prohibit smoking anywhere in the building.

2. We used all chairs, individual seating (got rid of the sofas) because American strangers do not like to sit next to American strangers. This is observable in reception areas you visit: the last places to be used are the ones on multiple seating pieces with two or more places.

3. Because of the significant number of cataract cases among the patients who come to these doctors, the following seating characteristics were necessary:

a. Eighteen-inch seat lip height with no more than one-inch drop from lip to seat bottom. Repeated anthropometric and human factors studies of seating show that when lip height is less than eighteen inches and seat drop from the lip is more than one inch, older persons find it very difficult to get up out of the chair. (*Note:* This seat height and drop should be used for public seating only in situations in which a significant proportion of the sitters are elderly.)

b. The seating surface itself must be not smooth and/or glossy; it should be textured, not rough, but with a definite corrugation. Otherwise the older patients will not be able to easily remain upright while sitting for two reasons. First, it takes more strength to remain upright on a glossy surface. Second, their visual perception is measurably impaired by the cataract or other problem (or they would not be there to see the eye surgeons in the first place) and this limits the ability to remain sitting upright, even for relatively short periods.

4. The desperate need for more seating in this limited space dictated that as many chairs be put into it as possible. Therefore they had to be ganged to conserve space. Another reason for ganging is that the chairs stay in place better so that the minimal aisle tolerances are preserved.

5. This was a very low-budget job. The chair chosen was one designed by Robin Day in England, but produced under license in the United States. It has a molded polypropylene seat and back in one piece, and the seating surface is slightly corrugated, as required. The use of polypropylene offers an added dividend: this plastic does have a slight give or deflection when you sit in it, so it does bend a bit to accommodate body size and shape. Therefore, these chairs are quite a bit more comfortable than the more rigid shell chairs made from fiberglass reinforced polyes-

ter or nylon or other rigid plastics. This particular chair is good-looking and comes in five beautiful colors, which did not hurt the space a bit.

6. We were able to cram forty-five places to sit (chairs) into the space where there had only been twenty-three places to sit before on sofas and chairs combined. This was done without violating E. T. Hall's observation that a visitor's seat within ten feet of and facing the receptionist will make the receptionist feel involved with the visitor and obliged to converse; the doctors' receptionist is a busy person with other work to do. None of the forty-five chairs faces the receptionist directly.

Designer's Note 1

Obviously the preceding is not the best solution to this design problem—if the constraints were not there. However, the constraints were there, and this was the best solution we could come up with at the time. The doctors and their technicians were pleased with it and more patients can now sit on chairs.

Designer's Note 2

After looking at the problem and analyzing it, we suddenly realized that it was not the first time—we had done it with sofas, chairs, and tables twenty years before. At least the installation had lasted for twenty years

Figure 1. The doctor's waiting room—after.

without a major breakdown, though we will have to admit that the vinyl was a bit tattered after all that time and all that heavy use. Then, too, we realized that we had never heard of interdisciplinary inputs to interior design twenty years before.

References

Edward T. Hall, "The Hidden Dimension" (Garden City, N.Y.: Doubleday & Co., Inc., 1966), p. 123.

John Zeisel, "Interior Designers Discover Behavioral Research," *Design & Environment*, vol. 1, no. 3, Fall 1970, pp. 42–43.

Case Study 3 **_The Redesign of the Interior of Chicago–Read Mental Health Center_**

An American Society of Interior Designers Public Service Project

This project started with the submission of a proposal to Chicago–Read Mental Health Center and the Illinois Department of Mental Health for research to plan the redesign of the interiors, the actual redesign, and then for the evaluation of the design by the American Society of Interior Designers Illinois Chapter as a public service project. After the acceptance of the proposal by the then superintendent of the center, John T. Nelson, the chapter committee on the project interviewed the superintendent, various members of the staff, and a group of former patients to get their views on what was needed in the redesign; we also toured the buildings involved. We found plenty of interior problems.

Interior Problems Part of the interior problems arose from the fact that few of the buildings or spaces were being used for the exact purpose for which they were originally designed; our purpose was to redesign the spaces for the uses at the time and build in enough flexibility for future use changes.

It should be noted at this point that the center is organized so that all patients from the city of Chicago come first to it and then if they do not improve sufficiently after a stay of no more than sixty days, are sent to more specialized institutions for further treatment. When the project began the patient wards were set up on a geographic basis. Chicago, for the purpose of the center, was divided into regions and subregions; the organization of the wards reflected these geographic divisions. All patients from each region and subregion were placed in the corresponding ward in the center. This meant that there was no segregation of patients by type of illness or by race, though there was some segregation by sex.

One important result of this organization of the center was that any interior used by patients must be designed so that it will withstand the use that results from the fact that patients with all types of mental maladies will use it, and inevitably in some cases, abuse it.

Universal Problems

One problem was universal in every area we visited: the draperies were a shambles, torn, missing, or drooping. The hardware was first class, but we felt that the method of attaching the drapes to the rods might be the problem. Snap tape drapes that simply unsnap and pull off the travelers would be the solution. If they were used and a patient grabs a drapery, it simply unsnaps instead of tearing. Also, the draperies had originally been installed with hanging cords to traverse them with; we suggested that the cords be eliminated and that new rods and draperies be made and installed for hand traversing. We also recommended that flame retardant drapery materials be used.

Another universal problem was broken and burnt furniture. Although some of the well-made solid walnut frame, heavy vinyl (channeled) upholstered chairs had stood up fairly well, evidently no replacement program for burnt backs and seats had been put into action, though replacement backs and seats were available from the manufacturer. The burns were from cigarettes, of course.

Several staff members pointed out that chairs are preferable to couches in this setting because couches offer more crevasses to hide dirt and burning cigarettes, and because patients are less likely to sleep in chairs than they are on couches. However, another overriding reason for using chairs can be found in the writings of Kiyo Izumi and Humphry Osmond on mental hospital design. One of their seating design goals is to eliminate unwanted confrontations and interactions among patients; they used two simple methods toward this goal.

One was to eliminate any seating piece for more than one person so that any patient would not be forced to sit next to another patient. The other was to provide more chairs in the common room areas than there were patients to sit in them; in this way there were always enough chairs, and even if patients claimed certain chairs as their own (as often happens in institutions), every patient had been provided with a private place to sit down. Additionally, chairs are much more movable than multi-person seating pieces, allowing individual patients to interact or not, as they wish.

Not Enough Chairs

At Chicago–Read there were not enough chairs; in one ward we observed that the doctor in charge had to keep waking sleeping patients in their rooms in order to get them to go to the television room, where there was not enough seating to make television viewing inviting. One reason for the lack of seating was probably the lack of a repair program for seating pieces.

We recommended that wood frame chairs with replaceable seats and backs be used. They were to have fire retardant fabrics, fire retardant foam, and an open space between the seat and back so that dirt and burning cigarettes could be seen and would not fall into the typical crevice of a fully upholstered piece. We also specified contrasting fabric colors, so that the dreary appearance of the common spaces might be improved somewhat.

Wall Problems

One of the prime reasons for the overall dingy appearance of the whole facility could be blamed on the previously specified wall vinyls. There seems to be no known way to keep these from being torn, given the diverse types of patients who are admitted to this facility. The torn vinyls gave the place a run-down look and we felt that it would be a waste of time and money to replace them only to have the same thing happen again and again.

Another wall-related problem was the lack of good signage, a glaring design omission. It was virtually impossible for the staff, let alone the sometimes confused patients, to find their way about, or know where they were. Various authors, including Hall, Osmond, and Izumi, have written about the importance of the self-orientation of the mental patient, and in this facility the staff admitted that they themselves had to use maps to be able to find their way around.

As a combination answer to the signage, orientation, and wall vinyl problems we recommended the use of lively colors of epoxy paint after the wall vinyls (anyhow the remains of them) had been removed. Actually, what we specified was a system where the desired color is painted on the wall and then a clear epoxy chemically compatible with the base color coat is put on over it. We also recommended that the signage also be applied as a base coat, using supergraphics, and that the signage for the various wards be color coded. A further necessity, we felt, was metal corner protectors, preferably made of stainless steel.

No Patterns

We added one design caution, as Izumi suggests, that *no* patterns be used anywhere in the institution more complicated than normal wood grains. He gives the reason for this recommendation as the possibility that mental patients are likely to conjure up disturbing illusions from strong patterns on an interior surface. An example he gives is the possibility of knotty pine producing illusions of eyes staring at the patient.

Nursing Stations

The Chicago–Read nursing stations were the subject of many comments from the staff and from former patients. Nursing stations become a barrier to staff-patient interaction when the staff uses them as a place to hide. One former patient described using the pay telephone in the patient kitchen area to call the nursing station because she could get no response by standing at the counter in front of it. This type of counter was cited by several of the former patients we interviewed as a bar to patient-staff interaction

To make the staff more accessible to the patients, both former patients and staff members suggested (and we concurred) that it might be helpful to remove the barrier and place a staff desk or desks in the middle of the television viewing area, which is now in front of the nursing station counter in each ward. This would make the staff more accessible to the patients.

Other Problems

Several comments were made about the lack of bulletin boards in all of the offices in the center, but this lack was especially evident in the nursing stations. Several people suggested that one wall of each nursing station be covered with bulletin board material. We felt that bulletin boards should also be provided in each office space and treatment space to prevent the evident disfiguring of walls throughout the facility, resulting in part from the various methods of putting notices on the walls (which also played a part in the torn wall vinyl situation).

Discolored and dirty ceilings were evident throughout; one of the former patients suggested that this might be the result of the issuance of an inadequate cleaning material to the maintenance staff.

Pay phone booths were another problem. The walls were dirty, covered with writing, and no sound deadening material seemed to be used. Since it is unlikely that typical sound deadening material would stay on the walls very long, we suggested pierced metal surfaced acoustic materials (used in some outdoor booths), and we felt that it should be possible to make the booths a bit more private than they were. We suggested scratch pads for the booths as well as wall-attached ash trays; former patients asked for a place to sit down in each booth.

In addition to the epoxy-paint system mentioned earlier, we suggested that patient-produced art be utilized as least in the bedrooms, and perhaps in the TV viewing spaces as well.

Storage problems were serious in the bedroom areas for two principal reasons: first, because the rather small bedroom chests, hardly larger than a typical night stand, were being destroyed by the patients, and second, because many of the closets and wardrobes were unusable because of lost keys. We suggested putting drawers underneath each bed. The staff maintained that key control had been improved and that would ease the situation.

A frequently mentioned difficulty in staff functioning was the obvious shortage of storage space on the wards; we suggested as a partial remedy the addition of lockers in each nursing station for both patients and staff.

We suggested name tag slots and name tags for patient rooms to improve patient self-esteem; this is suggested in the literature, especially by Edward R. Ostrander and Lorraine Hiatt.

Mirrors were broken and missing throughout the institution; we suggested unbreakable mirrors, and for the many broken windows we suggested mirrors made of polycarbonate to stop the continual damage.

Central Intake

The Central Intake area, where all patients go first, seemed too crowded. During our initial visit to the area we felt that more of the nearby rooms might be used to relieve the crowding, though this might require more reception staff than were involved at that time. However, increased staff here might have some therapeutic value in that entering patients would have more people around during the long waits that seem to characterize entrance to this institution (as well as to most others).

Corridors

We felt that one area of the institution seemed ripe for some sort of transformation—the corridors. They were spacious, replete with nice views of the outside, and barren. This barren state seemed to contribute to the depressing aura of the entire facility. While we thought that colors and supergraphics on the wall would help, we also thought that a more comprehensive design solution might lie in another direction. We felt that the corridors might be used for activities other than just getting people and things from one place to another.

We suggested the Borda Wing of the South County Hospital, Wakefield, R.I., as a possible model for use of the corridors for various activities; it was obvious that Chicago–Read needed more space for various functions and we thought that some of these could go on in the lightly used corridors.

In the Borda Wing, the corridors were turned into areas for the following activities: informal medical consultations with patients' families, places where families could visit and have snacks with patients, a small library, water fountains, game and writing space, and phone booths. While these were not the activities that would necessarily be appropriate for Chicago–Read, since South County is a general medical hospital rather than a mental health institution, more activity in the corridors would have had the effect of changing the sterile look of the corridor space, and proper allocation of functions would have relieved the general shortage of space.

Former Patients' Reactions

Former patients' reactions to the interiors of the institution reflected many of the preceding comments, but several of their suggestions were different and deserve mention. They felt that patients should be allowed to have parakeets and/or other birds in cages and that birdhouses should be placed outside the windows so that patients might watch birds nesting, and so on. They also felt that the redesign of the interiors should reflect the fact that the facility had been designed for far fewer patients than it then housed; they also felt that the separation of the more psychopathic and criminal patients from the rest might help.

Former patients also suggested a redesign of the telephone system so that patients could receive calls then being aborted when a sick patient answered the pay phone and then hung up without saying anything or calling anyone to the phone.

Perhaps the most important design element the former patients stressed was the condition of the lighting of the interior spaces. They termed the lighting depressing and felt that the quality of interior lighting is an important factor for the patients in the total atmosphere of the center.

One of the staff suggested that some of the necessary maintenance work, especially on interior furnishings, be done by the patients and that they be rewarded with small amounts of money; this would seem to be an administrative and therapeutic question beyond the scope of interior design. However, this suggestion might have merit in that in this way patients might have more of a sense of "ownership" and concern for the interior furnishings; also the suggestion did underline the necessity for maintenance performed with more regularity and effectiveness than had existed in the past.

Staff Reactions

After the redesign had been completed, we held a meeting with the staff of Chicago–Read Mental Health Center; their comments follow.

The visiting team from the Joint Commission on Hospital Accreditation had commented favorably on the colors used (very strong). Although some staff had predicted an increase in fighting among the patients because of the increased color stimuli, in fact, fighting has decreased since the redesign has been implemented and this decrease persists. Both patients and staff respond more favorably to the new colors used, and this response persists.

The interior surfaces and furnishings have received better care and more careful use since the redesign has been accomplished; further, patients and staff feel better about Chicago–Read now.

The staff likes vinyl upholstery best; it is much easier to maintain because of the numerous urination and defecation accidents; these make it very difficult to clean the olefin upholstered pieces. Where olefin upholstery is used, it stretches, and its nubby texture makes it hard to clean, especially when such "accidents" occur.

There has been a reduction in broken glass since the redesign and this reduction persists. Where polycarbonate has been used (both for mirrors and for windows), it scratches and discolors readily if anything is used to clean it except water.

The heavy-appearing wood furniture furnished along with the redesign is not picked up and thrown as much now because of its bulky look.

The wood furniture is much easier to repair than the old furniture, both wood and metal (it was specified so that it would be); the metal tubular furniture which they had previously could not be successfully welded. About one-third of the new furniture has had to be repaired, although there is general agreement among the staff that the new furniture is much better and more durable than the old furniture, as well as being easier to repair.

Since the heating system at Chicago–Read is dry-electric, the resulting atmosphere tends to dry wood furniture out, making it split, splinter, and fall apart if it is not sealed properly. This happened to a few pieces, but they all have been successfully repaired by the manufacturer.

One staff member suggested that all tables in the Center should be solid blocks of wood so that patients could not remove table legs and use them as weapons. Tables with "butcher block" tops have held up well. Staff members felt that they were "easy to clean" and "very attractive."

Patients sleep on the two-seater sofas used, but, of course, their beds are not available to them when this happens.

The staff plan to number night stands, closets, and chests so that keys can be given to patients, though they feel that they must have a general master key for each category. They also emphasized that each lock and key must have a legible number on it that cannot be rubbed off.

The patients still take incandescent light bulbs out of their sockets and throw them. (We repeated a recommendation made previously that they consider using more fluorescents with light spectrums close to that of natural sunlight both to solve the throwing problem and to improve the lighting atmosphere of the facility.)

At least one manic patient picked up a lamp and tried to use it as a weapon; all lamps should be bolted down. This incident took place on a Friday, the day when patients from the houses of correction are admitted. We had only bolted lamps to benches that were used on the periphery of each day room area.

As recommended, the drapes were hand traversed with no cords or pulleys; no problem with this specification was reported in any area of the center.

No fire safety hazard was noted for the drapes, and the suggested snap tapes used on the drapes instead of typical drapery pins allowed the drapes to fall when grabbed by patients instead of tearing as they had before. Cigarette burns show on the carpet; however, since the carpet merely chars, no fire safety hazard was noted.

Staff have had some success repairing carpet burns by using a scalpel to scrape off the charred portions of the carpet pile and then recoloring the backing with marker pens. The carpet withstands the traffic and cleans well, except for the cigarette burns. It is the specified type, a closely woven through-the-back velvet with looped uncut pile of acrylic-modacrylic fiber. Today the carpet choice would probably be a third- or fourth-generation nylon carpet with static control, but it would be the same type of weave in the same type of configuration.

A mistake was made in the carpet installation; instead of using metal binder bars, the installer used a rubber or vinyl compound which did not hold its position; the compound used tends to rise and people trip over it.

The typical observation was made that sharp edges are dangerous for some patients, especially epileptic and geriatric ones.

The general reaction to the specified epoxy-surface wall paint was excellent. In the hallways especially, this combination over the former wall vinyls has held up "miraculously." Some walls still had the first application of the newer finish when these conversations were held, though others have had to be repaired. Although there have been some difficulties in repairing the epoxy-surface finish, the finish itself was termed "fantastic." It is so tough that walls are being damaged instead of the newer finish.

However, some staff objected to the "offensive" odor of epoxy when it is being applied, and there seemed to be an internal conspiracy to try to sabotage the walls to make work for the institution's painters. Incidentally, when epoxy could not be obtained fast enough for some repairs, ordinary flat paint was used instead; the flat paint smudged and could not be cleaned well.

Evaluation Method   To find out what was needed in the redesign, a study had been conducted, and after the redesign had been completed, another study was done to measure how well we had succeeded.

First, the items shown in Figure 1 were administered to 106 staff members and patients.

Figure 1. Questionnaire Items for Evaluating Physical Facilities

	Excellent	Good	Fair	Poor	Bad
1. Overall quality of lighting					
2. Light from windows					
3. Color of walls					
4. Color of floors					
5. Physical condition of the mirrors					
6. Physical condition of the furniture					
7. Physical condition of the draperies					
8. Physical condition of the walls					
9. Physical condition of the windows					
10. Physical condition of the ceilings					
11. Physical condition of the phone booths					
12. Maintenance of the furniture					
13. Maintenance of the draperies					
14. Maintenance of the walls					
15. Maintenance of the windows					
16. Maintenance of the ceilings					
17. Maintenance of the phone booths					
18. Facilities to store patients' clothing					
19. Facilities to store patients' personal items					
20. Facilities to store staff clothing					
21. Facilities to store supplies					
22. Facilities to store equipment					
23. Overall sound quality of Chicago-Read					
24. Noise isolation from outdoors					
25. Noise isolation among rooms in a unit					

	Excellent	Good	Fair	Poor	Bad
26. Other sound considerations (specify)					
27. Directional signs in the halls					
28. Identification numbers & names on the rooms					
29. Names and identification within the units					
30. Identification of each building					

After redesign had been completed the original questionnaire was readministered.

The original questionnaire stated the item and gave the respondent five choices in rating each item: excellent, good, fair, poor, and bad. Due to the low response in both extremes, the top two categories and the bottom two categories were collapsed. The descriptive ratings hereafter will be entitled good, fair, and poor.

There was a judgmental sample drawn of staff and patients before the redesign was started and another after all work had been completed. Since the passage of time had changed the identity of patients and staff, a repeated measures design was not considered. However, the same questionnaire was administered to the same ward before and after redesign.

It was decided that a cross tabulation approach would be an accurate approach to analyzing data of this nature. Two of the original tables are displayed in Tables 1 and 2 and the figures underlined were used in the main tables.

Table 1. Pre-Redesign—Item 1

	Staff	Patient
	1	12
Good	5.9%	80.0%
	10	3
Fair	58.8	20.0
	6	0
Poor	35.3	0.0
	$X^2 = 19.03$, p = .0001	

Table 2. Post-Redesign—Item 1

	Staff	Patient
	33	9
Good	63.5%	64.3%
	12	2
Fair	23.1	14.3
	1	3
Poor	13.5	21.4
	$X^2 = .87$, p = .65	

Although chi square has been reported it is necessary to point out that use of this statistic as procedure assumes that a random sample was drawn from a defined population. These samples were not random samples and were drawn at the discretion of the staff on duty on both occasions when the questionnaires were administered.

Observations   A number of observations might be made concerning the preceding data obtained from the results of the questionnaires:

1. Findings like this may be just statistical artifacts; we do have different samples and different sample sizes (pre-design: 56 staff and 50 patients; post-design: 62 staff and 15 patients), and further, we are really getting data from two different populations.

2. To the extent that the data do show authentic differences as a possible result of design, there was clear improvement in staff attitudes toward the interior environment *after* the design was accomplished. See Tables 1 and 2.

3. The results of the pre-design questionnaires show a much greater disparity between the views of the patients and those of the staff concerning the interior environment than did the post-design ones. This may be due to either:

    a. The smaller number of post-design questionnaires received, 77 total as compared to the 106 pre-design questionnaires received, or

    b. The turnover of the staff and patients questioned during the four-year period between the administrations of the questionnaires, 1972 to 1976.

    (See Figures 2, 3, 4, and 5.)

4. Perhaps the most important possibility illumined by the results is that there *can* be a wide difference between the way mental health center staff views an interior environment and the way patients view an interior environment. This possibility suggests that the views of *both* patients *and* staff should be considered in the planning of mental health treatment facilities.

5. For cross-checking opinions, the differences in the result of comparing the views of those who saw items as "good" as compared with those who saw them as "bad" may be useful in interior planning—

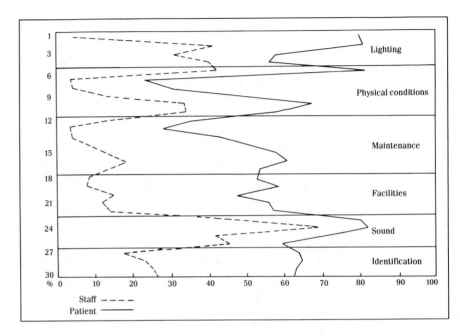

Figure 2. Pre-Redesign: What Percent Said Good

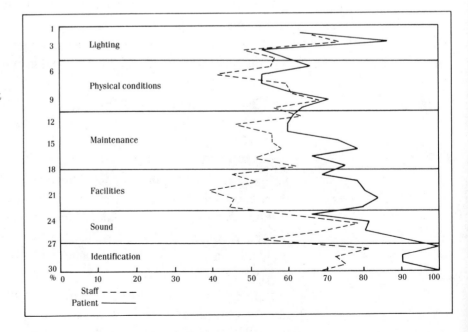

Figure 3. Post-Redesign: What Percent Said Good

Figure 4. Pre-Design: What Percent Said Bad

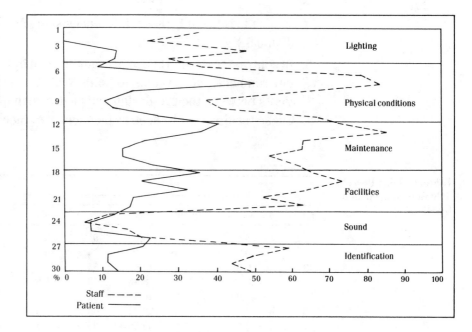

Figure 5. Post-Redesign: What Percent Said Bad

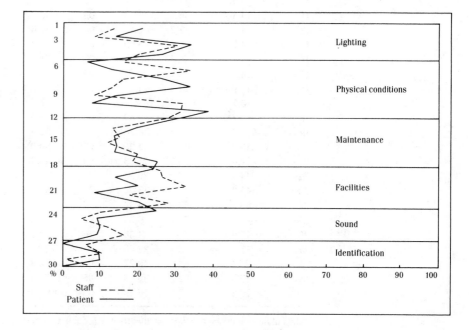

though in this study these differences seem small. (See Figures 2, 3, 4, and 5.)

6. In contrast to the marked improvement seen by the staff in the interior environment, there seems to be little change in the views of the patients between the pre-design and post-design questionnaire results. These results must be seen as inconclusive since the identities of both

Table 3. What Percent Said Good (Excellent or Good)

Item	Pre Staff	Pre Patient	Pre X^2	Pre p	Post Staff	Post Patient	Post X^2	Post p
1	5.9	80.0	19.03	.05*	63.5	64.3	0.87	.64*
2	40.7	81.6	21.21	.05	74.6	86.7	3.07	.22*
3	30.8	57.4	12.89	.05	48.3	53.3	0.36	.84*
4	40.0	56.3	3.46	.18	56.9	60.0	0.09	.70*
5	42.0	81.3	16.53	.05	55.7	66.7	1.04	.59*
6	3.6	23.4	20.34	.05	41.9	53.3	2.45	.29*
7	3.7	31.0	15.60	.05	59.7	53.3	0.91	.63*
8	14.3	46.8	20.57	.05	61.7	60.0	4.67	.10*
9	33.3	67.4	13.28	.05	69.4	71.4	0.86	.65*
10	34.5	57.4	10.83	.05	56.7	64.3	1.61	.44*
11	14.5	36.4	16.23	.05	63.2	61.5	3.38	.18*
12	3.6	27.7	15.15	.05	46.6	60.0	1.24	.54*
13	3.7	42.9	28.09	.05	55.9	60.0	0.83	.66*
14	9.3	51.1	25.32	.05	56.1	73.3	1.67	.43*
15	14.3	58.7	28.31	.05	57.9	78.6	3.09	.21*
16	18.9	61.4	21.27	.05	51.7	66.7	1.09	.57*
17	13.7	53.5	19.14	.05	62.3	75.0	2.69	.26*
18	8.7	52.9	9.63	.05*	45.8	69.2	3.10	.21*
19	7.7	58.3	34.23	.05	52.5	78.6	3.26	.19*
20	15.4	47.5	12.25	.05	39.0	80.0	6.50	.04*
21	12.0	56.5	21.33	.05	46.6	83.3	5.50	.06*
22	14.6	57.1	20.94	.05	44.1	80.0	5.19	.07*
23	49.0	79.1	13.02	.05	63.9	66.7	2.56	.27*
24	68.0	82.2	4.34	.11	78.3	81.8	0.63	.72*
25	41.2	72.7	9.54	.05	67.8	80.0	0.69	.71*
26	45.0	59.1	1.56	.46	53.7	90.9	5.71	.06*
27	17.3	63.6	22.66	.05	81.4	100.0	2.43	.29*
28	23.1	64.3	19.22	.05	72.4	90.0	2.08	.34*
29	25.0	62.8	16.69	.05	75.0	90.0	4.67	.10*
30	26.4	62.2	16.79	.05	69.0	100.0	4.62	.10*

*The chi square measure might be slightly inflated due to a zero or low cell count in the original table from which this measure was drawn.

staff and patients had changed during the intervening four-year period. (See Tables 3 and 4.)

7. While the results of the pre-design questionnaires show easily rec-
    ognizable differences between the views of the staff and the views of
    the patients on the quality of the interior environment it should be
    noted that the post-design questionnaire results show much less dif-
    ference between those same views of patients and staff. (See Figures
    2 and 3.)

Table 4. What Percent Said Bad (Bad or Poor)

Item	Pre				Post			
	Staff	Patient	X²	p	Staff	Patient	X²	p
1	35.3	0.0	19.03	.05	13.5	21.4	0.87	.65
2	22.2	0.0	21.21	.05	8.5	13.3	3.07	.26
3	48.1	14.9	12.89	.05	31.7	33.3	0.36	.84
4	27.3	14.6	3.46	.18	20.7	26.7	0.69	.71
5	36.0	8.3	16.53	.05	16.4	6.7	1.04	.59
6	78.6	36.2	20.34	.05	33.9	13.3	2.45	.29
7	83.3	50.0	15.60	.05	16.1	26.7	0.91	.63
8	60.7	19.1	20.57	.05	13.3	33.3	4.67	.10
9	37.0	10.9	13.28	.05	8.1	14.3	0.86	.65
10	41.8	12.8	10.83	.05	21.7	7.1	1.61	.45
11	65.5	25.0	16.23	.05	21.1	38.5	3.38	.18
12	72.7	40.4	15.15	.05	27.6	26.7	1.24	.54
13	85.2	35.7	28.09	.05	13.6	20.0	0.83	.66
14	63.0	21.3	25.32	.05	15.8	13.3	1.67	.43
15	62.5	15.2	28.31	.05	12.3	14.3	3.09	.21
16	54.7	15.9	21.27	.05	20.0	13.3	1.09	.58
17	60.8	23.3	19.14	.05	18.9	25.0	2.69	.26
18	65.2	35.3	9.63	.05*	25.4	23.1	3.10	.21
19	73.1	20.8	34.23	.05	26.2	14.3	3.26	.20
20	63.5	32.5	12.29	.05	32.2	20.0	6.50	.04
21	52.0	17.9	21.33	.05	17.2	8.3	5.50	.06
22	62.5	17.1	20.94	.05	28.8	20.0	5.19	.07
23	12.2	14.0	13.02	.05	11.5	25.0	2.56	.28
24	4.0	6.7	4.34	.11	5.0	9.0	0.63	.73
25	15.7	6.8	9.54	.05	11.9	10.0	0.69	.71
26	20.0	22.7	1.56	.46	16.7	9.1	5.71	.06
27	59.6	20.5	22.66	.05	6.8	0.0	2.43	.29
28	50.0	11.9	19.82	.05	10.3	10.0	2.08	.35
29	44.2	11.6	16.69	.05	1.7	10.0	4.67	.10
30	49.1	13.3	16.79	.05	8.6	0.0	4.62	.10

*The chi square measure might be slightly inflated due to a zero or low cell count in the original
table from which this measure was drawn.

Getting Design Information from the User

Let's go back a bit. How and why did we pick this particular method to get the design information we needed at Chicago–Read?

If you are commissioned to design an interior, and if you feel that you need information on user needs and wants, the procedure you use will depend on how much money the client is willing to pay for this process.

Ideally in the present state of the art, you would first administer questionnaires to the users. From the answers to these questionnaires you would not only get a general idea of needs and wants but you would also learn of certain acute individual needs. You would then interview generally to check the questionnaire answers and you would also interview intensively those individuals showing acute situations to find out just what those acute needs are and how they may be satisfied.

Let us say that you found out from the questionnaire answers that Amy Smith's replies reveal that Amy feels that she needs more privacy in her work station as a confidential secretary to a vice-president. You would interview her to find out whether the problem is visual privacy or audio privacy, or perhaps both.

Some people are very conscious today of another kind of privacy—olfactory privacy. Some individuals are allergic to tobacco smoke or maybe they do not like the body odors of the worker nearest to them. You might find out that the privacy of being protected from objectionable odors is at the root of Amy's problem.

Another matter that can be checked initially with questionnaires is ergonomic fit. Do the workplace and its furnishings fit the person using them? Is the chair fitted with enough adjustments of sufficient range so that it is comfortable for the user? Are the work surfaces large enough for workers to do their jobs? Is there storage space for personal items? Is there enough filing space and does it fit the materials in use? Are there enough drawers of the right kind in the desk pedestals? Firm initial answers to these questions can provide the designer with the necessary ammunition to get to the nitty gritty of what is needed for each individual.

A third component should be added to the questionnaires and interviews: observation. As to when the observation should take place, knowledgeable practitioners are divided. Some say that you should observe before you distribute questionnaires in order to find out what design issues you can see before you make up the questions; others say that you should use observation as a tool to determine acute needs after you have unearthed them in the questionnaire answers. This practitioner would say that you might do it both times, if your client is willing to pay the bill, to make certain that the design job is getting as much information as possible. In any case, the 35-millimeter single lens reflex camera is a great tool for recording observations.

However, you cannot always use all three methods. Where substantial portions of the user population are heavily drugged or have limited reading and writing abilities (as in mental hospitals and mental retardation treatment sites, for instance), you may have to leave out the questionnaires and depend on interviews and observation as your means to obtain user information.

At Chicago–Read we were able only to administer a very simple questionnaire at the beginning and end of the work because of the difficulty of working with the patients and a very busy overworked staff. Note that the questionnaire we used only has five words to rate the interior environment: excellent, good, fair, poor, and bad. These words were not chosen lightly. They were picked because everybody who can hear and read has much the same idea of what those words mean. Therefore, you can be reasonably sure that the results you get represent what the people who answer think.

Quite a few people who make up questionnaires on the environment do not agree with this use of just five words. Some of these people use a device called the "semantic differential." Essentially this method places two words of opposite meaning on a line with five or seven spaces between them and asks the person being questioned to put a mark in the space that represents his feeling about the quality of the environment being tested. For instance one question might look like this:

ordered —— —— —— —— —— —— —— chaotic

(This is an actual example from a "tested" semantic differential scale.)

A mark in the middle space would show a neutral feeling and as the marks get closer on either side to each word they indicate more and more agreement with that word—if the answerer knows the meaning of those words. The results are then subjected to statistical analysis to find out the relative strength of feeling about various aspects of the environment.

This method, in my opinion, has a fatal flaw. When you go beyond the simplicity of excellent, good, fair, poor, and bad, people really differ on what more complicated words mean, and if there is no general agreement on meaning, the results become meaningless, too. So, I strongly recommend the five key words as a good method of finding out what you want to know for design.

At Chicago–Read we used the same questionnaire before we did the design work as we did to find out what staff and patients felt about the completed job. We could not control who got the questionnaires because at both times the center was embroiled in political controversies. Therefore, we had to hand the questionnaires to administrators; they picked the patients and staff to receive them. Furthermore, because the center is a limited-stay institution (average length of stay: twenty-eight days) we are sure that we did not get the reactions of the same patients four years later and the normal staff turnover probably means that we did not get the same staff to answer the second questionnaire either.

With that disclaimer in mind, look back at Figure 2 with the results of the first questionnaire. You can see that this questionnaire showed that there can be a wide difference between the way mental health center staff views an interior and the way patients view an interior. Since that can be true, you should get the ideas and reactions of *both* staff and patients before you try to redesign a mental health center, as we said before. In fact, you had better find out about the needs and wants of the users of any space you design *before* you design it. Decide which one of the three—questionnaires, interviews, and observation—or what combination of the three will best serve your needs and fit your budget. These are the methods that have been most useful for me.

Acknowledgment   This study was supported in part by a grant from the Educational Foundation of the Illinois Chapter of the American Society of Interior Designers. The author also wishes to thank Robert Sommer for his help in preparing the questionnaire and also Thomas W. Madron, Carolyn C. Marks, and Roy D. Hedges for their help in analyzing the results of the questionnaires.

As a public service project at first of the Midwest Chapter of the National Society of Interior Designers, and then of the Illinois Chapter of the American Society of Interior Designers, many members gave much time and talent to this enterprise, but Ruth Leibovitz as job captain must be singled out for services far beyond the call of duty; she was also chairperson of the committee from start to finish. Jerry Jerrard, Ethel Samuels, and this writer as coordinating designer also served from beginning to end. Others involved included Joan Brown, Carol Caz, Priscilla Custin, Elie Feldman, Irving Kaplan, Rosalie Krone, and Pat Levine.

Case Study 4 *Community Hospital— Springfield, Ohio*

For the interior design and space planning of Community Hospital's $11 million addition and remodeling program in Springfield, Ohio, human factors principles were used to determine the choice of colors, textures, and types of interior furnishings superimposed on the usual criteria of taste and aesthetics. Unfortunately, human factors principles could not be applied to the building forms, since these were determined by the fact that the existing structure was to be reused, which largely defined the shape of the addition as well.

Generally speaking, the use of human factors principles consisted of putting each interior design choice in the context of its use and the reactions of those who were to experience each choice or use it.

Color Selection

In terms of wall and ceiling color selection, the strongest colors were used in the underground portions of the addition where laboratory and X-ray facilities had been located by the architects, Schreiber-Little and Associates, AIA, of Springfield, Ohio. Since this area is windowless, it followed that bright, sunny colors would compensate for the lack of light from windows. Otherwise this part of the work environment would not have the proper visual climate for normal working activities in the below ground spaces.

Also, beginning with this underground section, all storage spaces were done in a strong epoxy white so that dirt could be immediately evident even on casual inspection, and also so that it might be easier to identify stored items against the high reflectance value of white at any lighting level.

At the principal entrance, a real effort was made to avoid the usual shiny "eye-ease green and white" combination that most people associate with hospitals. A predominately gold carpet with flecks of brown was selected for some areas, a blue-green one for others, and an orange and brown combination called India Spice was also used. The walls were covered with a fire-rated vinyl with the natural look of grasscloth.

For long wear and cleanability, the upholstery in the reception and waiting areas near the entrance is woven from 100 percent nylon treated with a stain repeller in golds, blue-green, and oranges, depending on the color of the carpet. The rough texture of these heavy covers provides ventilation where people have to sit for long periods and provides a welcome contrast to the usual institutional look.

All draperies on this floor, which contains administrative, reception, and office areas, are made of natural colored, flame retardant, roughly woven casement cloth.

The reception furniture is simply designed architectural modern; a slightly different style in the same vein was used for the office furniture. There was a choice of carefully chosen and ergonomically correct desk tops from oiled oak melamine laminate to light walnut; all of those offered for selection fell within the recommended 30 to 50 percent light reflectance range and are matte surfaces, rather than shiny ones, to greatly reduce glare. In most areas glare from work surfaces has been eliminated by the combination of these selected tops with careful lighting design.

Work Station Analysis and Seating

Individual work station analysis using human factors principles produced the proper work surface size for each desk and table keyed to the task.

All seating was chosen for selection with two principal criteria being critical:

1. Comfort produced by the combination of shape, size, filling, and cover (cover textures provide necessary ventilation for seated tasks of long duration).

2. Comfort produced by the range of adjustability of seat height, tension, and back height. Chairs with insufficient adjustability will be uncomfortable for the people who use them if an individual happens to be in the size range not covered by the adjustability of the chair. (For adjustability ranges for working office chairs, see the chapter on "Sitting Down.")

Incidentally, since no comprehensive data exist concerning the comfort of actual chairs now in the marketplace, we did make some crude comfort tests of office chairs readily available within the budget limitations of this hospital to determine which chairs would be offered for employee selection. We also checked their ranges of adjustability.

To continue the warmth engendered by the carpet in the public and office areas we used the same three-color combination for alternating color schemes in the eighty-nine patient rooms. By using the same quality of carpet throughout the hospital and by using the same three-color combination, we were, of course, able to obtain a lower price for the hospital because of the larger quantity of the same three colors. Alternating color printed on the same ground cloth we had used on the entrance floor for draperies were used for the patient rooms, producing a similar quantity price saving.

The carpet in both areas had to pass the Hill-Burton Act standards for flammability in effect at the time, of course, and it needed to be eminently cleanable; we used a woven-through-the-back, acrylic-modacrylic blended, round wire carpet that had one additional feature a hospital needs: a waterproof back to confine spills and stains to the pile, thus eliminating the necessity for replacing the underlay when the predictable heavy stain occurs. Pneumacel, composed of gas-filled fibers, was the separate underlay. It met Hill-Burton standards for flammability, too, but is now no longer manufactured.

Today we would probably use a tightly-woven third- or fourth-generation delustered nylon (with static control), utilizing the soil-hiding properties and long wear of this fiber. Underneath, rubberized all-hair underlay would be the first choice. As an experienced carpet installer once said, "We've been using all-hair for more than one hundred years and haven't had major trouble with it." Today both the carpet and the underlay would have to pass the Flooring Radiant Panel Test developed by the National Bureau of Standards, U.S. Department of Commerce.

The Endless Tunnel

Naturally, we were faced with the classic institutional design problem: absolutely straight 200-foot-long corridors. Mayer Spivack has documented the effect of the typical institutional corridor that appears to be endless: feelings of despondency and despair on the part of the human beings who must use it. Not wanting to foster such feelings in patients or staff, we managed to largely avoid the endless tunnel look by dividing the corridors into thirds with mildly contrasting colors on each third of the walls and a neutral color on the floor.

Chairs versus Sofas

Having observed the typical American reluctance to sit next to a stranger on a sofa (if any seat on a sofa is occupied, the rest of them will not be until every single chair in the same area is filled first), we originally planned all lounge and reception areas with single seat chairs. We did this for another very good reason: that single chairs, being easily movable, provide the greatest flexibility for group seating; people who want to sit next to each other are able to easily move the chairs. It is difficult to predict the size and/or composition of groups who will occupy a hospital waiting area or patient lounge at any given time.

Our original plan was followed except for one part of the hospital; in the "showplace" waiting area, the reception room near the main entrance, we were overruled by the hospital administration who demanded sofas and, of course, got them.

Maintenance Triumphs

Although our resulting seating arrangement still contained quite a few single chairs to make the best of the situation and still was reasonably flexible, later we were overruled again, this time in the classic manner, by the maintenance department of the hospital.

They insist on placing the chairs and sofas around the perimeters of all the spaces so that those who wait can only talk to the persons on either side of them, not the position most conducive for conversation; thus conversation is only possible between two seated people, not three or four or more.

This may make it easier to clean the spaces, but it certainly inhibits interaction among the human beings who must occupy these spaces through no controllable decision of their own. For one thing, these arrangements seem "sacred" and almost no one will move the seating in a public reception area unless it is obviously arranged for group conversation in the first place. The way the janitors place the seating, it becomes just like airports, and so far, our efforts to get administrators to overrule the maintenance people have been futile.

Color Notes

Although the hospital management originally objected to our bright, sunny colors in the underground portion, they finally saw the light on that one. Additionally, in two other areas we specified a color without argument or discussion: the operating room walls, and the fronts of the counters in the hospital employees' cafeteria. The color choice for these two diverse areas was the same: turquoise, selected according to the theories of Darell Boyd Harmon and arising from the same visual reasoning for two different places. The rationale is the same for both, according to Harmon (see Harmon's theories).

One More
Necessity

As you probably have sensed from the foregoing, we have not really discussed one other necessity: a cooperative client. The ergonomic approach to design problems is different from the traditional one; the interior designer must make sure that the client fully understands the importance and the benefits of the human factors input to the client's problems. Without that full understanding the interior designer cannot function at full effectiveness.

Case Study 5 *Behavioral Design of the Northwest Regional Offices of The Federal Aviation Administration*

Figure 1. The new building for the FAA, Los Angeles. (Sam A. Sloan photo)

*Sloan's Methods
Are Tested*

Sam A. Sloan's methods (see "Life in the Office") were tested when his People Space Architecture Company was commissioned to design behaviorally the new Northwest Regional Offices of the Federal Aviation Administration through a contract with General Services Administration. Robert Sommer, Dennis E. Green, and the author acted as Sloan's consultants.

The first meeting of this design team lasted four and a half days, with pauses only to sleep and eat; some of us didn't know each other very well when we started, and we had never worked together as a team before, but by the end of this first marathon session, we knew each other much better and were working well together.

For any interdisciplinary team to be effective, some sort of initial consciousness raising session such as this is absolutely necessary, though some teams omit the procedure. It is the author's conviction that the later effectiveness of this team could not have occurred if this session had not been held in this way.

The first day was spent almost entirely inspecting and photographing the FAA offices in use at that time, in order to get visual evidence of how people worked and to identify some of the problems. Photography is most important as a behavioral design tool, and during this design process it proved to be very useful. We did not have to depend entirely on hastily written notes, and careful study of our "before" photos revealed problems and design opportunities which might otherwise have been overlooked.

The members of the team thus formed felt that offices must be designed to satisfy the wants and desires of people. We abhor the designer on an ego trip, who functions in the mode of the archetypal Scandinavian "form giver," imposing a design straitjacket on the luckless workers from a lofty position on high. Frequently this procedure results in a uniformity which, while it may be aesthetically pleasing to the designer, does not involve the workers or necessarily satisfy their needs, since they have no chance to share their views. Dennis Green has refined the philosophy of the team in a ten-point statement that he calls "User Participation: The Power of the Process." In putting the team's philosophy into effect, we hope to:

1. Relieve the worker's potential anxiety that results from meeting the unknown

2. Act as a self-actualizing process, in which creative activity is stressed as normal rather than abnormal

3. Produce a physical design more related to the balance of the worker's aspired values, desired values, and actual values

4. Create a setting in which a total range of values and preferences can be uncovered and in which the employee's point of view can be shown as a positive force in the design process

5. Provide a more democratic climate and an emphasis on individual responsibility as an important ethical base

6. Create an awareness of what the design process is and provide practical experience for the participant that can be applied in a wide range of activities

7. Dispel the employee's idea that "nobody cares about how I feel and therefore I'm probably not worth very much"

8. Arrive at a much better relationship between artifacts and individual human beings' ergonomic fit

9. Deal realistically and openly with conflict and resolve it through positive complementarity rather than negativistic compromise

10. Provide a logical framework in which interdisciplinary actions can complement each other rather than contend for dominance

Green also originated the "social water hole" theory of how an office actually works, and he has applied this theory to practical design. He feels that, in addition to its utilitarian aspects:

The office is also a vital human gathering place where people congregate not only to perform a work task, but also to share their daily experiences. In today's office environment, we can find people as much concerned about their own personal problems and aspirations as they are about the routine work tasks. Discussion for the day often centers not around work itself, but about the individual accomplishments and tragedies of the worker and his family and friends. Even political and religious haggling competes with the functional activities of regular work flow.

Green points out that the meeting and gathering places of the past—the marketplace, the town hall, the church, mosque, temple, or synagogue, and the village fountain or "water hole"—no longer function as they once did, if they are even still in existence. In an impersonal urban society the office now assumes the social role that these gathering places once had. He believes that unless individual social needs are satisfied by user participation in the design process, the value of design cannot rise above the merely functional, remaining largely mechanical and cosmetic.

Design Procedure   There were approximately four hundred employees of the Northwest Region of the Federal Aviation Administration in Seattle, Washington. The project of designing offices for them tested the hypothesis that people working in an office can participate in designing their own working environments with confidence and direction. Their individual physical, social, and territorial requirements, determined by adroit questioning and observation, can be translated into design issues and requirements with the aid of a computer and can then be woven into the total design. However, the usual communications survey is not enough.

To accurately assess the contemporary needs, the design team determined that the investigation of seventy-four design issues or requirements identified by a careful examination would provide the necessary data. This data would be used not only for the meaningful development and arrangements of working spaces but also for each individual's selection of artifacts and tools as an integral part of his or her participation in the design of his or her own work station. Before specifically investigating the seventy-four items, we found it necessary to evaluate the FAA's previous facilities to identify workers' environmental concerns and also to provide the design team with a basis for comparison of workers' reactions to the new offices. After implementation, this same analysis of environmental quality could be made to ascertain the effects of carefully devised individual research and user participation in design on the actual quality of the built environment. The initial questionnaire and its results appear in Figure 1.

From the results of the questionnaire, completed by the 185 employees then working, it was possible to make certain gross physical assessments of the existing FAA offices. The facilities had poor to bad acoustics, fair to poor air temperature and comfort, good to fair lighting, fair space and furnishings, and fair to poor equipment.

After completion and tabulation of the first questionnaire, we held interviews that included a more detailed and individualized seven-page questionnaire. It provided enough information on each individual so that

▓ MAJORITY RESPONSE   ◣ SECONDARY RESPONSE

This is your opportunity to help us do a better job of planning facilities. Please give us your best opinion of the following list of items in this room by making an appropriate check (✔) on the rating lines. And if you rate something on the poor side, try to tell us what the problem is.

THE CHARACTERISTIC BEING EVALUATED

EXCELLENT GOOD FAIR POOR BAD

WHAT IS THE PROBLEM?

SOUND
Overall sound quality of work station
Ability to hear/be heard
Noise isolation from outdoors
Noise isolation between work stations
Other sound considerations (specify)

CLIMATE
Overall climate quality of work station
Freshness of air
Temperature of air
Draft-free-ness of air
Orientation to exterior walls/windows
Other climate considerations (specify)

LIGHTING
Overall lighting quality of work station
Light from windows
Room lighting
Color of walls, floors, etc.
Glare-free-ness of surfaces
Other lighting considerations (specify)

SPACE
Overall "space" quality of work station
Length, width, & height of work station
Arrangement of furniture
Work surface height & size
Other "space" considerations (specify)
Floor coverings

EQUIPMENT
Overall quality of equipment
Comfort of furniture
Facilities to store garments
Facilities to store supplies
Other equipment

COMMENTS: Perhaps we have missed something in the above list that you'd like to comment on. Please do so below or on the back of this questionnaire. We want to know in what ways this building "turns you on"—or off!

Figure 2. Synthesis Sheet

acute needs could be identified and then checked through cross-analysis on a computer. These acute needs are flags that warn the designer to check out the other issues within the same category. Thus, when Mary Jones reveals an acute need for privacy, the designer can check her answers to questions on various types of privacy needs—audial, visual, security, or smoking. In this way the answers from the questionnaire and interview become design tools to enable the designer to satisfy individual human needs.

In addition to the privacy criteria, the seventy-four design issues and requirements analyzed included the following:

1. Personal proximity needs on a highly social to antisocial scale; color preferences—bright, medium, or none; territorial needs; motility or mobility characteristics; hierarchical orientation; aggressive-nonaggressive traits; need for living plants; extent of disablement, if any; acuteness of sight and hearing; sensitivity to temperature change, noise, and visual distraction; adequacy of artifacts and tools such as desks, files, chairs, tables, wall-mounted items, machines, and storage cabinets.

2. Maintenance: volume of waste and dirt; extent of interior and exterior traffic.

3. Reuse preference for specific artifacts and tools.

4. Requirements for group work and social space.

5. Comfort ratings for seating and work surfaces.

Simultaneously with this part of the study, the widest possible range of artifacts and tools was developed within space and budget limitations. In this selection process heavy emphasis was placed on the ergonomic characteristics of the artifacts offered so that, as the workers change, the artifacts or tools can be adjusted to the requirements of successive users.

In an unused section of a hangar near the new facilities, each individual designed his or her own work station with a member of the design team. Each piece of furniture offered was available so that a work station could be arranged in its actual pattern to verify its workability. The floor was carpeted and a ceiling installed to simulate that in the new building.

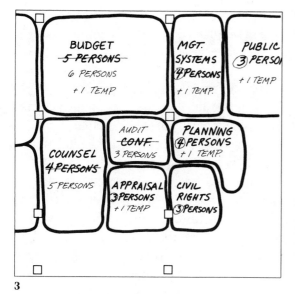

3

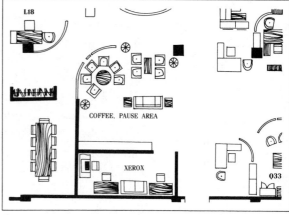

4

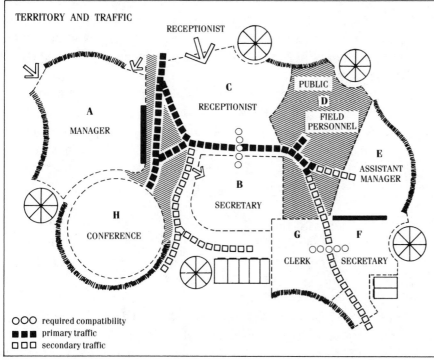

5

Figures 3, 4, and 5.
Stages of the development of the interior space planning at FAA-Seattle. (Courtesy of Sam A. Sloan)

Typical furniture combinations were developed for executive, supervisory, secretarial, and technician tasks at each work station. This was an attempt to reflect the personal requirements of the individual occupying the station.

Simultaneously, group space was developed with a proper compromise between individual and group requirements. The major design issues of group orientation are territory and traffic. Personable people can provide a fence for less sociable workmates, and people needing privacy should be placed so that they will not easily be disturbed.

In the design of group space and individual work stations, we attempt to actualize the basic needs of each worker. Each artifact and tool was run through an ergonomic or human-factors sieve to determine whether or not it met the necessary criteria for comfort and safety. Desk surfaces were checked so that they are glarefree and reflect properly to permit the worker to concentrate without creating problems. Chair fabrics must be not only long-wearing and easily cleaned but also woven so that the surface provides necessary ventilation. Chair heights and backs must be adjustable so that they can accommodate the expected range of workers. Different sizes and shapes of work surfaces, as well as varying drawer combinations, are offered so that task requirements can be individually satisfied.

With thirteen desks, fifteen chairs, six credenzas, sixteen colors of fabric, a full range of telephone colors, and even six different in and out baskets available for each person's choice, the power of selection was real, and was exercised. These choices are not just the means of satisfying personal whims; by making these choices the worker participated in the design of his or her own workplace.

Research

User satisfaction with the built and furnished office space determined the success of the design process. It was then deemed valuable to conduct post-occupancy evaluation of the success (or failure) of the self-actualization process effort. Moreover, it was decided that comparative analysis of another similar office design, using the more traditional methods without user involvement, would help to document reasons for considering a change in professional design processes for federally commissioned office space. The Western Regional Office of the Federal Aviation Administration in Hawthorne (Los Angeles) was selected for comparative evaluation inasmuch as it was about the same size and accommodated a comparable number of employees as the Seattle FAA headquarters building.

A survey was conducted in both offices after one year of occupancy. Office personnel were asked in a fourteen-page questionnaire to compare their new working conditions with their old ones. Approximately 80 percent of the people tested cooperated. The data were analyzed according to the chi square test for statistical relevance and found to have less than a 5 percent degree of relevance by chance. What follows is the synthesis of that research effort undertaken by GSA and the People Space Architecture Company in behalf of the FAA.

Fourteen Issues Affecting User Satisfaction

Building Aesthetics

This particular design issue (as a rule) demands so much priority from management and the professional design consultant that it virtually eliminates all but intuitive gestures to other important issues. Yet, the user populace of Seattle gave an overall voice of 65 percent satisfaction with their building, while in Los Angeles only 51 percent were satisfied with the aesthetic quality of their structure. The American Institute of Architects, on the other hand, has given repeated acclaim to the Los Angeles building and refused to give recognition to the Seattle structure. The reason given by an AIA jury member refusing to award design excellence to the Seattle building was the residential quality or "lack of discipline and control of the interiors," which, interestingly enough, was the very reason why the Seattle user population voiced greater approval of their building. They were given interior choices, and they exercised the privilege with relish.

It suffices to say that the building aesthetic as a design issue ranks much higher on the priority scale for management and architects than it does for the employees in a building. Furthermore, as the individual users considered the building aesthetic on a more personal scale, it became apparent that they were much more critical—voicing 88 percent approval of the overall quality of the Seattle building, 67 percent approval of the exterior skin of the structure, and only 41 percent satisfaction with the aesthetic quality of the entrance lobby.

Sound/Noise   The acoustics of a building have become a genuine concern for building designers in the twentieth century. Until recently, however, the effort has been to curtail and contain sound rather than to manufacture ambient sounds into the working environment. The "white sound system" was placed in the Seattle structure to create an ambient overtone in an effort to mask irritating noises. The results of this $40,000 effort were disappointing to say the least in that Seattle users gave only 37 percent approval of the acoustical quality of their space, a mere 1 percent improvement over their previous office spaces where six to eight trains practically drove through the structure on a daily scheduled basis.

It is interesting to note that people with long tenure in their present jobs were much more critical of the sound/noise problem than others. Another interesting factor is the apparent difference between women and men in their tolerance of noise. Females were less critical of noise than were their male counterparts. Older persons seemed to tolerate noise in their working environment less than the younger workers. The highest degree of tolerance was shown in the 20 to 30 age group. Administrators were far more critical and less tolerant of noise in their working environment than nonadministrators.

Climatic Comfort   As a general rule approximately one-third of the cost of building is in the mechanical systems designed to provide climatic comfort to the occupants. For years designers have thought that the issue of climatic comfort was the most critical of all design issues if building occupants were to be satisfied.

In both the Los Angeles structure and the Seattle structure there were highly controlled, well-balanced mechanical systems with little variance in temperature or humidity. In Seattle 54 percent of the people voiced satisfaction with the climatic comfort while only 40 percent were satisfied in Los Angeles. Women showed much greater sensitivity to the climatic variables than men. They expressed on a per capita basis nearly twice the degree of discomfort as the men. Of note is the measurably higher degree of satisfaction expressed by those in Seattle who participated in the interior design process even though they neither considered nor had any effect upon the design of the mechanical systems.

On a humorous note: taller people expressed greater satisfaction than shorter people—presumably because heat rises and consequently it's warmer up where they are. More seriously, people who sat close to windows expressed a much greater degree of satisfaction with the interior climate. Yet the greatest range of temperature variation during a day's occupancy of a structure occurs at the window wall.

Light Adequacy

More research has been done in lighting and its effects on the uses of office spaces than any other design problem. Yet the required lighting levels in America are far above most other countries. When this research was carried out the "president's war on energy waste" was under way and every other light fixture was blacked out in the Los Angeles structure. The measured light levels in the Los Angeles building varied from 200 foot-candles at the window-wall to 50 foot-candles in the core offices to as low as 15 foot-candles in the corridors.

On the whole, users of both buildings expressed amazing tolerance to the lighting levels. Men expressed a slightly greater tolerance than women to lighting conditions. The greatest expression of dissatisfaction came from those with more than ten years' tenure at their present jobs.

Of note once again is the greater satisfaction expressed by those who participated in the Seattle interior design process even though they neither considered nor had any effect on the lighting systems. Very active participants gave 92 percent approval to the lighting, while moderately active participants gave 78 percent approval and slightly active participants 74 percent approval.

Space Quality

Each person evaluates space in his own way, with his own set of priorities intrinsic to his hierarchical position in the office, physical location in the building, and tenure in his job. Space is good if it "feels" good, bad if it "feels" bad. Oddly enough, the only way to find out how people feel about space is to ask them. We asked about the length, width, and height of personal and group spaces as well as about the arrangement and surface orientation of the furnishings.

The response by users indicated an apparent overall dissatisfaction with space quality. Mainly, they complained about the openness and the lack of personal "turf" delineation. The space quality in both Seattle and Los Angeles, however, improved substantially from the old quarters to the new. Women were more discerning about space quality than were the men. Middle-age people were more satisfied than older or younger people.

Once again those who participated actively in the Seattle interior design program registered an 82 percent satisfaction with their space quality, while the overall average for Seattle users was only 67 percent.

Equipment

The ergonomic fit of an office particularly depends on the satisfaction of individual users with the equipment they must use daily. Questions were based on user satisfaction with desks, chairs, and credenzas as well as with typewriters, storage units, and the actual convenience of "convenience" outlets.

It was initially thought that a pattern of less or more satisfaction with the equipment might develop in direct relationship to a person's height, weight, and physical condition. This did not prove to be the case. It appeared that lighter people in Seattle were less satisfied with their equipment than heavy people; however, that trend reversed itself in Los Angeles. Taller people in Seattle appeared to register a higher degree of satisfaction with their equipment reflecting the greater adjustability of it. However, once again, the Los Angeles responses did not underwrite that pattern.

In Seattle every user was offered the opportunity to select his or her own desk chair while in Los Angeles the same chair was given to everyone. To obtain the chairs in the marketplace to allow a choice in Seattle we had difficulty finding what we wanted.

For instance, the range of adjustment of seat height for a stenographic chair should be from 13⅔ inches to 20⅔ inches or more. The closest fit we could find in a decent quality available steno chair was a range of seat height adjustment from 15½ inches to 20½ inches. The chairs we selected had a separate seat and back; the back itself was not only adjustable in height but also swiveled vertically to follow the user's curve in the lumbar region or the small of the back. These physical and mechanical characteristics were probably important in the measured feelings of steno chair adequacy, which turned out to be much greater in Seattle than in Los Angeles.

The non-steno desk chair, or the executive swivel chair as it is colloquially known, showed easily discernable features to explain the measured difference in adequacy between Seattle and Los Angeles. The non-steno chairs bought at Los Angeles did not have a lumbar support adequate enough to ensure comfort; this resulted in early complaints and a standard purchase order had to be made up for buying separate additional cushions to make up for the deficiency.

On the other hand, the non-steno chairs we specified for Seattle had an invisible lumbar support for the small of the back that basically consisted of a block of much firmer foam in that specific region. When the user sits in this chair, the user depresses the softer foam elsewhere but the firmer foam in the lumbar region does not depress as much and becomes the lumbar support.

By coincidence, the chair we specified at Seattle was also bid at Los Angeles and we were told that the difference in bid prices between the lumbar-defective chair bought and the Seattle one that works well was exactly 25 cents on chairs that were bid at about $100 each. The extra cushions cost much more than that and the discomfort interrupted work and caused distress as well.

There were marked differences among the feelings of adequacy of the desk at the two offices. Seattle people showed up as believing that their desks were more nearly adequate, even though we were frustrated again

Figure 6. This is the comfortable chair used in Seattle; it didn't need extra cushions. (Steelcase photo)

in our specifying process at Seattle because we could not find available the kit of parts we needed to make sure that each desk was fitted both to the individual person and to that individual's task. We also wanted a desk that would be adjustable in height in a minimum range of 26 to 31 inches, as indicated by the ergonomic literature for the main part of the desk, and a separately adjustable typing portion for the steno desks that would adjust from 21 to 27 inches in height as a minimum range, as is also indicated in the ergonomic literature. Such adjustability was not available in the marketplace at that time; the only desks we could find showed little beyond the usual one or one and one-half inch height adjustments, and unfortunately, the main and typing portions of the steno desks were only adjustable together, not separately.

However, we were able to do things in our desk specification that may have helped in making the Seattle people feel better about the adequacy of their desks. The first thing was that we made sure that the tops of the work surfaces at Seattle were not glaring; we did this of course by specifying matte or dull surfaces that do not glare.

The second thing was that we made sure that the work surface tops only reflected between 30 percent and 50 percent of the light that hits them, as is recommended in the ergonomic literature.

The third thing we did was to try as best we could with the extremely limited options available to try to size the work surface to meet individual work requirements. We were only able to do this in a limited way because not really that many sizes and configurations were available in the marketplace.

The fourth thing we did should be routine in every work surface and desk specification process—we of course tried to meet the storage requirements by varying types, sizes, and numbers of drawers beneath the work surface.

Now for some reactions to another movable item—the screens. The overall sound quality of the work stations was perceived as better at Seattle than at Los Angeles. This was a separate question on the questionnaire, but the answers to six other associated questions about ability to hear and be heard, noise isolation from the outdoors and from other work stations, as well as freedom from distracting noises and freedom from distracting conversations—the answers to all these strongly support the measured greater satisfaction with the overall sound quality of the work stations at Seattle.

Satisfaction is also indicated to be substantially greater at Seattle in terms of visual privacy—in fact the percentage of respondents in the excellent and good categories on both audial and visual privacy is almost doubled at Seattle over Los Angeles. We feel that the differences in indicated satisfaction may be due to better screen specification at Seattle in terms of ability to absorb sound, and also in terms of height and size.

We also feel that the careful development of group work space—who is next to whom and how far from whom—that put the screens in their carefully plotted places may have helped to produce a sound and sight environment in Seattle that was perceived by the users as better.

Color/Texture

Building aesthetics and color/texture are the two issues normally given the most attention in the more traditional design processes. It is not surprising that the overall expression of satisfaction is higher in Los Angeles than in Seattle for two reasons. One reason is the overall control of color use in the Los Angeles offices with one floor yellow, another blue, and so on—a homogeneous blend of color. The other reason is the transition from the tremendous mess in the original quarters in Hawthorne to the crisp new quarters of the new building.

Seattle people were disappointed with the architecturally avant garde, raw, exposed concrete walls of their building. The registration of satisfaction with the use of color and color combinations at a personal level in Seattle was very high; however, managers and supervisors registered higher satisfaction levels with the use of color and color combinations than their clerical counterparts in both cities. The big surprise with this issue came in the participation responses. People who actively participated in Seattle voiced less satisfaction than those who did not actively participate. This was one of only two issues where participation in the design process did not create a higher degree of acceptance and satisfaction with the final results of the planning.

Space Arrangement

Questions for this issue were based on the relationships of people and the ease of movement between people. Nearness to support facilities and other conveniences also served as a basis for evaluation of this issue.

The expression of satisfaction with this issue was well below the overall average of satisfaction on all other issues. The Seattle people expressed 50 percent satisfaction and the Los Angeles people only 43 percent satisfaction with space arrangements. Those with longer tenure both at their present job and in government service gave substantially lower ratings than those with less tenure.

In both cases, the workforces acknowledged an improvement in space arrangement from their previous quarters where there was less openness than in their new quarters.

Communication

The ability to communicate is a paramount issue in offices. In another study done in an insurance office building, People Space Architecture Company documented that each individual conducted an average of sixteen conversations per hour, or 38 percent of his or her working time. The ease with which these work and social interactions can be conducted provides a good measure of the functionability of the office space.

Little variation was registered from the overall average by any of the types of people other than the substantially higher satisfaction levels recorded by those who participated actively in the design process. Active participants in the Seattle design process voiced 81 percent approval of their ability to communicate as compared to an average 50 percent expression of satisfaction by others.

Privacy

Privacy as a design issue is an almost impossible criterion to satisfy for most individuals. In both Los Angeles and Seattle the previous office structures afforded a greater degree of privacy. The open plan office is virtually impossible to make satisfactory to people on the basis of privacy.

Visual and acoustical privacy are quite different in character and must be dealt with separately in the design process. Nevertheless a person evaluates privacy in an overview without separating those elements. Privacy is also the pinnacle of all personal requirements in the design game of compromises between individual and corporate needs.

Women expressed a greater need for privacy than men. This would appear to overturn an age-old concept that men need more privacy than women in office situations. The very old and the very young of an office workforce indicated greater need for privacy and less satisfaction with the privacy conditions offered in both regional headquarters buildings. It has always been thought by many designers that the longer a person serves a department or holds tenure at his particular job the more privacy requirement he develops. This research tends to refute that concept, showing that people new at their jobs have a greater need for privacy. They expressed less satisfaction with the privacy conditions that prevailed than those with longer tenure.

Those participating actively in the design process registered a higher degree of satisfaction, or perhaps it would be called tolerance of their privacy conditions. A truly strange pattern revealed shows that the respondents spending less time actually occupying their work stations indicated less satisfaction and voiced more criticism about their lack of privacy than their fellow workmates spending more time at their desks.

Personalization

The personalization of a person's territory goes hand in hand with privacy. The ability to express oneself in the total fabric of the environment constitutes this issue. Management policies are directly related to this issue inasmuch as management decides and regulates the degree of change allowed.

In Los Angeles management was very restrictive about personal items displayed as opposed to a more relaxed attitude by Seattle management. The overall average satisfaction with the personalization of the environment was very low in both buildings, each showing a decline in satisfaction with the transition from the old offices to the new. The under-20 and the over-60 age groups were once again the most critical, while managers naturally registered higher satisfaction levels with their policies than those under them. In a seemingly repetitive pattern, those with more than ten years' tenure at their present jobs were substantially less satisfied than others.

Those actively participating in the Seattle design process registered a higher degree of satisfaction (48 percent) with their ability to personalize their work stations than those who were moderately (36 percent) or slightly active (11 percent) in the design process.

Management Policy

It would seem natural that a move from offices with random spaces and a general lack of discipline into new quarters with carefully delineated spaces and a feeling of discipline would precipitate a noticeable drop in satisfaction with management policies. Indeed that was the reaction of both the Los Angeles and the Seattle FAA workforces in this research project.

This was one issue on which participation in the design decision process had little effect. In fact, those who did not participate at all in the Seattle office design process registered the same degree of satisfaction as those who participated actively.

Government employees display a general shyness in their criticism of their superiors in research questionnaires. The comments we fielded "off the record" indicated a covertly developed counterculture in the non-management workers. This was particularly apparent in Los Angeles where stringent measures were taken to "keep it clean" in the office environment. The workforce viewed the "Mr. Clean Award" given monthly as a game played by management. Several departments tried in earnest not to win the award.

Job Performance

Shyness is an unknown trait when you query a government employee about his ability to perform his job. Job performance averaged a full 20 percent over other ratings given in response to our questionnaire.

Of interest, however, is the fact that the ability to perform the work tasks only improved 7 percent in Seattle and in Los Angeles "no improvement" was registered. This makes it pertinent to ask the question: Why a new building at all? Indeed, the answer is neither simple nor clear. While the Los Angeles workforce registered a 14 percent improvement in overall environmental qualities, they concurrently indicated "no improvement" in their ability to perform their work tasks. Similarly, the Seattle workforce gave a rating of 12 percent overall improvement in environmental conditions while indicating only a 7 percent increase with their ability to perform their required tasks in the new offices.

Building Safety

There are two types of response to the question of building safety. One is the response to actual safety in accordance with requirements for fire codes and exiting, health standards, and climatic controls. The other type of response is an intuitive response of perceived safety in a building.

Most interesting of all responses to this issue is the marked drop in perceived safety indicated by users in Los Angeles. They left a series of quonset huts labeled as "firetraps" to move into a modern high-rise (six-story) office building. Their indicated satisfaction with the building's safety dropped from 50 percent to 33 percent. Two out of three people feel unsafe in the new Los Angeles FAA office headquarters structure. This is a serious problem that deserves further attention.

Once again, people participating actively in the design process registered substantially higher levels of satisfaction with the building's safety than those who had less participation in the design process. Heavier people felt less safe than lighter people. Males felt slightly more safe than females. The over-60 employees registered a substantially lower sense of satisfaction with building safety than the under-60 employees.

Age

Forty-four percent of the Los Angeles workforce is between 30 and 50 years of age. Exactly one-half of the Seattle workforce is between 30 and 50 years of age. Consistently, this age group finds less fault with and shows more appreciation for the environmental amenities afforded them by the organization. The under-20 age group represents only 3 to 4 percent of the workforce and appears to be the most demanding and dissatisfied element of the workforce. The over-60 sector of the office population also represents a generally disenchanted minority regarding environmental satisfaction.

The older element of the workforce in Seattle showed a definite psychological decline in acceptance of environmental conditions regarding the move from the old quarters to the new. An example is the 75 percent satisfied response to the privacy conditions in the old structure, with that action dwindling to a 13 percent satisfaction response to privacy conditions within the new structure.

Gender

There appears to be little overall difference in the way that females judge their environment as opposed to males. A few items seem worth mentioning. Women seem to tolerate noise a little better while showing less tolerance for climatic variations. The female worker is generally more critical of her environment, grading lower on most issues, while still maintaining an almost direct proportion to her male counterpart in the before and after evaluations.

Women rate themselves higher in job performance, are less comfortable with building safety, and indicate a need for more privacy than men in their working environment.

Men are less discerning about the quality of their space and their equipment as well as the color and texture qualities of their environment. The one issue that men seem to show more concern about than women is that of management policies as they relate to use of the environment.

Job Type

In both Seattle and Los Angeles the manager-supervisor echelon of the workforce indicated an overall 10 percent greater satisfaction with the working conditions than the technical-clerical personnel. The nonmanagerial types were more critical of building aesthetics, space quality, and color and arrangement conditions.

It was surprising that exactly one-half of the employees considered themselves "supervisors." Another 18 percent considered themselves managerial in Seattle. Analysis of the work, however, would show that the average employee of the FAA deals more on a one-to-one basis with the public than employees of most other governmental agencies. Consequently more self-supervision is required of them than of most office workers.

Collar Color

Approximately one out of three FAA employees consider themselves "administrative" in their execution of daily activities. There is little difference in the overall satisfaction expressed by nonadministrative vis-à-vis administrative evaluation of the working environment.

Administrative types were less tolerant of noise and in Seattle rated themselves considerably lower in satisfaction with their ability to perform their jobs. Oddly enough, it was the nonadministrative types who complained most about the "lack of privacy."

Tenure in Government

An amazing 76 percent of the Los Angeles workforce have been in government service for ten years or longer. Sixty-seven percent of Seattle's workforce have been bureaucrats for over ten years. This does not, however, seem to affect their degree of criticism or level of satisfaction with their working environment. Those who have been in government service between two years and six years seem to indicate a consistently higher degree of satisfaction with their working environment

Tenure of FAA Employment

Once again it seems amazing that over 50 percent of the workforce have been with the parent organization for more than ten years. This does not, however, seem to develop a more critical or less satisfied worker. In fact, those with less than one year's tenure with the FAA are more critical and less satisfied on nearly every issue concerning their working environment.

Tenure at Present Job

There is a strong indication that tenure in a particular task has a directly proportionate relation to environmental satisfaction. Satisfaction with the working conditions seems to start quite low and grow to a peak that occurs between four and six years, then drops again to a lower level. One of the few issues that conflict with that pattern is the privacy issue in Los Angeles. This could be attributed to the move into a new "open office" environmental situation.

Less than one in four employees has been at his or her present work task more than four years. It would be interesting to know how many persons were promoted within their own task oriented workgroup as compared to promotions laterally into new task areas.

Time Spent at Desk

An average 60 percent of the FAA workforce in these two regional offices indicated that they spend 100 percent of their time at their desks. There is virtually no variation between the satisfaction results in general as compared to those registered by this occupation majority.

A single note of interest regarding this issue is the fact that those in Seattle who spend the least time at their desks are the most demanding of privacy and the least satisfied with everything except building safety.

Proximity to Windows

Exterior orientation was an early issue recognized as important to many people by our design and research team. In the Seattle design process special effort to ferret out and satisfy those who truly needed the exterior orientation produced a degree of difference in their response in regard to satisfaction with the environment. The analysis was made by examining those working within ten feet of the windows. The difference was a 17 percent greater expression of satisfaction with environmental issues by Seattleites sitting close to the windows than by their Los Angeles counterparts.

Those along the window were far more satisfied and much less critical of the climatic comfort of the environment than others. Those farthest from the windows, usually along the inner core of the structure, expressed greater satisfaction with privacy conditions. People closest to the windows gave higher ratings regarding the "quality" of their space. Another important point is the high degree of acceptance to light adequacy given by people along the windows.

One group, more than twenty working together, informally told us that if they could not have their workplaces next to windows they would quit their jobs. Somewhat surprised by this reaction, we had a discussion with them and found the group to be composed entirely of qualified aircraft pilots, both active and inactive; they wanted to know the weather visually at all times.

Physical Condition

Only 5 percent of the Seattle respondents indicated any physical impairment. In Los Angeles 6 percent indicated they had physical disabilities.

In Seattle the disabled felt more unsafe in their building. Further, they expressed "no satisfaction" with privacy conditions although it is difficult to know whether or not they required more privacy because of their disability. However, they were more complimentary about the lighting adequacy. Those in Seattle who were handicapped were given special attention during the design process.

In Los Angeles an expression of dissatisfaction with the equipment was registered by those who considered themselves disabled. Those with walking problems were severely critical of privacy conditions. Oddly enough, those with sight problems and hearing problems expressed dissatisfaction with the sound and noise conditions, while those with hearing problems expressed approval on the same issue. From a research standpoint we can only conclude that a little deafness is helpful in the "open-space" planned office.

Weight

About 50 percent of the respondents weighed between 150 and 200 pounds. There were absolutely no departures from the norm registered on any issue by these people.

The only significant response by lighter people (under 100 pounds) made in concert between Seattle and Los Angeles was a lower expression of satisfaction with building safety.

The only departure from the overall average response made by heavier (over 200 pounds) persons was the expression of greater acceptance of management policies. Might viewing this fact from a different vantage point reveal that management policies are being determined by people over 200 pounds?

Height

The height of an individual produced little variation in response to the environmental issues. Generally the people under five feet in height responded with a much lower degree of satisfaction on nearly all issues than others did.

Of interest is the fact that most equipment and furnishings are built for the "average" person, 5' 5" to 6' 0" in height and 150 to 200 pounds in weight. In Seattle, these people did in fact give the greatest expression of satisfaction with their equipment, but in Los Angeles the "most satisfied" included the over six foot group along with the average person of average weight and height.

Comments and Conclusions

It was impossible to tie down, in either Los Angeles or Seattle, actual building and furnishing costs, moving expenses, and down-time due to the move. The records for these elements are distributed through several layers of bureaucratic agencies with the cost amortized over several fiscal years. It would require an expensive audit to ferret out this information. It was decided to forgo this portion of the exercise.

Some general comments regarding the space planning process and costs might help to answer the question: "Was the Seattle effort very expensive?" The answer is that these methods were not expensive, even though they were comprehensive. The cost ranged from one-quarter to one-half of the cost of traditional methods of design.

Since user involvement in the design process produces greater satisfaction to the user and is less expensive to the agency, it would seem reasonable to expect this design procedure to be used in planning all government office buildings; however, the canons of tradition in the design and construction industry are hard to change. Most architectural firms specializing in government work would be unable to qualify for contracts requiring sociometric and psychometric investigation as an integral part of the design process.

Other points to discuss are the questions of: "What effect does a new building have upon user-satisfaction with his work environment?" and: "Does the new building affect the ability of the employee to perform his work task?" It would appear from this research that a new building, while it may solve other aesthetic, functional, and economic problems for the agency in question, does not substantially improve the ability of the workforce to perform their job tasks. Neither does a new structure create a substantial increase in satisfaction with the fourteen design issues we have investigated.

In Los Angeles a new structure was built for the FAA using a traditional Beaux Arts method of design and construction. In Seattle a modern, user-advocacy design process was employed to space plan offices in a new structure built for the FAA by the county government.

A comparison of the responses to our research questionnaire given by the two workforces shows that satisfaction with the work environment and job productivity are not substantially improved by moving to these new buildings. However, our research does prove that satisfaction with the work environment and job productivity are substantially improved when office personnel are included in the design process as they were in Seattle. Comparison shows that being included in the design process is what makes the difference in the attitude the user population displays towards our nation's office buildings.

New buildings are very expensive to build in today's inflated construction industry. The fact that new buildings do not improve worker attitudes, which was brought out by the research report, may not be stimulating to the nation's economy or to the construction industry, but it should be of interest to the nation's taxpayers, currently overburdened with the high cost of regulatory agencies in our government.

Participation

The participation factor is not really valid as research data for the Los Angeles respondents inasmuch as there was no control of the administration of the design process. Only 2 percent of the Los Angeles workforce said they had participated actively. Seventy percent said they had no participation in the process. The comparative differences, however, point out that those with "no participation" in Los Angeles scored nearly every issue substantially lower than those participating to any degree. The prognosis here is that this very difference accounts for the 12 percent less overall expression of satisfaction with the working environment registered by the Los Angeles workforce.

Our results indicated that very active participation in the design process improves the satisfaction level while maintaining a low dissatisfaction response. Interestingly enough "no participation" develops identical satisfaction and dissatisfaction responses as "moderate participation."

The most important piece of information in this study for designers and managers is that "slight participation" in the space design and furniture selection process elicits the lowest levels of satisfaction and the greatest expression of dissatisfaction. The message seems to be: "If you are going to get involved, make it honest and meaningful!"

Aftermath

However, there is more. We are a "radical design group." According to T. George Harris in *New York* magazine:[1]

> When a radical design group consulted Seattle white-collar workers about office furniture and layout for a new Federal Aviation Administration building, morale and satisfaction soared. Compared with FAA workers in a fancier building in Los Angeles, Sommer reports, the Seattle workers were significantly happier, more pleased with everything—from their jobs to the air conditioning system. . . .
>
> There, variety has now been institutionalized so that the regulations writers will have trouble taking control back from the office workers; a new employee can go off to a storage room to pick his or her desk and chair from a motley inventory. . . .
>
> All the evidence simply points to a new role for architects and designers: to work as consultants to the actual users of office space, rather than pushing on with their snobs' role as builders of monuments to themselves and as promoters for the hard-edged image of corporate clients.

Acknowledgment

The help of Sam A. Sloan, President, People Space Architecture Company, in gathering the material for and writing this case history is gratefully acknowledged.

[1]Harris, T. George, "Psychology of the New York Work Space," *New York*, vol. 10, no. 44, pp. 51–54, October 31, 1977. (T. George Harris is the former editor of *Psychology Today*.)

Case Study 6 — *Comprehensive Interior Design Process: GSA's 6100 Corridor*

Building on the procedures used by Sam Sloan and his team for the design of the Federal Aviation Administration's Northwest Regional Office in Seattle, Hunter/Miller + Associates, of Alexandria, Virginia, carried the office design process to a new pinnacle of comprehensiveness with their "Comprehensive Interior Environmental Design Project—6100 Corridor GSA Central Office Building." Both Sloan's project and the one done by Hunter/Miller + Associates were done under contract to the General Services Administration.

The Design Process

How did such an all-inclusive design process come to happen? Well, the instigator was Jay Solomon, at that time the administrator of GSA. He made it happen because he very much wanted it to happen, and you have to know that the 6100 Corridor not only contained Jay Solomon's own office but also the offices of his chief assistants and associates in the GSA; in other words, there are not any "Indians" on 6100, only chiefs and their satraps.

This made the process even more difficult, because in the user participation design process it is typically the chiefs who refuse to have anything to do with it; the peons are forced to fill out the questionnaires while the chief's secretary "does" the office.

True to form is this statement from Jeff Miller, president of Hunter/Miller + Associates:

Unfortunately, much of the data gathering process coincided with an unusually demanding period of time for the occupants of the corridor. Initially, user response to the questionnaire was poor; but, with the involvement and support of Mr. Solomon, eventually 95 percent of the users completed a questionnaire.

Hunter/Miller + Associates had done all the right things—even in the proper sequence. First, they created an HMA-GSA team so that no wires would get crossed. It consisted of Jeff Miller, Jerre Bradshaw, and Beth Baughman from HMA; and Richard Iselin, chief of Interior Planning, Public Buildings Service; Joel Rudick, chief of Interior Planning and Design, PBS-Central; and Kathryn Hindman, confidential assistant to Mr. Solomon, on the GSA side.

Then the data gathering "process began with a self-administered user questionnaire . . . which covered . . . work and paper flow, job satisfaction and satisfaction with the office environment" down to even minor items of furniture, as well as the arrangement of it. It included a self-inventory of furniture which in addition to listing each item, asked the respondent detailed questions about his/her satisfaction with all aspects of each item; it also asked respondents "to draw their 'ideal' work station" according to Jeff Miller.

After the questionnaires came back and after the data from them had been compiled, Hunter/Miller + Associates carefully observed the users at work and then "conducted extensive interviews with a majority of the occupants in order to clarify information uncovered in both observations and analysis of questionnaire data."

However, two things about the questionnaires made this project different from others and probably set the tone for cooperation and participation of the users in the design process:

1. They were *really* comprehensive.
2. They were written in plain, slangy language, not academese, designese, or bureaucratese.

Each person's questionnaire was forty-three pages long and divided into seven sections:

1. Administrative data
2. Existing work station
3. Work flow
4. Activities
5. Ideal work station

6. Satisfaction with environment
7. Job satisfaction

To get an idea of the language used and how really comprehensive the questions were, take a look at the section on the respondent's desk chair in the sample questionnaires.

After the questionnaires had been administered and returned, the information on them gave HMA a solid and comprehensive basis for interviewing each respondent to discuss needs and wants expressed on the questionnaires. The interviews were designed so that HMA could come up with concrete equipment and layout recommendations for every worker on the 6100 Corridor.

These interviews, summarized here in Jeff Miller's words, also gave HMA a chance to discuss the goals of the project and how they might be attained. One of the concerns uncovered in the interviews was that "users prefer working in private offices. They are not sure that they can adapt to open planning." Yet GSA management wanted open planning and "a plan that insures high visibility for employees." Therefore, HMA knew that they "must provide users with the same visual and acoustical privacy as was existent on the Corridor."

GSA management wanted to increase space utilization: "Users cited the need for adequate space as a major priority in the office environment." HMA solved this problem by recommending systems furniture with increased storage capabilities—vertically above work stations.

"Users noted noise control their number one priority in the office design." HMA then knew that they must have several alternate solutions ready for the final plan; they knew that they must keep noise at existing levels or below if the plan was to be satisfactory to the users.

Although HMA carefully measured light levels and found them acceptable, they found that "users currently supplement fluorescent ceiling light with decorative lamps"; HMA proposed an alternative task/ambiant lighting system.

Other concerns were noted and dealt with during the interviews, such as accessibility for the handicapped; security of both personal and government property; and the general appearance of the offices.

During this period of interviewing, HMA people made themselves available for discussion and answering questions from any user at definite times and in addition, kept user comment forms available at all times

Hunter/Miller +
Associates
Environmental Designers and Consultants

2
COMPREHENSIVE INTERIOR ENVIRONMENTAL DESIGN PROJECT
6100 Corridor - GSA Central Office Building
GSA Region 3 - Project Nó. 7492

Name: _____   **Date completed:** _____

COLOR/MATERIAL:

CONDITION:

◯ new   ◯ good   ◯ fair   ◯ not good   ◯ not usable (damaged)

REMARKS: Rate your present additional work surface and its efficiency.
If you have more than one additional work surface, designate which work
surface you are referring to.

◯ Really fits my needs well

◯ Work surface is adequate

◯ Work surface is inadequate for my needs

◯ Too small - I need a _____"Long x _____"Wide

◯ Too large - I need a _____"Long x _____"Wide

◯ Wrong type - I need a _____

◯ Not enough drawers/storage - I need the following
   drawers, _____

◯ I need lockable work surface storage

◯ I don't like its appearance

◯ It's hard to clean

◯ It doesn't offer any flexibility

◯ It's a safety hazard

◯ Other, describe _____

If you do not presently have additional work surface(s) but feel that
you need one, describe what you need and how you would use it.

B. Seating

1. Describe your present <u>desk chair</u> and indicate quantity (if more
    than one).

◯ **Armless posture chair**

   ◯ with wheels   ◯ swivels   ◯ tilts
   ◯ without wheels   ◯ does not swivel ◯ does not tilt

◯ **Armless chair**

   ◯ with wheels   ◯ swivels   ◯ tilts
   ◯ without wheels   ◯ does not swivel ◯ does not tilt

◯ **Arm Chair**

   ◯ with wheels   ◯ swivels   ◯ tilts
   ◯ without wheels   ◯ does not swivel ◯ does not tilt

◯ **High back executive chair**

   ◯ with wheels   ◯ swivels   ◯ tilts
   ◯ without wheels   ◯ does not swivel ◯ does not tilt

◯ **Other (describe)**

Hunter/Miller +
Associates
Environmental Designers and Consultants

2

COMPREHENSIVE INTERIOR ENVIRONMENTAL DESIGN . PROJECT
6100 Corridor - GSA Central Office Building
GSA Region 3 - Project No. 7492

Name: _____   Date completed: _____

The seat is _____" above the floor.

COLOR/MATERIAL:

CONDITION:

○ new   ○ good   ○ fair   ○ not good   ○ not usable (damaged)

REMARKS: Rate your present desk chair(s). If you have more than one
chair, designate which chair you are referring to.

○ really fits my needs well   ○ adequate

○ inadequate for my needs

    ○ needs wheels   ○ too wide

    ○ shouldn't have wheels   ○ it hurts my rear end

    ○ needs arms   ○ too small

    ○ shouldn't have arms   ○ too narrow

    ○ arms too high   ○ wrong type, I need a _____

    ○ arms too low   ○ seat too high, make it _____" lower

    ○ can't adjust seat height   ○ seat too low, make it _____" higher

    ○ it hurts my legs   ○ back too high, make it _____" lower

    ○ it hurts my back   ○ back too low, make it _____" higher

    ○ can't adjust back ○ height ○   ○ I don't like its appearance

            tension ○ position ○   ○ I don't like the finish/material,
                           should be _____

    ○ should tilt backward and forward

    ○ shouldn't tilt backward and forward   ○ hard to clean

    ○ should swivel totally around   ○ it doesn't offer any flexibility

    ○ shouldn't swivel totally around   ○ it's a safety hazard

    ○ too large   ○ other, describe _____

2. Describe your present guest chair(s) and indicate quantity (if
more than one).

    ○ Armless chair

        ○ with wheels   ○ swivels   ○ tilts

        ○ without wheels   ○ does not swivel ○ does not tilt

to make it easy for the inhabitants of the 6100 Corridor to give HMA design information and feedback.

Adjacency diagrams, including listings of support areas, were also developed and from the information obtained in the questionnaires and interviews, the very critical User Verification Forms were prepared. As you can see from the illustrations, these forms were a thorough and comprehensive listing of space and equipment needs of each user, even including physical classifications and handicaps.

However, the procedure connected with these forms provided that each user personally verify the information contained in them and sign the form; his/her supervisor was likewise required to verify and sign each user's form. Of course, this involved a bit of negotiation of user's wants and needs against the realities of GSA guidelines and available space and equipment. Only five out of seventy-seven users interviewed (less than 7 percent) made equipment requests that could not be granted in full.

Afterword

So, there you have it. The issue is power. Should interior designers have the power to tell the users what they can have? Or, should the users be able to tell the interior designer what they need and want and get it? We cannot have it both ways.

In many places tightfisted management will not permit their workers to have anything to say about their surroundings and furniture. The two examples in this volume, the FAA in Seattle and the 6100 Corridor, were both funded by a U.S. government agency, the General Services Administration. We do not have published examples from industry and this is significant because of the hierarchical structure of most American industrial firms prohibits giving that much power to the workers.

Yet, both of these examples of GSA-funded projects are examples of something else, the emerging process of programming. Programming is essentially finding out what spaces are needed, what spaces need to be next to one another, and what tools the workers need to do their job. This process can produce whole buildings from scratch, and where the process is used carefully, it does. As you can see, it is also the essential process of user-oriented interior design.

Is programming the future of interior design?

Form 1: ADMINISTRATIVE DATA

Hunter/Miller + Associates
Environmental Designers and Consultants
ADMINISTRATIVE DATA

COMPREHENSIVE INTERIOR
ENVIRONMENTAL DESIGN PROJECT
6100 Corridor
GSA Central Office Building

3rd Rev.
2nd Rev.
1st Rev.

1

NAME: Vacant   POSITION CODE: 11000-01   DATE: 9 August 1978

ADMINISTRATIVE DATA

OFFICE: Deputy Administrator

SUB-GROUP: N/A

POSITION: Deputy Administrator

GS LEVEL: GS4

ERGONOMIC DATA

AGE CATEGORY:

HANDED:

ANTHROPOMETRY:

PHYSICAL LIMITATIONS:

PROGRAMMED AREA

WORKSTATION TYPE: H

SUPPORT REQUIREMENTS: None

NET ALLOCATED AREA: 408 S.F.

% NET CIRCULATION: 81.6S.F.

GROSS USABLE AREA: 489.6 S.F.

ENVIRONMENTAL CHARACTERISTICS

FORM: Private Office

FLEXIBILITY: Layout & dimensional flexibility

SECURITY CONTROL: Confidential material

OTHER:

FUNCTION

USE: Work Station

USER: Senior Executive

SPECIAL EQUIPMENT & MILLWORK:

HVAC

TEMPERATURE: HVAC Individual Control

AIR:

FINISHES

CEILING TYPE:

WALL TYPE:

WALL FINISH:

FLOOR FINISH: Carpeting

BASE:

WINDOW COVERING:

SPECIAL FINISHES:

PLUMBING

WATER SUPPLY: None

ELECTRICAL

OUTLETS: 110V Duplex

COMMUNICATION:

LIGHT INTENSITY: 50 Foot Candles

LIGHT FIXTURES:

Form 2: PRESCRIPTIVE SPECIFICATIONS

Hunter/Miller + Associates
Environmental Designers and Consultants
PRESCRIPTIVE SPECIFICATIONS

COMPREHENSIVE INTERIOR
ENVIRONMENTAL DESIGN PROJECT
6100 Corridor
GSA Central Office Building

3rd Rev.
2nd Rev.
1st Rev.

2

NAME: Vacant   POSITION CODE: 11000-01   DATE: 9 August 1978

WORK SURFACE	SQUARE INCHES	MIN. DEPTH	TYPE
PRIMARY	3024	36"	
SECONDARY	1872	24"	
TERTIARY			

FILE STORAGE	LINEAR INCHES	REMARKS	S
LETTER			
LEGAL	30		x
EDP			

OPEN SHELF STORAGE	LINEAR INCHES	REMARKS	S
BOOKS(9")			
BINDERS(12")			
EDP(15")			
LTR FILE(12")			
LGL FILE(15")			
MISC SUPPLY			

DRAWER STORAGE	CUBIC INCHES	REMARKS	S
PENCIL(2 1/2"H)	750		
BOX(6"H)	2160		x

CLOSED SHELF STORAGE	LINEAR INCHES	REMARKS	S
BOOKS(9")	48		x
BINDERS(12")			
EDP(15")			
LTR FILE(12")			
LGL FILE(15")			
MISC SUPPLY	36		x

VISUAL AIDS	SQUARE INCHES	REMARKS	
TACKABLE			
MAG/LIQ CHALK			

SEATING	DESCRIPTION	REMARKS	QTY.
DESK	Arm		1
GUEST	Arm		2
CONVERSATION		Seat 5-6	

MISCELLANEOUS	DIMENSIONS	REMARKS	S
Coffee table to be determined			
(2) end tables to be determined			
(2) lamps to be determined			

Hunter/Miller + Associates
Environmental Designers and Consultants
ADMINISTRATIVE DATA

COMPREHENSIVE INTERIOR
ENVIRONMENTAL DESIGN PROJECT
6100 Corridor
GSA Central Office Building

3rd Rev.
2nd Rev.
1st Rev. 8/11/78

1

NAME: Vacant   POSITION CODE: #11000-02   DATE: 26 July 1978

ADMINISTRATIVE DATA

OFFICE: Deputy Administrator

SUB-GROUP: N/A

POSITION: Special Assistant

GS LEVEL: GS-17

ERGONOMIC DATA

AGE CATEGORY:

HANDED:

ANTHROPOMETRY:

PHYSICAL LIMITATIONS:

PROGRAMMED AREA

WORKSTATION TYPE: F

SUPPORT REQUIREMENTS: None

NET ALLOCATED AREA: 210 S.F.

% NET CIRCULATION: 42S.F.

GROSS USABLE AREA: 339.3S.F.

ENVIRONMENTAL CHARACTERISTICS

FORM: Open Private Space

FLEXIBILITY: Layout & Dimensional
              Flexibility

SECURITY CONTROL: Conf. material, personal
                  property

OTHER: None

FUNCTION

USE: Work Station

USER: Senior Executive

SPECIAL EQUIPMENT & MILLWORK: None

HVAC

TEMPERATURE: HVAC, Individual Control

AIR: Building Standard

FINISHES

CEILING TYPE: To Be Determined

WALL TYPE: To Be Determined

WALL FINISH: To Be Determined

FLOOR FINISH: Carpeting

BASE: To Be Determined

WINDOW COVERING: To Be Determined

SPECIAL FINISHES: To Be Determined

PLUMBING

WATER SUPPLY: None

ELECTRICAL

OUTLETS: 110 V duplex

COMMUNICATION: To Be Determined

LIGHT INTENSITY: 50 Foot Candles

LIGHT FIXTURES: To Be Determined

Hunter/Miller + Associates
Environmental Designers and Consultants
PRESCRIPTIVE SPECIFICATIONS

COMPREHENSIVE INTERIOR
ENVIRONMENTAL DESIGN PROJECT
6100 Corridor
GSA Central Office Building

3rd Rev.
2nd Rev.
1st Rev. 8/11/78

2

NAME: Vacant   POSITION CODE: #11000-02   DATE: 26 July 1978

WORK SURFACE	SQUARE INCHES	MIN. DEPTH	TYPE
PRIMARY	2592	30"	
SECONDARY	1728	24"	
TERTIARY	1728	24"	

FILE STORAGE	LINEAR INCHES	REMARKS	S
LETTER			
LEGAL	60		X
EDP			

OPEN SHELF STORAGE	LINEAR INCHES	REMARKS	S
BOOKS (9")	36		
BINDERS (12")	36		
EDP (15")			
LTR FILE (12")			
LGL FILE (15")			
MISC SUPPLY			

DRAWER STORAGE	CUBIC INCHES	REMARKS	S
PENCIL (2 1/2"H)	750		X
BOX (6"H)	2160	Minimum 2 Drawers	X

CLOSED SHELF STORAGE	LINEAR INCHES	REMARKS	S
BOOKS (9")	30		X
BINDERS (12")			
EDP (15")			
LTR FILE (12")			
LGL FILE (15")			
MISC SUPPLY			

VISUAL AIDS	SQUARE INCHES	REMARKS	
TACKABLE			
MAG/LIQ CHALK			

SEATING	DESCRIPTION	REMARKS	QTY.
DESK	arm	Casters/swivel/tilt	1
GUEST	arm		3
CONVERSATION			

MISCELLANEOUS	DIMENSIONS	REMARKS	S

Hunter/Miller + Associates
Environmental Designers and Consultants
ADMINISTRATIVE DATA

COMPREHENSIVE INTERIOR
ENVIRONMENTAL DESIGN PROJECT
6100 Corridor
GSA Central Office Building

3rd Rev.
2nd Rev.
1st Rev. 11 Aug. 78   **1**

NAME: Vacant   POSITION CODE: #11000-03   DATE: 26 July 1978

ADMINISTRATIVE DATA

OFFICE: Deputy Administrator

SUB-GROUP: N/A

POSITION: Executive Assistant

GS LEVEL: GS-16, Supervisor

ERGONOMIC DATA

AGE CATEGORY:

HANDED:

ANTHROPOMETRY:

PHYSICAL LIMITATIONS:

PROGRAMMED AREA

WORKSTATION TYPE: F

SUPPORT REQUIREMENTS: None

NET ALLOCATED AREA: 210 S.F.

% NET CIRCULATION: 42 S.F.

GROSS USABLE AREA: 252 S.F.

ENVIRONMENTAL CHARACTERISTICS

FORM: Open Private Space

FLEXIBILITY: Layout & Dimensional

SECURITY CONTROL: Personal Property

OTHER: None

FUNCTION

USE: Work Station

USER: Senior Executive

SPECIAL EQUIPMENT & MILLWORK: None

HVAC

TEMPERATURE: HVAC, Individual Control

AIR: Building Standard

FINISHES

CEILING TYPE: To Be Determined

WALL TYPE: To Be Determined

WALL FINISH: To Be Determined

FLOOR FINISH: Carpeting

BASE: To Be Determined

WINDOW COVERING: To Be Determined

SPECIAL FINISHES: To Be Determined

PLUMBING

WATER SUPPLY: None

ELECTRICAL

OUTLETS: 110 V duplex

COMMUNICATION: To Be Determined

LIGHT INTENSITY: 50 Foot Candles

LIGHT FIXTURES: To Be Determined

Hunter/Miller + Associates
Environmental Designers and Consultants
PRESCRIPTIVE SPECIFICATIONS

COMPREHENSIVE INTERIOR
ENVIRONMENTAL DESIGN PROJECT
6100 Corridor
GSA Central Office Building

3rd Rev.
2nd Rev.
1st Rev. 8/11/78   **2**

NAME: Vacant   POSITION CODE: #11000-03   DATE: 26 July 1978

WORK SURFACE	SQUARE INCHES	MIN. DEPTH	TYPE
PRIMARY	2592	30"	
SECONDARY	1728	24"	
TERTIARY	1728	24"	

FILE STORAGE	LINEAR INCHES	REMARKS	S
LETTER			
LEGAL	60		x
EDP			

OPEN SHELF STORAGE	LINEAR INCHES	REMARKS	S
BOOKS(9")	126		
BINDERS(12")			
EDP(15")			
LTR FILE(12")			
LGL FILE(15")			
MISC SUPPLY			

DRAWER STORAGE	CUBIC INCHES	REMARKS	S
PENCIL(2 1/2"H)	750		
BOX(6"H)	2160	min. 2 drawers	x

CLOSED SHELF STORAGE	LINEAR INCHES	REMARKS	S
BOOKS(9")	36		x
BINDERS(12")			
EDP(15")			
LTR FILE(12")			
LGL FILE(15")			
MISC 36x24	36		x

VISUAL AIDS	SQUARE INCHES	REMARKS	
TACKABLE			
MAG/LIQ CHALK			

SEATING	DESCRIPTION	REMARKS	QTY.
DESK	arm	Casters/swivel/tilt	1
GUEST	arm		3
CONVERSATION			

MISCELLANEOUS	DIMENSIONS	REMARKS	S

Index